THE SECRETS OF HAPPY FAMILIES

THE SECRETS OF HAPPY FAMILIES

Improve Your Mornings, Rethink Family Dinner,
Fight Smarter, Go Out and Play,
and Much More

BRUCE FEILER

WILLIAM MORROW

An Imprint of HarperCollins*Publishers*

For Eden and Tybee

Wherever you go
Whatever you do
Always remember . . .

All happy families are alike; each unhappy family is unhappy in its own way.

—LEO TOLSTOY

CONTENTS

THE SECRETS OF HAPPY FAMILIES

INTRODUCTION

Why We Need New Thinking for Families

IT WAS THE first night of our annual family get-together in August. For four generations my family had been gathering every summer on Tybee Island, Georgia, just east of Savannah. We held raucous family meals of steamed shrimp, corn on the cob, and mudslinging over politics. We worked together on eccentric art projects using bottle caps and misplaced dominoes. We got stung by jellyfish.

My grandfather had taught us blackjack in that place. I had my first kiss there. My wife, Linda, had so embraced the island she suggested we name one of our twin daughters Tybee for this quirky paradise. Our other daughter was named for her own magical garden, Eden.

But now that paradise was on edge.

Linda and I were the first to arrive. Our girls had recently turned five years old, meaning we had survived the parental death march of sippy cups and diaper caddies. But now we were flummoxed by a new set of challenges—getting the family up and out the door every morning, wrangling our kids to sit through dinner once in a while, remembering to flirt with each other occasionally. On top of that, I had forgotten to pack the girls' stuffed animals that morning, meaning I would be sleeping on the cold side of the bed at exactly the moment we were supposed to be having vacation sex.

My sister and brother-in-law, who arrived next, faced their own trials—prying their adolescent son from his Nintendo; pushing his tween sister to do her chores; preparing their kids for the onset of bullying, cliques, and peer pressure.

My older brother, who came last, warned us that it was time to have some tricky conversations about Mom and Dad. Had the moment come to switch Dad to a wheelchair full-time? Was Mom's eyesight so weak she should stop driving at night? Should they sell their house and move closer to us? Should they sell their house and move farther from us!

I felt like a piece of bologna in the sandwich generation, squeezed between aging parents and rising children.

Sure enough, all the tension soon boiled over. As we gathered for dinner, I noticed something out of the corner of my eye. My nephew was texting under the table. I knew I shouldn't say anything, but I couldn't stop myself and asked him to put his phone away.

Kaboom! A mushroom cloud erupted. My sister snapped at me not to parent her son; my mother huffed that all the grandchildren could have better manners; my father pointed out that my daughters were the ones balancing spoons on their noses; my brother harrumphed that it was impossible to have an adult conversation anymore; and my wife threw up her hands and went to retrieve ice cream for the girls *exactly as her mother would have done.*

"But they haven't even finished their vegetables," I complained.

"But Mom promised us banana splits!" they cried, dissolving into sobs.

"That's it, girls," I said. "We're going to bed!" That sent the girls sprinting to the far side of the house, and eventually everyone retreated to separate rooms.

Later that night my father called me to his bedside. There was a quiver in his voice, a palpable sense of fear I could never remember hearing before.

"Our family is falling apart," he said.

"No, it's not," I said instinctively. "It's stronger than ever."

But lying in bed that night, I wondered: *Was he right?* Were we descending the slippery slope of dysfunction? What is the secret sauce that holds families together? What are the ingredients that make some families effective, resilient, functioning, happy?

Like everyone we knew, Linda and I were baffled by these questions. Now that our children were becoming their own people, the challenges of developing a family culture seemed more nebulous and more acute. Our girls were in the golden years of childhood—from the first step to the first kiss; from potty training to the prom—when we would have our best hope of cultivating a family identity. But while the world overflows with advice about breast-feeding, sleeping, and tantrums, smart thinking about later childhood is harder to find.

Maybe it's because those problems are gnarlier. Navigating nap time is child's play compared to navigating screen time. How do you teach kids discipline while making sure they have fun along the way? Is it possible to develop timeless values in a 24/7 world that prizes novelty and coarseness? How do couples find time to nurture each other while spending so much time nurturing our kids?

Whenever Linda and I have these questions, we turn to our parents, even though their experience is so outdated it's almost quaint. Or we turn to Facebook, even though our friends are as clueless as we are. Magazines and TV chat shows offer mostly empty platitudes. How-to manuals with their chirpy banalities pile up unread next to our beds. Even our metaphors are outdated. Sandwich generation? Linda wouldn't dare serve processed luncheon meat to our kids. So what are we, then, just schmears of organic hummus in a vegetarian wrap?

These days, the old rules no longer apply, but new ones have yet to be written.

The next morning I turned to Linda: So whom do we call to make sure our family works?

A NEW DAY FOR FAMILIES

It turns out to be an astonishingly good time to ask that question. The last fifty years have seen a wholesale revolution in what it means to be a family. We have blended families, patchwork families, adoptive families. We have nuclear families that live in separate houses as well as divorced families that nest in the same house. We have families with one parent, two parents, three parents, or more, and families with one, two, or three faiths, and some with none.

No matter what kind of family you are part of, an enormous new body of research shows that your family is central to your overall happiness and well-being. Study after study confirms that the number one predictor of life satisfaction comes from spending time with people you care about and who also care about you. Simply put, happiness is other people, and the other people we hang around with most are our family.

So how do we make sure we're doing that effectively? The last decade has seen a stunning breakthrough in knowledge about how to make families, along with other small groups, run more smoothly. Myth-shattering research from neuroscience to genetics has completely reshaped our understanding of how parents should discipline their children, what to talk about at family dinner, and how adult siblings can have difficult conversations. Cutting-edge innovation in social networking and business has transformed how people work in groups. Trendsetting programs from the U.S. military and professional sports have introduced remarkable techniques for making teams function more efficiently and bounce back from setbacks more quickly.

But most of these revolutionary ideas remain ghettoized in their subcultures, where they are hidden from the people—the families—who need them most.

This book is designed to make a dent in that problem.

I have tried to write the book I have most wanted to read as a spouse, parent, uncle, sibling, and adult child. I've broken down families into the things we all do—love, fight, eat, play; fool around, spend money, make pivotal life decisions—and tried to discover ways to do them better. I have sought out the most illuminating experiences, the smartest people, and the most effective families I could find as a way to assemble best practices of families today. My goal was to put together a playbook for happy families.

Most of these ideas have been hiding in plain sight. I took a course from the founder of the Harvard Negotiation Project on how to fight smart. I visited ESPN to find out what the best coaches know about building successful teams. I worked with Green Berets to design a perfect family reunion. I got some advice from Warren Buffett's banker about how to set up an allowance. I sat down with top game designers in Silicon Valley to see how we can make family vacations more fun.

And on one of my favorite days, I visited the set of *Modern Family*. The most popular show on American television captures many of the crosscurrents in families today. There's a suburban family battling everything from technology to dating. There's a gay couple with an adopted Vietnamese daughter. There's a grumpy grandfather with a Colombian trophy wife and a day-trading, lovelorn son.

A key part of *Modern Family*'s success is that no matter how outrageous the characters act or how loony a story is, the writers pull a string just before the final commercial and the family comes together in a reassuring hug. I'd sure like one of those strings! I talked to the cast and creators about what the success of *Modern Family* says about modern families and whether we should all live our lives more like a sitcom.

In the course of this research, I also encountered a shocking array of outdated advice and ill-informed recommendations, and this book became something of a crusade against a few fashionable trends.

The first is the family improvement industry. Of the nearly two hundred books I read, the ones by therapists, counselors, child-rearing experts, or other traditional "authorities" on family life were by far the least helpful. It's not that they were poorly written. It's that they seemed tired and out-of-date. The questions they asked seemed retread from thirty or even forty years ago; the answers seemed stale. A century after Freud, this once-innovative field seems to offer few original ideas.

At the same time, nearly everything else about contemporary life is being remade and reimagined. Where are the fresh ideas for families? Early on, I set the goal of speaking with the leading lights of technology, business, sports, and the military about the innovative ideas they bring home to their families. I made a parallel goal of not speaking with any therapists. (For the record, I violated that goal only once, when I met with a Belgian sex therapist.)

The second trend is the happiness movement. Anyone who's stepped into a bookstore or scanned the Internet in recent years knows a new field emerged in the early twenty-first century called positive psychology. Pioneered by a group of visionary scholars, the movement shifted attention away from the long-standing focus on individuals with mental illnesses or other pathologies and concentrated on high-functioning individuals and what the rest of us could learn from them. The field exploded, and I, like many, have learned a tremendous amount from this exciting literature.

But as even the leading practitioners of positive psychology have complained, all the attention on individual happiness has also made our culture more shallow and self-centered. A primary tenet of most happiness books, for example, is to figure out what makes us happy. Yet among the things proven to make us the least happy are raising children, tending aging parents, and doing household chores. That's 80 percent of my waking hours!

We need to take the central premise of the happiness movement—its focus on those who do it right—and apply it to the area of our lives that's been scandalously overlooked: our families.

Finally, the parenting wars. The last few years have seen an outpouring of books, articles, and magazine covers wrangling over the issue of what's the proper way to raise children. Be strict like the Chinese; no, be lax like the French; spank 'em like they did in the good 'ol days of the good 'ol U.S. of A. These debates are fiery, passionate, and oddly familiar. Isn't the tough-minded Tiger Mom just the inverse of the permissive Dr. Spock?

The authors of those books have an ideology they want to promote. I don't. I don't have a country I'm trying to emulate. I don't have a mascot. I have a question: What do happy families do right and how can the rest of us learn to make our families happier?

And I have a conviction: No matter what I find, I'm not going to reduce it to a list of five, six, or seven things you absolutely must do to create the perfect family. In 1989, Stephen Covey published *The 7 Habits of Highly Effective People*, one of the most successful self-help books ever written. It has sold more than twenty-five million copies. The book spawned countless imitators seeking to identify "5 Easy Steps" or "Six Simple Truths." The Internet, with its emphasis on bite-size wisdom, has only accelerated this trend. As every blogger, Tweeter, and Pinterest poster knows, readers love lists. I've certainly digested my share of such lists (and generated more than a few myself), but secretly I hate them. They stress me out because I'm always worried I'm going to forget number 4 or disagree with number 2.

So in this book I've tried to go to the opposite extreme. I've strived to generate a fresh gathering of best practices for each of the subjects I tackled. Not just parenting, but also marriage, sex, money, sports, and grandparenting. My goal was to create The List to End All Lists, more than two hundred bold new ideas for improving your family. While that might seem overwhelming, please hear me out.

A collection like this is liberating, I believe, because it's obvious no one can attend to them all. If you're like Linda and me, a few will make you uncomfortable. *Do I have to use the word* vagina *when giving my daughters a bath instead of the more demure* privates? A few you might not agree with at first. *What do you mean I should cancel date night?* And a few you might simply reject. *Let your kids decide their own punishments?*

But if you're also like us, you'll be shocked by how much you didn't know and jazzed to get started trying out some new techniques. I'm almost prepared to guarantee that you've never encountered at least three-quarters of the ideas in this book. (With us, I'd put the figure at 90 percent.) And I'm betting at least a few of them will be useful. My hope is that if you take just one idea from each chapter in this book, your family will be transformed in less than a week.

And who among us doesn't want that? For all the lip service we pay to families in our culture, most of us have a nagging fear we're not doing it as well as we might. We know our families are the single biggest influence on our well-being, yet we spend surprisingly little time trying to improve them. Just listen to the conversations we have all the time: We're busy; we're harried; we're overwhelmed. We feel time slipping away. Having beaten the biological clock to have our kids, now we race a different ticking clock to help convert those kids into a family.

And we can. Everything I've learned persuades me it's possible to give our children a strong family culture they can carry with them throughout their lives. It's possible to include grandparents, siblings, even bumbling Uncle Joe in an extended community of love and support. It's possible to have a happy family.

Nearly a century and a half ago, the great Russian novelist Leo Tolstoy began *Anna Karenina* with one of the most famous lines in all of world literature. "All happy families are alike; each unhappy family is unhappy in its own way." When I first encountered this line, I thought the first half, in particular, was inane. Of course all happy families are not alike: Some are large, some are small; some are boisterous, some are quiet; some are traditional, some are nontraditional.

Writing this book has changed my mind. Recent scholarship has allowed us, for the first time in history, to identify some building blocks that high-functioning families share; to understand the techniques effective families use to overcome challenges; to pinpoint the skills each of us needs to conduct ourselves more successfully in this most maddening of human institutions. Is it possible, all these years later, to say Tolstoy was right: All happy families do have certain things in common?

That answer, I believe, is yes. Come, let me show you why.

PART ONE

ADAPT ALL THE TIME

1

THE AGILE FAMILY MANIFESTO

A Twenty-First-Century Plan to Reduce Chaos and Increase Happiness

THE TENSION BUILDS up all through the week. This kid refuses to make her bed. That one won't put down the iPhone. "Wasn't it your time to take out the trash?" "Hey, I told you, stop taking my gum!" "Mommmmmmm!"

By Sunday evening, the family is ready for relief.

At just after 7:00 P.M., the sun was setting on the town of Hidden Springs, Idaho, population 2,280, just north of Boise. Two horses were running along a serpentine ridge. Some kids were finishing a pickup baseball game in Dry Creek Valley. But inside a neo-traditional, three-story, caramel-colored house, the six members of the Starr family were sitting down to the most important business of their week: their weekly family meeting.

The Starrs are a typical American family with their share of typical American family issues. David, a balding, roly-poly man with a mustache and goatee, is a software engineer. He's part of the new breed of deeply involved dads who's constantly tinkering with how his family runs. He also has Asperger's syndrome, making it difficult for him to read other people's emotions. He and his wife, Eleanor, are an impressive couple, because she is a woman of almost pure emotion, a flame-haired earth mother eager to spread love and fresh-baked corn bread to the neighbors. A few years after their wedding, David took an emotional assessment test and scored 8 out of 100; Eleanor scored 98. "How do we get along?" they wondered.

On top of this combustibility, they quickly added four children in five years—Mason (now fifteen), Cutter (thirteen), Isabelle (eleven), and Bowman (ten). One had Asperger's syndrome, another had ADHD; one was laid-back, another had low self-esteem; one was a star math student who tutored on this side of town; another was a great lacrosse player who had practice on that side of town. "We were living in complete chaos," Eleanor said.

Like many parents, the Starrs were trapped in that endless tension between the sunny, smooth-running household they aspired to have and the exhausting, earsplitting one they actually lived in. That gap is invariably widest in the hour after the kids get up in the morning, and the hour before they go to bed—the twin war zones of modern family life.

"When you're living in a house where six people are trying to brush their teeth at the same time and everyone is fighting, nobody is happy," Eleanor said. "I was trying the whole 'love them and everything will work out' philosophy, but it wasn't working. 'For the love God,' I finally said, 'I can't take this anymore.'"

What convinced her to make a change was the day David asked each of their kids to describe their mom. Their answer: "She yells a lot."

What the Starrs did next, though, was surprising. Instead of turning to their parents or friends, or trying to find advice in books or on television, they looked to David's workplace. They turned to a cutting-edge program called "agile development" that was rapidly spreading from automobile manufacturers in Japan to software designers in Silicon Valley. Agile development is a system of group dynamics in which workers are organized into small teams, each team huddles briefly every morning, and the team convenes for a longer gathering at week's end to critique how it's functioning. In the workplace, these gatherings are called "review and retrospective"; in the home, the Starrs called them "family meetings."

As David wrote in an influential 2009 white paper "Agile Practices for Families," having weekly family meetings increased communication, improved productivity, lowered stress, and made everyone much happier to "be part of the family team."

When Linda and I adopted the agile blueprint with our daughters, weekly family meetings quickly became the single most impactful idea we introduced into our lives since the birth of our children. They became the centerpiece around which we organized our family. And they transformed our relationships with our kids—and each other—in ways we never could have imagined.

And the meetings did all this while lasting under twenty minutes.

"THE BEST THANKSGIVING WE EVER HAD"

The institution of the family has undergone dramatic changes in recent decades. From the decline of marriage to the rise of divorce, from the surge of women into the workplace to the novelty of men being more involved in raising children, nearly every aspect of domestic life has been transformed.

Yet through all this, the family has prevailed and has even grown in importance. A 2010 Pew study found that three-quarters of adults said their family was the most important element of their lives; the same number said they were "very satisfied" with their family life, and eight in ten said the family they have today is as close or closer than the one they grew up in.

That's the good news. Now, here's the bad news: Almost everyone feels completely overwhelmed by the pace and pressures of daily life, and that exhaustion is exacting an enormous toll on family well-being. Survey after survey shows that parents and children both list stress as their number one concern. This includes stress inside as well as outside the home. And if parents feel harried, it trickles down to their children. Studies have shown that parental stress weakens children's brains, depletes their immune systems, and increases their risk of obesity, mental illness, diabetes, allergies, even tooth decay.

And kids know it, too. In a survey of a thousand families, Ellen Galinsky, the head of the Families and Work Institute and the author of *Mind in the Making*, asked children, "If you were granted one wish about your parents, what would it be?" Most parents predicted their kids would say spending more time with them. They were wrong. The kids' number one wish was that their parents were less tired and less stressed.

How do we solve that problem, at least inside the home? Part of the challenge has to do with families constantly undergoing change. My favorite line about parenting is from my friend Justin, who has four children. "Everything is a phase," he says, "even the good parts." Just when kids start sleeping, they stop napping; just when they start walking, they begin throwing tantrums; just when they get used to soccer, they add piano lessons; just when they start putting themselves to bed, they begin having homework and needing their parents' help again; just when they get the hang of taking tests, along comes texting, dating, and online hazing. No wonder the great Harvard family theorist Salvador Minuchin said the most important characteristic of families is being "rapidly adaptable."

So has anyone out there figured out how to reduce stress and improve adaptability? Yes—in fact, an entire field has been devoted to this issue.

In the early 1980s, Jeff Sutherland, a former fighter pilot in Vietnam, was chief technologist at a large financial firm in New England when he began noticing how dysfunctional software development was. Companies followed the "waterfall model," in which executives issued ambitious orders from above and expected them to flow downward to the programmers below. Eighty-three percent of projects came in late, overbudget, or failed entirely. "I'm looking at this and thinking, 'This is worse than flying over North Vietnam,'" Jeff told me one afternoon at his home in Boston. "There only half the people got shot down!"

Jeff was determined to design a new system, in which ideas would not only flow down from the top but also percolate up from the bottom. Around 1990, he read thirty years of articles in *Harvard Business Review* before stumbling across one from 1986 called "The New New Product Development Game." The authors, Hirotaka Takeuchi and Ikujiro Nonaka, said the pace of business was quickening and argued that successful organizations were built around speed and flexibility. The paper highlighted Toyota and Canon and likened their tight-knit teams to rugby scrums. "We hit that paper and said, 'That's it!'" Sutherland said.

Jeff is credited with applying the word *scrum* to business. Later *scrum* fell under the umbrella term "agile development." Today, agile (the word is used as a collective) is standard practice in a hundred countries, and two-thirds of all software is developed using its philosophy. Odds are you used something today, from your cell phone to your search engine, that was built using agile practices.

In time, leading firms like GE and Facebook began using them in their executive suites, too.

In many ways, agile is part of the larger trend in society toward decentralizing power. The business guru Tom Peters said "agile organizations win" because they're not bound by fixed rules. They have the freedom to create new rules. A similar evolution has been happening in families for decades, as power has shifted from the exclusive domain of fathers to include mothers and, increasingly, children. Inevitably, fans of agile began to ask whether families could benefit from its practices.

"I began to see a lot of people using agile at home, especially with their children," Jeff told me. Jeff's own children were grown at the time, but he and his wife, Arlene, started using agile to help manage their weekends. They took me into their kitchen and showed me a giant flowchart hanging on the wall. The chart was divided into three columns: STUFF TO DO, THINGS IN PROGRESS, THINGS DONE. In the left-hand column, STUFF TO DO, they placed a series of Post-it notes—"animals," "grocery shopping," "Skype with Veronica." When either person begins working on an item, they move it from the first column to the second column; when they finish, they move the note to the third column.

Agile terminology describes this type of flowchart as an "information radiator." Having large, highly visible displays lets everyone on the team track everyone else's progress. "If you have something public like this in your home," Jeff said, "I guarantee you'll get twice as much done. Guarantee."

Their favorite example was their first agile Thanksgiving. "We got everybody together and made a list of what needed to be done," Arlene said. "Food needed to be bought, dishes needed to be prepared, the table needed to be set. Then we created a small team for each item."

"We had this hospitality team led by a nine-year-old," Jeff said. "Whenever the doorbell rang, he would grab people and run to the door. 'Hi! We're so happy you're here. Let us take your coats!' No one has ever felt so welcomed to our house. Everyone agreed it was the best Thanksgiving we ever had."

But of course it didn't go off without a glitch. The team assigned to set the table couldn't agree on how to arrange the place cards. One of the daughters-in-law prefers to sit alongside her spouse, while the Sutherlands prefer to split up the couples. The committee couldn't reach consensus, so they punted, producing a bottleneck at the table.

"This is where agile is particularly effective," Jeff said. "The next day, at our review meeting, we discussed what happened. First we named the problem. *The team doesn't agree on seating.* Then we proposed solutions for the next gathering. *We can seat couples together, split them up, or mix and match.* Then we built agreement, which was to switch off at alternate family functions."

So what lessons did they take away?

"Jeff and I each had difficult upbringings," Arlene said. "Our primary goal as parents was not to set up the same barriers for our children that our parents set up for us."

"That's where agile comes in," Jeff added. "People think it's natural to live in a world in where everyone is dysfunctional. It's not. It's normal for people to be satisfied. All you have to do is remove the barriers that are making you unhappy and you'll be a lot happier. That's what this system does."

In effect, what agile accomplishes is to accept that disorder and order live alongside each other. By acknowledging things will go wrong, then introducing a system to address those wrongs, you increase the odds that the system—in this case the family—can work right.

WHAT ARE YOU FORGETTING?

A similar goal motivated Eleanor and David Starr to make their Idaho home a happier place.

The first problem they attacked was the bedlam in the mornings. David, who had used an information radiator at work, suggested they use one at home. The family sat down and created a morning checklist. The document listed what every kid needed to accomplish before school. They tacked the note on the kitchen wall. Their first list looked like this:

**SELF-DIRECTED
MORNING CHECKLIST**

1. Take vitamins or medicine
2. Eat breakfast
3. Shower or wash face and neck
4. Take care of your hair
5. Do morning chores
6. Brush your teeth (two minutes)
7. Backpack, shoes, and socks

What are you having for lunch?
What are you taking to school today?
What are you forgetting?

For the first few weeks, nothing really happened. The kids wandered around in something of a daze, asking what they were supposed to be doing and generally complaining. "And every time they would start milling about," Eleanor told me, "I simply said, 'Check the list.' After a while, I became like a broken record. 'You need to check the list.'" Gradually the kids began gravitating to it without having to be told. "I would say it took about two weeks," Eleanor said. "We had to make a few modifications. The little one couldn't read, so we made some symbols for him. But eventually, it clicked."

Boy did it. When I showed up in the Starrs' kitchen at 6:00 A.M. that Monday, five years after this system had been implemented, I was amazed by what I saw. Eleanor came downstairs, made herself a cup of coffee, and sat down in a reclining chair. She remained there for the next ninety minutes as first her two oldest children came downstairs, checked the list, made themselves breakfast, checked the list again, made themselves lunch, checked the list, emptied and reloaded the dishwasher, rechecked the list, fed the pets, checked the list one final time, then gathered their belongings and made their way to the bus stop.

When I asked why they checked the list so often, she said they found it comforting on groggy mornings.

As soon as the older children were gone, the two youngest ones came downstairs and did the same things, though with different chores. With the logistics taken care of, Eleanor could concentrate on the softer side of mothering—asking about an upcoming test, smoothing over an anxiety, spreading a little love on their day. It was one of the most astonishing family dynamics I had ever seen.

I told Eleanor how impressive it was, but I strenuously said this system would never work in my house—our girls needed too much monitoring; they would never stop what they were doing and check off some list. Eleanor looked at me sympathetically. "That's what I thought," she said. "I told David, 'Leave your work out of my kitchen.' But I was wrong."

David beamed, then added, "You can't overestimate the satisfaction a person gets by doing this." He made a check mark in the air.

"Even in the workplace, adults love it. And with kids, it's heaven."

But if the morning list transformed one of the biggest pain points in their lives, the bigger change came when they implemented another agile practice.

"WHAT WENT REALLY WELL IN OUR FAMILY THIS WEEK?"

Just after dinner on Sunday night, ten-year-old Bowman plopped down at the kitchen table and began making a drumroll with his hands. This meant the family meeting was ready to begin, and gradually all of the other members sat down and added their hands to the percussion. The older two boys fought over a chair. Isabelle grabbed a Jolly Rancher, which Bowman snatched out of her hand. "Knock it off, you two," David said.

When everyone was settled, David asked the first question. "What went really well in our family this week?"

The core idea of agile development is that life is constantly changing, and we have to organize ourselves in ways to allow us to react to changes in real time. The centerpiece of the program is a weekly review session built on the principle of "inspect and adapt." Three questions traditionally get asked: (1) What have you done this week? (2) What are you going to do next week? (3) Are there any impediments in your way we can help you with?

The Starrs came up with a modified three questions for their family meeting.

1. What things went well in our family this week?
2. What things could we improve in our family?
3. What things will you commit to working on this week?

I was struck by how eager the children were to provide answers. In response to what went well, Cutter said they did a good job checking off chores; Mason said he and Bowman came up with a good solution when the Weedwacker broke; Eleanor said she and Mason were fighting less.

The answers to the second question—"What can still be improved?"—were even more revelatory. One child said the chores list got mixed up; another said finishing evening activities was getting harder. Eleanor said the children were not following the rule of no screen time during the week, and David threw in that there was entirely too much interrupting.

But the real magic occurred when they moved to the final question, "What will you commit to working on this week?" David listed all of the items on the "to be improved" list, and the family voted to focus on two: no screen time and no interrupting. The children then proposed possible remedies for controlling screen time. How about a secret password to turn on the television? Too complicated, they decided. How about just agreeing to follow the rule? Not tough enough. How about taping a sign over all the screens? Only if it's not ugly, Mom insisted. No problem; two kids were given the task of designing the signs.

They moved on to interrupting, and one kid had a bold suggestion. Push-ups! Everyone loved this idea, but how many? Two? Ten? Five? They settled on seven, but who got to decide when someone was officially interrupting? Again, a novel solution emerged. One parent or two children. To demonstrate, all four of the kids dropped to the floor and began counting push-ups.

"You guys are covered in a thin film of weird," David said. "So is that a wrap?"

"That's a wrap," they cried.

In his paper "Agile Practices for Families," David stressed the important differences between using agile at work and at home. Employees are paid to abide by the system; family members are not. Employees can be fired; children cannot.

Still, he insisted, the main benefit is the same: Agile provides a built-in mechanism for communication. "What works about the family meeting," he said, "is that it's a regularly scheduled time to draw attention to specific behaviors. If you don't have a safe environment to discuss problems, any plan to improve your family will go nowhere."

WELCOME TO OUR FAMILY MEETING

Back at home, Linda listened to my description of the agile family movement. After David's white paper was published online, he was asked to lead a few seminars at computer conferences, the trade press picked it up, and his ideas began to go viral. Blogs started popping up around the country. A how-to manual was published. Linda was skeptical but agreed to try at least some of the techniques.

The first thing we experimented with was a morning list. Mornings were a complete wreck in our house, with screams, threats, tears, and tantrums—and that was just the adults! We sat down with the girls and told them about our plan, including the news that they were now old enough to make their beds in the morning. We assembled our list, along with a homemade poster—er, information radiator—to make the whole thing more appealing. When I said I wanted everyone to be more cheerful in the mornings, the girls added to the list a phrase they'd heard from their cousins: "Joy! Rapture! Yay!" We taped the signs near the kitchen.

	MONDAY		TUESDAY		WEDNESDAY		THURSDAY		FRIDAY	
GET DRESSED	✓	@	✓	@	✓	@	✓	@	✓	@
MAKE BED	✓	@	✓	@	✓	@	✓	@	✓	@
OPEN SHUTTERS	✗	☹	✗	☹	✓	@	✓	@	✗	@
SET THE TABLE	✓	@	✓	@	✓	@	✓	✗	✓	@
DRINK MILK	✓	@	✓	@	✓	@	✓	@	✓	@
TAKE VITAMINS	✓	@	✓	@	✓	@	✓	@	✓	@
CLEAR THE TABLE	✓	@	✓	@	✓	@		@	✓	@
BRUSH TEETH	✓	@	✓	@	✓	@		@		@
BACKPACKS READY	✓	@	✓	@	✓	@	✓	@	✓	
COATS/MITTENS	✗	☹	✓	@	✓	@	✓	@	✓	@
JOY, RAPTURE, YAY!	✓	@	✓	@		@	✓	@	✓	@

My goal was to have the morning list reduce our commotion by 20 percent. In the first week alone, it was cut in half. I was stunned. I particularly noticed that the girls were strict in their self-judgments and didn't give themselves check marks they hadn't earned. Frowny faces were common. Linda was also impressed, and I could see her softening to these geeky ideas I was dragging home. The system wasn't perfect, of course. Neither one of us was sitting with our feet up discussing social studies, but I kept reminding myself the Starrs had a five-year head start, and their kids were a lot older.

After a month, our girls had mostly internalized the list and began to slack off with their check marks. We regressed every now and then and had to resort to our old habits of "hurry up, put on your shoes," "find your mittens, we're late." A few times I even forgot to print out the list. At three months, we held a revision session. We let the girls change the wording of a few items, removed some altogether (GET DRESSED), rearranged others (BRUSH YOUR HAIR went earlier), and experimented with bonus points. Ultimately we felt confident enough in our grasp of agile to proceed to the main event.

Our first family meeting was nowhere near as successful as the morning list. We started off well, adopting the Starr family's drumroll. Then we played an old theater game I love in which one person leads the others in saying "ma," alternating between faster and slower, before freezing and saying, "Welcome to our family meeting."

We then asked three questions:

1. What went right in your life this week?
2. What did not go right in your life?
3. What will you work on next week?

Here's where the problems began. Tybee complained she wasn't chosen to answer first. Eden mentioned how much she loved a playdate, which seemed irrelevant to the rest of us. I looked over and saw that Linda was flipping through a catalog. Not good. After a few more weeks of equally uninspired gatherings, I called David.

"You're focusing on the wrong thing," he said. "The purpose of the meeting is not to talk about each of you as individuals. It's to focus on how you're functioning as a family."

He was right. When else did we discuss this most basic thing: *how* we were a family. We redesigned our questions:

1. What worked well in our family this week?
2. What went wrong in our family this week?
3. What will we work on this coming week?

Suddenly amazing things started coming out of our daughters' mouths. The insights were minor, but hearing the girls articulate them left us gobsmacked. What worked well in our family this week? "Getting over our fears of riding a bike," "We've been doing much better making our beds without being asked." "Clearing our plates." What went wrong? "We didn't do our math sheets on time" "We didn't greet visitors at the door like Mom asked."

Like most parents, we found our daughters to be something of a Bermuda Triangle: words and thoughts would go in, but none ever came out, at least not revelatory ones. Their emotional lives were invisible to us. The family meeting provided that rare window into their innermost thoughts.

And the breakthroughs didn't stop there. The girls soon started directing their comments toward each other—and toward us. What didn't work well? "Daddy screamed too much in the morning." "Mommy, you forgot to get milk so we couldn't have French toast like you promised." What worked well this week? Eden: "I helped Tybee with her homework." Tybee: "We were supportive of Eden when she was sick." Who knew they were this self-aware!

The most satisfying moments came when we turned to the topic of what we would work on during the coming week. To my surprise, the girls loved this part. They suggested item after item. The lists grew so long we had to come up with a way of winnowing it down. We designed what I called an "Olympic-style" voting system, after the one used to select host cities for the Olympic Games. Everyone voted for their favorite items, then we eliminated the low vote-getter every round until we had two winners. The girls then proposed their own rewards and punishments. Say hello to five people this week, get an extra ten minutes of reading before bed. Kick someone, and you lose dessert for a month. Linda and I thought a week might be enough, but it turns out our daughters were little Stalins. Invariably we had to tone down their punishments.

Naturally there was a gap between the girls' off-the-charts maturity during these twenty-minute sessions and their actual behavior the rest of the week. But that didn't seem to matter. It felt to us as if we were laying massive underground cables that wouldn't fully light up their world for many years to come. Two years later, we were still holding these family meetings every Sunday evening. Linda began to count them among her most-treasured moments as a mom.

THE AGILE FAMILY MANIFESTO

So what did we learn?

The word *agile* entered the business lexicon on February 13, 2001. Jeff Sutherland and sixteen other designers met in Utah to find common ground about the variety of new techniques just gaining popularity. For two days, the men argued nonstop. Finally someone stood up and said, "Is there anything we can agree on?"

In less than an hour they had a twelve-point statement they called "The Agile Manifesto." Since then, it's been translated into fifty-eight languages.

After seeing agile techniques in action with multiple families, I believe the time is ripe for an "Agile Family Manifesto." I propose five planks.

1. *Solutions exist.* I first learned about agile from a friend in Silicon Valley when I turned to her one New Year's Eve and asked if she knew of anything in her world that could help my family. Agile development was the idea that made me believe there are hundreds of such innovations, in places we don't even think about, that can help families be happier. We don't just need to speak to family experts to improve our families; we can speak to anyone who's expert in making groups run more smoothly. That became a central premise of this project. Solutions are out there—we just have to go find them.

2. *Empower the children.* Our instinct as parents is to issue orders to our children. We think we know best; it's easier; who has time to argue? And besides, we're usually right! There's a reason few systems have been more "waterfall" than the family. But as all parents quickly discover, telling your kids the same thing over and over is not necessarily the best tactic. The single biggest lesson we can take away from agile practices is figuring out how to reverse the waterfall as often as we can. Let the children take a role in their own upbringing.

A significant amount of recent brain research backs this up. Scientists at the University of California and elsewhere found that kids who plan their own time, set weekly goals, and evaluate their own work build up their prefrontal cortex and other parts of the brain that help them exert greater cognitive control over their lives. These so-called executive skills aid children with self-discipline, avoiding distractions, and weighing the pros and cons of their choices.

By picking their own punishments, children become more internally driven to avoid them. By choosing their own rewards, children become more intrinsically motivated to achieve them. Let your kids take a greater role in raising themselves.

One takeaway I got from agile is that whenever I see friends with checklists—chores, schedules, allowance—I ask whether the adults or the kids are doing the checking off. Invariably it's the adults. The science suggests there's a better way. To achieve maximum benefits, have the children do the scoring. They'll develop a much finer sense of self-awareness. Even if this approach doesn't work on every occasion, it's about teaching your kids an approach to problem solving they can carry with them the rest of their lives.

As Eleanor Starr put it, "My whole goal is to make my children functioning adults. When they go to college, I don't want them calling me every day. I want their decision-making skills to be already in place."

3. *Parents aren't invincible.* Another instinct we have as parents is to build ourselves up as all-knowing in the eyes of our children. We pressure ourselves to be the answer person, the go-to authority, Mr. or Ms. Fix-it. But abundant evidence suggests that this type of leadership is no longer the best model. In 2012, scholars from MIT published groundbreaking research in *Harvard Business Review* about rethinking successful teams. After electronically monitoring small groups in many businesses on multiple continents, they concluded that the most effective teams are not dominated by a charismatic leader. Instead, members spend as much time talking to one another as to the leader, they meet face-to-face regularly, and everyone speaks in equal measure.

Sound familiar? "One thing that works in family meetings,"

David Starr told me, "is the kids are allowed to say whatever they want, even about the grown-ups. If I've come back from a trip and am having trouble reentering the routine, or if Mom hasn't been nice that week, this is their venue to express their frustration.

"Once I lost it with Bowman," he continued. "And that came out in the meeting when the other kids let me know my behavior was unacceptable. That was extremely powerful."

4. *Create a safe zone.* Every parent quickly learns that every child—and every adult—handles conflict differently. Some push back when criticized, some turn inward, some break down in tears. A key gift of the family meeting was to give us a designated space each week to overcome those differences. It was a safe zone, where everybody was on an equal footing, and no one could leave until a resolution was forged.

Linda definitely embraced this aspect of the family meeting. "When we're late for school or having a showdown in the supermarket," she said, "I don't have to worry about having a big discussion. We always have Sunday night."

5. *Build in flexibility.* The last item of the Agile Manifesto works just as well in the Agile Family Manifesto. "At regular intervals," the manifesto states, "the team reflects on how to become more effective, then tunes and adjusts its behavior accordingly."

Parents often create a few overarching rules and stick to them indefinitely. This philosophy presumes we can anticipate every problem that will arise over many years. We can't. If anything, modern technology shows us how fast change occurs. The Internet has certainly shown us that if you're doing the same thing today you were doing six months ago, you're likely doing something wrong. Parents can learn a lot from that.

The agile family philosophy accepts and embraces the ever-changing nature of family life. It's certainly not lax; think of all the public accountability. And it's not anything goes. But it anticipates that even the best designed system will need to be reengineered midstream. Perhaps the strongest endorsement I can give for agile family meetings is that our girls were five when we started; the Starrs were still doing it at ten, eleven, thirteen, and fifteen. We dealt with topics as minor as Valentine's candy; the Starrs dealt with issues as serious as sexually transmitted diseases. We have two kids, both of them girls; they have four kids, three of them boys. Our girls tend toward the verbal, artsy, highly emotional; their kids are largely numerate, techy, and introverted. The same template has worked well for both families.

As I was leaving the Starrs' home, I asked Eleanor and David what they thought was the most important lesson I should learn from the first agile family. "That we don't have all the answers," David said. "We've created a framework, but we're flexible within it. We try something; it might work; it might fail. The morning list we have now is our fifteenth iteration. We're communicating to the kids that it's okay to change."

Eleanor agreed. "In the media, families just are," she said. "But that's misleading. You have your job; you work on that. You have your garden, your hobbies, you work on those. Your family requires just as much work, if not more. The most important thing agile taught me is that you have to make a commitment to always keep working to improve your family. That's what no one believes until they start doing it themselves."

2

THE RIGHT WAY TO HAVE
FAMILY DINNER

Why What You Talk About Is More Important
Than What You Eat (or When You Eat It)

JOHN BESH IS a former U.S. Marine who is now a celebrity chef—the happy, handsome face of New Orleans cuisine. One day he was rummaging around in his home kitchen in Slidell, Louisiana, when he stumbled upon something that turned his stomach: a crumpled-up McDonald's bag. For John, a champion of local farming, this was an act of treason.

He carried the item to his wife, Jennifer, whom he's known since the two were elementary school classmates. "Really?" he said.

"Yes," she answered, unapologetically. Jennifer is a former lawyer who hates to cook. "When I married a chef, I thought I had it made," she told me. Raising four boys, ages seven to sixteen, with a husband who works nights, she just became so overwhelmed she picked up a quickie meal between sports practices.

"If you were half as concerned about what your boys eat as you are about what your customers eat," she told him, "we'd have a healthier family."

John was thunderstruck. He is a rare combination of good ol' boy (he still hunts and fishes) and cutting-edge (he learned molecular cuisine in Europe). He opened his first restaurant, the James Beard Award–winning August, in 2001. Today he runs nine of them, from the French Quarter to San Antonio. He's also a ubiquitous presence on cooking reality shows, has written two cookbooks, and makes scores of appearances supporting everyone from beleaguered fishermen in the Gulf of Mexico to U.S. Marines in the Persian Gulf.

As he put to me one spring afternoon while preparing shrimp and pasta in his kitchen, he was cooking for everyone in the world except for the people he cared about most in the world.

"That moment was a major turning point," John said. "I knew we needed a plan."

The scheme the Beshes came up with would have been unthinkable a generation ago, but it sprang from a question everyone seems to be asking these days: Is it time to give up on family dinner?

WHO NEEDS DINNER?

The last few years have seen an explosion of interest in family dinner. Everyone from Hollywood stars (Brad Pitt and Angelina Jolie, Tom Hanks and Rita Wilson) to Major League Baseball teams (the Boston Red Sox, the Los Angeles Dodgers) to TV personalities (Matt Lauer and Katie Couric) have joined the chorus encouraging families to eat more meals together. President Barack Obama has spoken often about having dinner every night with his daughters in the White House, calling it one of the advantages of "living above the office." President George W. Bush made a public service announcement with his mother. Bush said he always enjoyed family dinner when he was growing up, "So long as my mother wasn't cooking."

"It's not good to make fun of your mother," Barbara Bush injected, "even if you are president. But it is good to have dinner with your kids."

A recent wave of research shows that children who eat dinner with their families are less likely to drink, smoke, do drugs, get pregnant, commit suicide, and develop eating disorders. Additional research found that children who enjoy family meals have larger vocabularies, better manners, healthier diets, and higher self-esteem. The most comprehensive survey done on this topic, a University of Michigan report that examined how American children spent their time between 1981 and 1997, discovered that the amount of time children spent eating meals at home was the single biggest predictor of better academic achievement and fewer behavioral problems. Mealtime was more influential than time spent in school, studying, attending religious services, or playing sports.

"When you start to look at the research, which is staggering," Laurie David, the Oscar-winning producer of *An Inconvenient Truth* and the author of *The Family Dinner*, told me, "you realize all the things you worry about as a parent can be improved just by sitting down to regular dinners."

But as impressive as this research is, fewer and fewer families are actually eating dinner together. For starters, nearly everything in contemporary life conspires against regular nighttime meals. From longer work hours for parents to more homework for kids to "Let me just answer this text," dinnertime has become prime time for anything but eating. A study from UNICEF determined that Americans ranked twenty-three out of twenty-five countries when it came to fifteen-year-olds who eat dinner with their parents at least "several times a week." Fewer than two-thirds of Americans answered "yes," compared to more than 90 percent of Italians, French, Dutch, and Swiss.

The most head-shaking statistic I saw came from the Center on Everyday Lives of Families at UCLA, which has taped everything middle-class families have done over many years. The families in their study dined together only 17 percent of the time, *even when everybody was home.*

The Beshes can relate to these stresses. John grew up in a family of six kids, and dinner was a mandatory formality—napkins in your lap, ball caps off your head, no elbows on the table. His father, an airline pilot, "tossed around current events and asked us to dispense judgment." John said he first dreamed of becoming a chef as an eleven-year-old boy after his father was paralyzed in a biking accident, and John began helping prepare family meals. "Through food I found I could make people happy," he said.

Jennifer Besh grew up with similar rituals, though her four siblings were more raucous. "My sister was always arguing her constitutional rights."

So when the Beshes had their come-to-dinner showdown, they realized they wanted to reclaim their past but update it to meet their new reality. The first step: Stock the pantry.

"If you wait until you're hungry to think about dinner," John said, "you'll make bad choices." He immediately filled the house with supplies, which they could whip into hasty meals—pastas, grains, oils, spices. Jennifer began storing up proteins—chicken, shrimp, ground beef.

Next step: Plan ahead. They started sketching out weekly menus, with John agreeing to prep extra food, which Jennifer could then repurpose on hectic school nights.

"If you're cooking one chicken, cook two," Jennifer said. "If you're preparing pasta tonight, fix enough for tomorrow. If you're making hamburgers for Monday, make meatballs on the side for Thursday."

But their most radical step may have been the most effective. They gave up the fantasy of eating dinner together every night. They moved "family dinner" to "family breakfast." John took on this meal. "I realized if I was going to have quality time with my boys," he said, "it had to be early morning."

He developed a repertoire that incorporated all the kids' favorites—*pain perdu* (French toast), buttermilk pancakes, cheese grits, biscuits. If someone's in a hurry, he leaves breakfast wraps on the table.

Even more inventive is how the Beshes handled the evenings. With the boys eating school lunch as early as 10:30 A.M. (their school cafeteria is overcrowded), they come home hungry, and with sports practices starting as late as 5:30 P.M. (so working dads can coach), they're often not at home at the traditional dinner hour. So Jennifer began serving a large meal every afternoon at 4:00 P.M. After one of the boys says grace, she passes around her gerrymandered meal (Asian chicken salad from leftover chicken, Sloppy Joe sliders with that extra stash of beef from Monday), then everyone piles into the SUV and heads back out again.

When the family returns home around 7:30 P.M., she sends the boys to the shower, then gathers everyone back in the kitchen for dessert. Nine-year-old Jack told me this time is the best time of his day; his favorite treat: lemon icebox pie.

Notice the new routine: That's three "family dinners" in the course of a day, and not a one of them is *family dinnertime*.

"Instead of feeling guilty because you don't have the six o'clock thing," Jennifer said, "it's about coming together as a family whenever you have the time."

The Beshes' plan might not work for everyone. My wife threw up her hands when I mentioned dinner at 4:00 P.M. But the larger point still holds: Many of the benefits of family mealtime can be enjoyed without sitting down together every night. Even the folks at Columbia University's center on addiction, the ones responsible for a lot of the research on family dinner, say having joint meals as infrequently as once a week makes a difference.

Laurie David, in her book, gathered a number of inventive ideas to rethink the ritual:

- Can't have dinner together every night? Aim for once a week.
- Aren't home from work early enough? Gather everyone together at 8:00 P.M. for dessert, a bedtime snack, or just a chat about the day.
- Weekdays too busy? Aim for weekends.
- Don't have time to cook? Try Leftover Mondays, Chinese Takeout Tuesdays, or breakfast for dinner.

"The point is," David told me, "if you light a candle, or put a flower in a vase, or cover the table in craft paper and open up a box of crayons, you're showing respect for that meal. I, for one, find parenting challenging. I spend a lot of time beating myself up over everything I do wrong. I decided some years ago that family dinner would be the one thing I could do right."

John Besh made a similar decision, in his own way, and focuses his attention on Sundays. After church, John prepares a blowout meal for his brood. Relatives stop by, crawfish are boiled, jambalaya gets stirred. The family that's rarely been together all week now hangs out all afternoon. "To me, it's not a proper Sunday without everybody coming together," he said.

So what do those moments mean to him?

"I feel the same thing I felt when I cooked for my father," John said. "Happy. People are smiling, talking, laughing." He paused, then grabbed his youngest son, Andrew, and pulled him into his lap. "Give your daddy a kiss," he said.

IT'S NOT ABOUT THE DINNER; IT'S ABOUT THE FAMILY

The Beshes have rethought family dinner, but there's an even more radical idea out there: Forget the dinner entirely.

The person most associated with this view is among the more colorful people I met. Marshall Duke is wearing a Panama hat in his official Emory University photograph. He's taught psychology there since 1970 and is an expert in rituals and resilience. Marshall has appeared on every media outlet from *The Oprah Winfrey Show* to *Good Morning America*, but he's most comfortable where I met him on a Friday night, standing at the head of a Shabbat dinner surrounded by his wife, three children, and eight grandchildren.

"Okay, everybody, let's begin!" Marshall said, sounding like a camp counselor who had waited all winter for this moment. Marshall then pulled out a handful of traditional Jewish skullcaps and flung them, Frisbee-style, toward each of the grandchildren, who bobbed and wove in an attempt to land one on their heads. No one succeeded.

"Is this in the Torah?" I asked.

"No, it's in the Duke Family Hall of Fame," he said. "And that's much more important."

The candles were lit, wine and bread were blessed, then Marshall asked everyone to hold hands. "We would like to welcome our special guest tonight," he said, nodding toward me. "Brandon, we're happy you're home from college. J.D. had his teeth pulled, so we celebrate his bravery. And we have three birthdays to mark this week. Shira, anything special with you this week?"

"I got through finals," the twelve-year-old said.

"Great. Shabbat Shalom, everybody. Now, let's eat!"

In the mid-1990s, Marshall was asked to join a new initiative at Emory to explore myth and ritual in American families. "There was a lot of research at the time into the dissipation of the family," he said. "But we were more interested in what families could do to counteract those forces."

Not long after, Marshall's wife, Sara, a psychologist who works with children who have learning disabilities, made an observation about her students. "The ones who know a lot about their families tend to do better when they face challenges." Her husband was intrigued and, along with colleague Robyn Fivush, he set out to test Sara's hypothesis. They developed a measure called the "Do You Know?" scale that asked children to answer twenty questions, including:

- Do you know where your grandparents grew up?
- Do you know where your mom and dad went to high school?
- Do you know where your parents met?
- Do you know of an illness or something really terrible that happened in your family?
- Do you know what went on when you were being born?

Marshall and Robyn asked those questions of four dozen families in the summer of 2001, and also taped several of their dinner table conversations. They then compared the children's results to a battery of psychological tests and reached some overwhelming conclusions. The more children knew about their family's history, the stronger their sense of control over their lives, the higher their self-esteem, and the more successfully they believed their families functioned. The "Do You Know?" scale turned out to be the best single predictor of children's emotional health and happiness. "We were blown away," Marshall said.

And then something unexpected happened. Two months later was September 11. As citizens Marshall and Robyn were horrified, like everyone else, but as psychologists they knew they had been given a rare opportunity: All of the families they had studied had experienced the same trauma at the same time. They went back and reassessed the children. "Once again," Marshall said, "the ones who knew more about their families proved to be more resilient, meaning they could moderate the effects of stress."

Why does knowing where your grandmother went to school help a child overcome something as minor as a skinned knee or as major as a terrorist attack? And how can family meals and other rituals play a role in children gaining this knowledge?

"The answers have to do with a child's sense of being part of a larger family," Marshall said. Psychologists have found that every family has a unifying narrative, he explained, and those narratives take one of three shapes. First, there's the ascending family narrative that goes like this: "Son, when we came to this country, we had nothing. Our family worked. We opened a store. Your grandfather went to high school. Your father went to college. And now you . . ." Second is the descending narrative: "Sweetheart, we used to have it all. Then we lost everything. . . ."

"The most healthful narrative," Marshall continued, "is the third one. It's called the oscillating family narrative. 'Dear, let me tell you, we've had ups and downs in our family. We built a family business. Your grandfather was a pillar of the community. Your mother was on the board of the hospital. But we also had setbacks. You had an uncle who was once arrested. We had a house burn down. Your father lost a job. But no matter what happened, we always stuck together as a family.'"

Marshall says that children who have the most balance and self-confidence in their lives do so because of what he and Robyn call a strong "intergenerational self." They know they belong to something bigger than themselves.

"One of the central people in this equation is the grandmother," he said. "She'll say, 'You're having trouble with math, kid? Let me tell you, your father had trouble with math.' 'You don't want to practice piano? Boy, your aunt Laura didn't want to practice piano, either.'

"We call these the *bubbemeise*," he continued. "That's Yiddish for 'grandmother's fable.' Whatever problem the child is having, the grandmother has a story for it—even if it's made up!"

Marshall and Robyn point out that dinner is an ideal time to give kids this family history. Everyone's together; it's a safe environment; it's easier for children to hear about their family's ups and downs while they're in a nurturing environment doing something reassuring. And nothing is more reassuring than eating.

But dinner does not cause the benefits, he stressed. What generates the sense of attachment and emotional toughness is the process of hearing all those old stories and seeing yourself in the larger flow of your family. In other words, what we think of as family dinner is not really about the dinner. It's about the family.

Any number of occasions are opportunities to tell these stories, he said: holidays (Thanksgiving and Christmas); recurring family vacations (July Fourth on the beach, the annual ski weekend); or any ritualized activity that brings different generations together. Even a carpool or ride to the mall are moments, he said.

At the Dukes' Shabbat dinner, I asked everyone which family tradition they liked the most. Each answer was quirkier than the last. The Dukes' children told me about the four-day Thanksgiving weekend they've celebrated for over thirty years. It opens on Tuesday night, when they eat turkey sandwiches. Wednesday night they eat spaghetti, and everyone paints mustaches on their faces. On Thursday they hide cans of pumpkin sauce, bags of green beans, and a frozen turkey, so everyone can "hunt" for food like the Pilgrims did. Then on Friday they eat their Thanksgiving dinner. All weekend long, they have a color war, with the winning team getting a plastic duck.

"It's crazy," Marshall said, "there's no larger historical reason for any of it. But these traditions become part of your family."

Other rituals family members tossed out included a version of charades the family plays, or the provocative questions Marshall throws out at dinner. On this night, he brought up two studies. One found that people are friendlier when they're holding a cup of warm liquid instead of a cup of cold liquid. "Take note, Brandon," his father said, "you're better off picking up a girl in a coffee shop than a bar!" The other study found that when people sit inside a box they are less good at solving problems than when they sit outside. "You see, thinking outside the box is real!" Sara said.

But the most passion came when the grandchildren described their grandfather's annual gathering to make horseradish sauce for Passover. "We put on this awful Jewish music," one kid said. "Then we cut this disgusting horseradish root," another added. "Then we put it in the blender," a third said. "Then we dance around the table!" cried the youngest.

Marshall had a big smile on his face as his grandchildren spoke. "Do you hear this?" he said. "It's disgusting! It's hokey! It's odd! 'Grandpa,' they say, 'do I have to eat this?' And I say, 'Yup, gotta do it.' Why? Because rituals have to be created. We can't sit back and hope they'll just happen. We have to go out and make them happen.

"What I'm doing," he continued, "is establishing something my grandchildren will do with their children. There's not a doubt in my mind they'll do it. They'll say, 'Oh, my grandfather used to make us do this, so this is what it means to be part of our family."

HUNGER GAMES

By this point, I already had two surprising takeaways about family dinner. First, eating together every night is not as important as so many people say it is. Second, what you talk about matters even more than what you eat. But these discoveries led to a third question: What should we be talking about when we finally sit down at the table?

The Kennedys are an example of one extreme way of conducting dinnertime colloquies. One of the more renowned dinner tables is the one around which Jack, Robert, and Ted Kennedy (and their siblings) were raised. The patriarch, Joseph Kennedy Sr., raged at anyone who was late. The family stood when Rose Kennedy came to the table, then, from the way the children later described it, their father ran a seminar. Sometimes he asked everyone to recite a poem. ("The Midnight Ride of Paul Revere" was his favorite.) Other times he assigned a child to make a presentation on a controversial topic or to present a short biography of a public figure. Kennedy wanted controlled conflict, and he would tip off others in advance, so they could bone up on the topic and grill the presenter.

While those tactics may seem draconian today, researchers have amassed abundant evidence that similar techniques serve children well. Tens of thousands of family meals have been recorded, transcribed, and parsed over the last twenty-five years, with every "um," "drink your milk," and "you stole my fork" analyzed. Using Marshall's standard that a good family ritual should be fun, hokey, and memorable, I set out to assemble a menu of constructive mealtime activities, which I assigned to different days of the week. I dubbed them "The Hunger Games."

Monday: Word of the Day

The first thing I did was devise a simple formula: 10-50-1.

10. Aim for ten minutes of quality talk per meal. A surprising amount of mealtime conversation is about getting everyone fed. "I know it's hot. Just blow on it." "Could I have some more chicken?" "Don't talk with your mouth full." Researchers have determined that each meal can yield about ten minutes of substantial conversation. As meager as that sounds, it's also something of a relief. Even I can manage that!

50. Let your kids speak at least half the time. Adults do most of those ten minutes of quality talk, taking up around two-thirds of the conversation. That leaves only a third for all the children put together, or less than three and a half minutes per meal. Since a primary goal of family meals is socializing children, try to get the kids to do as much talking as possible.

1. Teach your kids one new word every meal. A large vocabulary is a great boost in life. Research shows that children with parents in the lowest income bracket hear 616 words in a typical hour, while children from parents at the opposite end hear 2,153 words. That's a gap of eight million words a year. As Ellen Galinsky said, "The difference between knowing three thousand words and knowing fifteen thousand words when you arrive at kindergarten is enormous." Once kids enroll in school, that importance only grows. A child in grades three through twelve is expected to learn around three thousand words a year.

The good news, Galinsky says, is that you can help. No matter your income level, start by speaking more like yourself to your kids. If anything, you should go out of your way to use words that are unfamiliar to them. When adults speak with babies, we naturally simplify our speech and elevate our pitch. This technique has been proven to be effective. But once your baby begins to speak, the same technique has the opposite effect.

Here are three simple games that can help build vocabulary:

- Throw out a word like *fruit, bird,* or *white,* and have everyone at the table come up with as many related words as possible. This simple game has been proven to boost creativity in children.
- Introduce a prefix (*a-, bi-, dis-*) or a suffix (*-er, -able, -ite*) and have everyone create new words.
- Bring a newspaper, magazine, or catalog to the table and ask everyone to find a word they don't know. Googling at dinner is allowed!

Tuesday: Autobiography Night

A valuable skill parents can give a child requires no special classes, no elaborate equipment, and no expensive tutor. It's the ability to tell a simple story about their lives. Beginning around age five, children develop the tools to describe past events, but these skills must be practiced. The family table is the perfect theater. Ask your child to recall a memorable experience, either from that day or the past. Then follow up with what psychologists call "elaborative questions." *Who? What? When? Where? Why?* These open-ended questions build memory and identity.

Don't think this matters? Researchers in Boston compared American parents with those from Korea, China, and Japan and found that American mothers asked more elaborative questions of their three-year-olds, supplemented their children's answers with additional details, and provided positive feedback to encourage more storytelling. By contrast, Asian mothers focused more on discipline and hard work. When the researchers checked back with the same children a few years later, they found that the American children recalled more about their past than did the Asian students, who remembered more about their daily routines.

As Marshall Duke discovered about children who know their history, the more kids remember about their own families, the more self-esteem and confidence they exhibit. With that in mind, devote a night to having kids tell stories from their own past, their "autobiography" if you will—the day they scored two goals at soccer, the night their mother made those awesome chocolate chip cookies. This game would work particularly well the night before a big test or game, as scientists have found recalling high points from their own lives boosts children's self-confidence.

Wednesday: Pain Points

Family meals are one of the few times when members of different ages can be on an equal plane. Researchers at the University of California noticed that when family members tell stories at dinnertime, others members join in, add details, correct facts, and generally help move the story along. Psychologists at UCLA labeled this process "co-narration." While joint storytelling can be frustrating for everyone to sit through, it actually helps family members work better in teams. This is true also when children work with siblings and parents to solve puzzles or untangle difficult situations at mealtime.

How can you trigger such conversations? One night a week, ask everyone to bring up a "pain point." It could be a child who has to do a school project with someone he doesn't like or Mom who has to take her father to the eye doctor at the same time that a parent-teacher conference is scheduled. Suddenly everyone teams up to dissect the dilemma and devise possible solutions, all elements of good problem-solving.

Thursday: Word Game Night

Can't you just have fun at dinner? Sure, but choose your games smartly, and you can help your kids build verbal skills, too. Family meals are what scholars call "speech events." They are laboratories where children learn to love language and use it properly. I test-drove dozens of word games with my girls, along with their friends, cousins, aunts, uncles, and grandparents. These four worked consistently with people of all ages:

- *Thesaurus Thursday.* Say a common word—such as *run, quickly, happy*—and have everyone come up with as many alternatives as possible.
- *The Alliteration Game.* Go around the table and ask everyone to make a sentence in which all the words begin with the same letter.

- *Fill in the blank.* Everyone comes up with a sentence for others to complete, like "The sport I most would like to learn is _____" or "When I look up into the sky, I think _____."
- *What's the difference between?* Someone tosses out a question, such as "What's the difference between New York and California?" or "What's the difference between a window and a door?" Everyone at the table has to give a different answer.

Friday: Bad & Good

Every Friday night in my family, we play a dinnertime game I played in my family growing up. It's called "Bad & Good," and the rules are simple. Everyone goes around and says what happened bad to them that day, then everyone goes around and says what happened good. The only mandates: You must have at least one bad and one good every day, and you're not allowed to knock anyone else's answer.

I was pleased to discover a growing body of research that reinforces the benefits of this type of exercise, which scholars call "tell about the day" activities. By watching others, including Mom and Dad, navigate ups and downs in real time, children develop empathy and solidarity with those around them.

But not everyone likes these games. I was stunned to find a PhD student in Washington, DC, who wrote a broadside attack on "Bad & Good." Lyn Fogle observed a single dad having dinner with his two boys over many months. He had read about "Bad & Good" in an article I wrote and started playing the game with his kids. Fogle thought the dad sometimes forced the game on the children. I can relate to that. My siblings and I sometimes complained when our parents made us play "Bad & Good," and my girls sometimes complain today. When I met Fogle for coffee, she pointed out that when children push back against a parental tactic, you should let them win, just to increase their sense of control over their lives.

Fair enough, but what should I do with this beloved family tradition? I asked Marshall Duke what he thought before I said good-bye that Friday night.

"First of all," he said, "I agree that if children are feeling a real trauma about something, you shouldn't force them to talk about it. We have good data on this.

"Otherwise, I respectfully disagree with Ms. Fogle," he continued. "To me, the most important thing we can give our children, at dinnertime or anytime, is a sense of perspective. Children take their cues from us. When they're young and they hear a loud noise, they don't look where the noise came from, they look at us. If you're not upset, they're not upset.

"It's the same when they get older," Marshall continued. "When a child tells you something bad happened at school, sometimes the best thing to say is 'Pass the ketchup.' It's your way of saying, there's no reason to panic. You can handle this, just like I handled things like this. Then, once you've taken the panic out of the air, once you've put the ketchup on your french fries, then you can begin the conversation."

"And what if my child doesn't want to play one of these games?" I asked.

"You say, 'Sorry, dear. Sometimes I didn't want to play this game when I was your age, but your grandmother made me do it. This is just what it means to be part of our family. Now, would you pass me the potatoes? And tell me, What happened bad to you today?'"

3

BRANDING YOUR FAMILY

The Power of a Family Mission Statement

D AVID KIDDER WAS a bachelor dad for the weekend. His wife, Johanna, was traveling on business, leaving him with three young boys. By early Saturday afternoon, he was showing signs of losing his wits. Jack, their six-year-old, was jumping on the sofa. Stephen, their four-year-old, was tugging at the refrigerator door. And Lucas, not quite two, had disappeared.

David was sprinting through the ground floor of their house in Mamaroneck, New York, just steps from the Long Island Sound. Within seconds, he issued a plaintive cry from the bathroom. "Oh, Lukie, what are you doing?"

Lucas had stripped himself down to his diaper, unfurled half a roll of toilet paper, and was stuffing the garland—and his clothes— into the toilet.

"Come on, we've got to get you cleaned up," David said. He sent the two older boys to the backyard, scooped up Lucas, and scurried up two flights of stairs to get him a new diaper and change of clothes.

As I followed David and this train of testosterone from one room to the next, I noticed the same decorative item hanging prominently in the kitchen, in the boys' room, and in the parents' suite upstairs. It was a framed piece of paper, cobalt blue, with KIDDER in bright vermillion letters in the center. Immediately under it was the phrase DO UNTO OTHERS. And all around the page was an array of short phrases with bolded words—FAITH, PURPOSE, KNOWLEDGE, JUSTICE.

"That's our belief board," David said. "Everything we believe as a family is on that sheet of paper."

Once David distracted Lucas with a set of keys, he was able to sit down and explain. A serial entrepreneur, David had started four different companies in technology, urban renewal, and mobile advertising. He also created a popular series of books called *The Intellectual Devotional* and wrote a manual for entrepreneurs. He has ideas—lots of them—and they spill out of him with infectious delight.

"The main thing I've learned in twenty years," he said, "is that young companies typically fail because they don't communicate their values. You have a charismatic leader with a bunch of beliefs, but those beliefs don't translate to the rest of the company."

So David created a playbook for his latest company. He called it his OS, or operating system, and it included everything from the purpose of the company, the values of the company, how to run meetings, and how to use e-mail. When he started, he and his wife had no children; by the time he finished, they had three. That's when he began to wonder if there might be a similar operating system for being a parent.

"I heard this TED talk by a guy who spent a decade studying work-life balance," David said. "He concluded most people have either a great family and an average career, or an incredible career and an average family. The only way to have both is to apply the same level of passion and energy to your family as you do to your work. There can be no asymmetry."

David decided the way to achieve symmetry was to create a playbook for his family.

"I consider the belief board like an OS for our lives," he said. "Our marriage, our kids, everything. Would you like to see it?" He stood up to get one. "Oh, no," he said, suddenly looking around. "Lucas, where are you?"

THE 7 HABITS OF HIGHLY EFFECTIVE FAMILIES

Every parent I know worries about teaching values to their children. How do we make sure they understand that some beliefs are timeless? How do we build a healthy family culture to make sure those qualities are passed on to our kids?

Parents have wondered about these questions for generations, but academics have largely ignored them. From the early 1900s, family studies focused instead on the weaknesses within families. Beginning in the 1960s, however, a few outlier scholars started trying to identify the traits healthy families have in common. Herbert Otto, of the University of Utah, made one of the first lists. It included: shared religious and moral values; consideration; common interests; love and happiness of children; working and playing together. Similar attempts were made by academics in Minnesota, Alabama, and Nebraska.

By 1989, there were enough of these lists that the U.S. Department of Health and Human Services invited a dozen researchers to a conference in Washington, DC, and asked them to find common ground on this issue. As the organizers stated on the eve of the conference, "Researchers, policy makers, and the media have focused considerable attention on how some families are failing. Much less attention has been paid to strong, healthy families, and the characteristics that make them successful."

Each scientist in attendance had already published a list of the qualities successful families share. For the first time, though, organizers closely reviewed two dozen of these lists to see if they could establish consensus. According to them, it was remarkably easy. The master list contained nine items:

- *Communication.* Family members talk to one another often, in a manner that's honest, clear, and open, even when they disagree.
- *Encouragement of individuals.* Strong families appreciate each member's uniqueness while cultivating a sense of belonging to the whole.
- *Commitment to the family.* Members of successful families make it clear to one another, and to the world, that their allegiance to their family is strong.
- *Religious/spiritual well-being.* Researchers concluded that a shared value system and moral code were common among highly functioning families. But they said these values were not contingent on membership in any denomination or frequent attendance at worship services.
- *Social connectedness.* Successful families are not isolated; they are connected to the wider society, and they reach out to friends and neighbors in crisis.
- *Adaptability.* Strong families are structured yet flexible, and they adjust their structure in response to stress.
- *Appreciativeness.* People in strong families care deeply for one another, and they express their feelings often.

Even if some members are not naturally expressive, they communicate their emotions by doing meaningful things for others.

- *Clear roles.* Members of successful families are aware of their responsibilities to the group.
- *Time together.* Members of strong families spend time together doing things they enjoy.

The conference results were published in a study called "Identifying Successful Families." While nothing specific came out of the project, it did coincide with (and perhaps help legitimize) a much more popular effort in this space, written by Stephen Covey. A management consultant in Utah, Covey had one foot in corporate America (he had a Harvard MBA) and another in the leadership of the Mormon Church. Frustrated with what he called the decline of character in society, he wrote *The 7 Habits of Highly Effective People*, which was published in 1989. The book mixes business-style analytics with revival-style positive thinking. It's been called the most influential business book of the twentieth century.

Covey, the father of nine and grandfather of fifty-two, was even more passionate about his family. In 1997, he repackaged his original ideas into a book called *The 7 Habits of Highly Effective Families*. The habits were the same, but the messaging was slightly different.

- Habit 1. *Be proactive.* Become an agent of change in your family.
- Habit 2. *Begin with the end in mind.* Know the type of family you want to build.
- Habit 3. *Put first things first.* Make family a priority in a turbulent world.

- Habit 4. *Think "win-win."* Move from "me" to "we."
- Habit 5. *Seek first to understand . . . then to be understood.* Solve family problems through communication.
- Habit 6. *Synergize.* Build family unity while also celebrating differences.
- Habit 7. *Sharpen the saw.* Renew the family spirit through traditions.

This list is strikingly similar to the master list put together at the conference in Washington, DC. But Covey proposed an idea not found on any other list I've seen. In his work as a management consultant, Covey often asked his corporate clients to write a one-sentence answer to the question "What is this organization's essential mission or purpose and what is its main strategy to accomplish that?" He then asked executives to read their answers out loud. Participants were usually shocked by how much their answers differed from one another's. Covey then helped them create a more unified mission statement.

Covey was not alone, of course. Companies had been identifying their core values and crystallizing their missions for decades. Organizational behavior exploded in popularity in the 1980s by focusing on how companies can build an effective team culture. Books like *In Search of Excellence* by Tom Peters and Robert Waterman Jr., published in 1982, became global phenomena.

One of Covey's real innovations was applying a similar process to families. He suggested that families create a family mission statement. "The goal," he wrote, "is to create a clear, compelling vision of what you and your family are all about." He said the family mission statement was like the flight plan of an airplane. "Good families—even great families—are off track 90 percent of the time," he wrote. What makes them good is they have a clear destination in mind, and they have a flight plan to get there. As a result, when they face the inevitable turbulence and human error, they keep coming back to their plan.

Covey said creating his own family's statement was the most transforming event in his family's history. He and his wife first looked over their marital covenant, in which they had included ten abilities they wanted their children to have. They then asked their kids a series of questions, including "What makes you want to come home?" and "What embarrasses you about our family?" Next the kids wrote their own statements. Their teenage son Sean, a high school football star, wrote, "We're one heck of a family, and we kick butt!" Finally they ended up with their single sentence.

The mission of our family is to create a nurturing place of faith, order, truth, love, happiness, and relaxation, and to provide opportunity for each individual to become responsibly independent, and effectively interdependent, in order to serve worthy purposes in society.

Covey lists a dozen examples of other families' mission statements. They range from the homiletic: *Our family mission: To love each other . . . To help each other . . . To believe in each other . . . To wisely use our time, talents, and resources to bless others . . . To worship together . . . Forever.*

To the sly: *No empty chairs.*

I had a range of reactions to this exercise. On the one hand, I found the whole thing a little corny. It seemed cumbersome, heavy-handed, and a tad humorless. Also, the pressure of fitting everything into a single sentence seemed liked a good way to end up with a long-winded sentence. On the other hand, I kinda loved the idea. I'm corny! I also thought Covey's idea captured something inherently true: How can we ask our children to uphold our family's values if we never articulate what those values are?

Around this time Linda came home one day complaining about some branding problem she was having at work. She cofounded and runs an organization called Endeavor that supports high-impact entrepreneurs around the world. For years, she has worked with branding gurus on Madison Avenue who help the organization identify its central mission and core values. It was a powerful, even emotional, process for everyone on her team.

That's when it hit me: What if we tried something similar with our family? What if we tried to create our own brand, so to speak? It could include a family mission statement like the one Covey proposed. It could include a list of shared values, maybe even a swoosh or some other cool logo.

Linda pointed out that brands have an external purpose families don't exactly have. We weren't selling running shoes, after all. But as I had seen with Linda's organization, brands also have an internal purpose. They force everyone to sit down, talk about what they believe in, and articulate a common vision. Could that process help us define for our girls, and ourselves, the values we actually believed in? There was only one way to find out.

"I BELIEVE WORDS MATTER, EVEN A FEW WORDS"

Once David Kidder decided to create a playbook for his family, he and his wife stayed up one night creating a list of their shared values. They came up with thirty. Over a period of weeks, they whittled those down to a one-sentence manifesto.

The purpose of our lives is to contribute our unique, God-given gifts to have an extraordinary positive impact on the lives of others and the world.

"That's the entire purpose of being a Kidder, right there, in one definition," David said.

But they kept going and created an additional list of ten supporting qualities, what branding experts would call their core values. I asked David if he considered putting together a twenty-page booklet, like the one he has for his company. "No, because I think the hardest thing to do is to make something simple," he said. "Managers manage what happens; leaders create a reality and lead everyone toward it." He added, dryly, "Plus, it's easy to overdo these things."

The first value on the list was FAITH: *We pursue our INDIVIDUAL journey with God.* "We want our kids to know they are spiritual beings," David explained. "I can't choose to define who is God to them, but I want them to have a relationship with God. Because when things go wrong in their career, their marriage, their body— and things will go wrong—they're going to find themselves at some point alone with God."

The second value was FAMILY: *We love, respect, and are loyal to one another, and build family TRADITIONS.* "We know that one day our boys will grow up and may get pulled in different directions," David said. "So we set up very specific traditions we do every year—a big ski trip, a place we go every summer, a specific set of things we do every Christmas. We want to create grooves in their minds that attach them to our family."

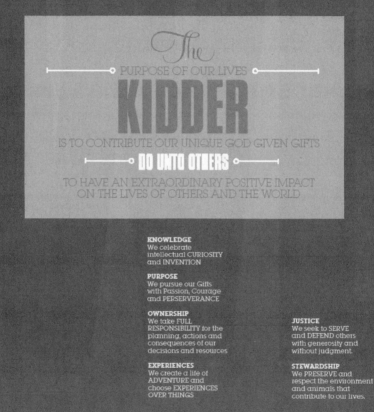

FAITH
We pursue our
INDIVIDUAL
Journey with God

FAMILY
We Love, Respect
and are Loyal to
Each Other, and build
Family and TRADITIONS

ATTITUDE
We are GRATEFUL,
FORGIVING, optimistic
and polite

HEALTH
We make good
decisions about how
we treat our minds
and bodies

The
PURPOSE OF OUR LIVES
KIDDER
IS TO CONTRIBUTE OUR UNIQUE GOD GIVEN GIFTS
DO UNTO OTHERS
TO HAVE AN EXTRAORDINARY POSITIVE IMPACT
ON THE LIVES OF OTHERS AND THE WORLD

KNOWLEDGE
We celebrate
intellectual CURIOSITY
and INVENTION

PURPOSE
We pursue our Gifts
with Passion, Courage
and PERSERVERANCE

OWNERSHIP
We take FULL
RESPONSIBILITY for the
planning, actions and
consequences of our
decisions and resources

JUSTICE
We seek to SERVE
and DEFEND others
with generosity and
without judgment.

EXPERIENCES
We create a life of
ADVENTURE and
choose EXPERIENCES
OVER THINGS

STEWARDSHIP
We PRESERVE and
respect the environment
and animals that
contribute to our lives.

Another entry that intrigued me said *We are* GRATEFUL, FOR-GIVING, *optimistic, and polite.* "We know that one of the best ways someone can be happy is to be grateful," David said. "So every night before the boys go to bed, we pray with them, and have them think about what they're grateful for. It's one of the greatest psychological triggers for having a healthy attitude."

I wondered if David worried that his belief board might be a bit too much. Was he creating some utopian ideal? "Maybe," he said, "but it's not meant to be that. It's meant to put in writing what we believe. Look, my dad is an amazing guy, but if you asked me what he believed as a parent, I wouldn't be able to tell you. I want my sons to know what their parents believed."

And what's the biggest benefit to having such a document?

"At the end of the day," he said, "you want your children to be truly happy. And that's what this board is trying to do. I believe words matter, even a few words. Maybe they'll matter when the kids are young; maybe they'll matter when they're eighty. Who knows? But this puts onto one piece of paper all the words that matter to their parents."

BUILT TO LAST

Before Linda and I began identifying our core values, I got some advice from two more people. The first is the country's leading expert on creating great company culture.

Jim Collins is a lifelong student of business management. He is the coauthor of *Built to Last: Successful Habits of Visionary Companies*, which was a best seller for six years, and he also wrote *Good to Great: Why Some Companies Make the Leap . . . and Others Don't*, which has sold more than five million copies.

A consistent theme in Collins's writing is that successful organizations identify what they excel at and exploit those strengths. Being a charismatic leader is easy, he wrote in *Built to Last*. It's far harder to build an organization "that can prosper far beyond the presence of any single leader."

As a parent, I found this idea particularly relevant—and worrying. Setting a good example for your children is hard enough, but how do you get them to internalize your values and carry them forward?

Collins, as it happens, is something of an extended member of my family, having been a lifelong mentor to my brother, who was his student at Stanford Business School. He was kind enough to talk to me about how his research can be applied to families.

"What I'm most interested in is any enduring, great human entity," Collins said. "That could be a religion, a company, a nation, or a family. And they all have this duality in them, which is 'preserve the core/stimulate progress.' What makes an entity enduring is that on the one hand, it's based on a set of core values. Those values are long lasting, and they provide a glue that transcends time and geography.

"And on the flip side," he continued, "while preserving that core, the entity is always struggling to evolve and remain relevant. That's what 'stimulate progress' is all about. It's a way of adapting your daily practices to make sure you're successful in the moment."

I loved this idea, especially because it sounded a lot like the agile family practices my family had already been experimenting with. Agile techniques are particularly effective at "stimulating progress." They offer a regular opportunity to tinker with the day-to-day mechanisms of our lives. But to be truly effective we had to move on to perhaps the harder side of the equation: "preserving the core." What advice did Collins have about that?

"If you're trying to identify your family's core values," he said, "the most important thing is to identify what your values actually are, not what you think they should be. If you come at this whole thing as 'we should have value X' and you don't, the process will fail. Only if they're deeply authentic can you hold on to them when it's inconvenient, and that's when you know it's core.

"A core value," he continued, "is something so central you would say, 'Even if it's harmful to us, we would still hold on to this value. Even if we had to pay penalties, even if we had to punish our children for violating it, even if we had to deny them something that would bring them pleasure, we would still hold to it.' That's what you need to keep in mind as you're making your family brand: It will work only if it stands for something."

KEEP MOVING FORWARD

The second person I talked to was Sean Covey. Sean is the fourth of Stephen Covey's nine children (the one who said his family's mission statement should be "We kick butt"). He's also the author of *The 7 Habits of Happy Kids* and is a leadership coach in the company started by his father. Sean turned out to be an ideal coach. A onetime quarterback at Brigham Young University, he's got a bit of the rebel in him. He told me that when his father first said they would be creating a family mission statement, he thought, This is one of Dad's weird things. He also said his personal mission in life was to travel with Led Zeppelin. But as a teenager he came to love the process of making the statement, and he later made one with his own eight children.

He offered me three pieces of advice.

One, keep it short. "The key is coming up with something

pithy and dramatic," he said. "Like three words, or one, or ten. I have a friend whose statement is like the U.S. Constitution. It works for him, but he's an exception." Sean's family chose a line from the animated film *Meet the Robinsons*: "Keep moving forward."

Two, make the drafting of it a special occasion. "You might want to go to a hotel, have a wonderful dinner, or do something that's a big deal so you create a memory associated with the process."

And three, post it in a prominent place. "I think it would be really meaningful for your daughters to grow up in a home where they could point to the mantel or the wall and say, 'This is what our family is about.'"

WHAT WORDS BEST DESCRIBE OUR FAMILY?

The time had come. First I made a list of values that might trigger a conversation between Linda and me. This was going to be an attempt to grease the wheel, because Linda was still somewhat reluctant to participate in this exercise. I could hear her saying to our girls, "Just another of Dad's weird things."

I picked a few words from *In Search of Excellence* and some from *Good to Great*. After reading that the KIPP charter schools, a network of college-preparatory public schools, started a pioneering program of "character reporter cards," I took all eight items on the list of qualities they evaluated for. And I took the entire list of 24 Character Strengths identified by Martin Seligman, the father of positive psychology. I ended up with eighty items, which I typed up in no particular order:

1. Agility
2. Courage
3. Passion
4. Curiosity
5. Inventiveness
6. Perseverance
7. Faith
8. Responsibility
9. Justice
10. Service
11. Stewardship
12. Purpose
13. Persistence
14. Positivity
15. Enthusiasm
16. Emotional
17. Excellence
18. Energetic
19. Excitement
20. Growth
21. Creativity
22. Imagination
23. Vitality
24. Uniqueness
25. Surprise
26. Independence
27. Community
28. Limitless
29. Diversity
30. Innovation
31. Entrepreneurial
32. Wow
33. Enthusiastic
34. Good citizenship
35. Trust
36. Integrity
37. Engagement
38. Commitment
39. Adventurous
40. Travel
41. Insatiable
42. Change
43. Question authority
44. Happiness
45. Pay it forward
46. Don't look back
47. Push through
48. Optimistic
49. Zest
50. Grit
51. Gratitude
52. Appreciative
53. Self-control
54. Politeness
55. Hope
56. Open-mindedness
57. Love to learn
58. Wisdom
59. Knowledge
60. Bravery
61. Kindness
62. Leadership

63. Forgiveness
64. Modesty
65. Prudence
66. Spirituality
67. Mindful
68. Being present
69. Discipline
70. Aggressive
71. Adaptive
72. Helpful
73. Cooperative
74. Supportive
75. Determined
76. Proactive
77. Protective
78. Quirky
79. Individualistic
80. Colorful

On a Friday night, I read the list to Linda, and we began cross-ing out items that didn't apply to us. Discipline is great, but a core family value? Question authority? We might come to regret that. Linda was surprisingly aggressive in knocking off items (includ-ing aggressive, which she crossed off twice). But I sensed we were turning a corner when she grabbed the paper out of my hands and scribbled additions into the margins. "We think outside the box." "We live lives of passion." She clearly gravitated toward the kind of upbeat sayings that most captured her voice.

Already the process seemed like a success. Not since we were married had we had such a direct conversation about the type of family we wanted to be.

Next we told Eden and Tybee we were having a pajama party that Saturday night, complete with popcorn and s'mores. They loved that idea, of course. When I discovered they'd never eaten popcorn that didn't come from a movie theater or a microwave, I went to the store to buy Jiffy Pop, a staple in my family growing up. As I was leaving, I remembered that Jiffy Pop has a high failure rate, so I decided I'd better have two. Sure enough, I burned the first one, filling the house with acrid smoke. We were well on our way to a memorable experience.

Once we assembled in Linda's and my bed, I taped a giant flip chart to the door. Then I read through the list of values, along with some questions I had modified from *7 Habits*.

What words best describe our family?
What is most important to our family?
What are our strengths as a family?
What sayings best capture our family?

We all took turns writing down answers. Soon enough, the sheet was filled with words: *teamwork, creativity, tell stories, be good people, travel games.* But then the energy shifted. The girls really came alive when they started shouting out our favorite expressions, including Linda's classic "We don't like dilemmas; we like solutions," and my recent addition, "We push through. We believe!" Then Eden cried out, "May your first word be *adventure* and your last word *love!*"

Suddenly the air sucked out of the room. When the girls were six weeks old, we held a small gathering to introduce them to our friends. I gave a brief toast, which ended with the wish, "May your first word be *adventure* and your last word *love.*" We spent years trying to make the first part come true. Every trip to the supermarket, drugstore, or playground became, "Let's go on an adventure!" Sure enough, *adventure* was one of the first words they mastered, their little lips curling charmingly around its syllables.

"That's it!" Linda said. "That's our family mission statement."

The girls started jumping up and down.

BRAND US

We weren't done yet. In the coming days, Linda and I tweaked the wording of a few phrases, and sifted through the other ideas to come up with twenty expressions that complemented the main one. "We dream undreamable dreams." "We are joy, rapture, yay!" "We are travelers not tourists." We pulled the girls back in and used our Olympic-style voting system to pare the list to ten. Jim Collins had warned me we shouldn't have more than five core values, but Linda insisted that we needed this many. We could always shrink it later. At least we were still shorter than the U.S. Constitution!

Now what? Sean Covey converted his statement into a crest and painted it on a wall in his family's home, but I knew Linda would never agree to that. Still, I wanted to do something visual. I asked around the neighborhood and came up with a short list of graphic designers. When one of them, Peter Kruty, wrote back that he was the father of two young kids and was intrigued, I made an appointment.

Peter suggested we come up with a symbol that captured our family. Linda and I walked through the house with the kids and discussed options, including a knickknack we had bought on a family trip and a quilt someone gave us when the girls were born. Finally we settled on a chambered nautilus I had given Linda when we got engaged. Soon we had a visual face for our family.

MAY OUR FIRST WORD BE

ADVENTURE

AND OUR LAST WORD

LOVE

We live lives of passion

We dream undreamable dreams

We are travelers not tourists

We help others to fly

We love to learn

We don't like dilemmas;
we like solutions

We push through. We believe!

We know it's okay to make mistakes

We bring people together

We are joy, rapture, yay!

So what exactly had we created?

First, we had a clear ideal. A central tenet of the family strengths movement, going back to the 1960s, has been a focus on what families should do and less on what they shouldn't do. A similar philosophy has recently been gaining currency in parenting circles. Alan Kazdin, a psychologist who heads the Yale University Parenting Center, has pioneered what he calls "parent management." His core idea is that parents should spend more time identifying and rewarding good behavior instead of endlessly punishing bad behavior.

This sounds simple, but it's not. Kazdin says parents need to specify the positive conduct they want to see more of. "You guys are doing so well playing together today!" "Great job, sticking with that math homework." Even more important, parents need to create a home environment where children know exactly what's expected of them.

The family brand is a clear, articulate vision of what we want our family to be and what values we want our children to uphold.

Second, we had a visual identity. One lesson learned by the first generation of happiness research is that expressing gratitude is a powerful way to feel happier. Gratitude journals, writing notes of appreciation, and counting your blessings (as David Kidder does with his kids) are all proven to increase happiness. But a less well-known technique has an even greater effect. It's called visualization.

Laura King, a professor at the University of Missouri-Columbia, asked subjects to spend a few minutes every day writing a narrative description of their "best possible selves." The experience dramatically boosted their optimism. When researchers compared that technique to simply expressing gratitude, the visualization exercise had a more immediate and more sustained impact on people's well-being.

Creating a family identity is the collective equivalent of imagining your best possible self. It forces you to conceive, construct, then put in a public place a written ideal of what you want your family to be. It may not be for everyone, but for us it was the most revealing and most exciting thing we had found to express our "best possible family."

Finally, we created a touchstone. A few weeks after we finished our document, Tybee's teacher called. Our daughter had been gossiping with another child about a classmate. Visions of teenage mean girls flashed before our eyes. Unsure what to do, Linda and I sat down and talked with Tybee. This was the first time we had turned my office into the "principal's office."

Tybee looked at us warily. Linda described the telephone call, and Tybee carefully said that two other girls had started this, and she had just gone over to listen. Linda asked if any part of our recent conversation about values seemed to fit here. Tybee cocked her head, picked up a copy of our poster on my desk, and pointed to one of the entries, "We bring people together." Suddenly we had a way into the conversation.

A month later, the girls got into some dispute at dinner about the last piece of chocolate in the Tupperware. The fight quickly deteriorated into screams and insults. Linda stepped in. "What does Mommy like to say?" Eden thought for a second, then sprinted to the document on the mantel, pointing to the line "We don't like dilemmas; we like solutions."

Jim Collins, in a way, had predicted this outcome. When I asked him where he thought this exercise might take us, he described a self-imposed clarity for dealing with life. "And one thing we know about life," he continued, "is it's going to hit you in random and unexpected ways—some good, some bad." If you don't have your own frame, he said, you'll be whipsawed by life. If you do, you're more likely to succeed.

PART TWO

TALK. A LOT

4

FIGHT SMART

The Harvard Handbook for Resolving Conflict

THE FIGHT GOES something like this. Linda walks into my office soon after the girls are asleep. She's had a bad day. She was late getting out of the house with them this morning; she had a tense meeting at work; she had no luck finding a sitter for Saturday night; and now she has to prepare a presentation for tomorrow.

My day hasn't been much better. I dealt with an overflowing toilet all morning; my conference call went poorly; I spent an hour on the phone with my dad's doctor; and now I have to stay up past midnight to meet a deadline.

"So do we have things to talk about?" she asks. You know that look you sometimes get from your spouse, the one that says with a wink and a grin, "Are you coming to bed early?" This isn't that look. This is the look that says, "I need a colonoscopy?"

"Yes," I say. "We have lots to talk about."

She sits down and crosses her arms. I put my feet on the desk. Cocked in these poses, we look like two prizefighters, stripped down and oiled up, waiting for the slightest wisecrack to send us both flying into a tizzy.

I call it the 7:42 P.M. fight. It's the time of the day when we deal with the detritus of our lives. Who's waking up early with the kids? Who's reserving the plane tickets for Thanksgiving? Who's buying milk for the pancakes this weekend? Who's waiting at home for the cable guy? Who's ordering the new shin guards? Who gets to work out tonight? And, by the way, am I ever going to see you naked again?

Tonight's installment is about the girls' upcoming birthday party. Linda wants to serve pizza; I want to serve pretzels.

"But we have to give everybody lunch," she says. "Parents will expect it. And besides, you never go to birthday parties, what do you know?"

"But we're already spending a fortune on the puppet show," I say. "Pizza is unoriginal. And the party starts at ten A.M., anyway. Can't we just give them snacks?"

After fifteen minutes of back-and-forth, Linda crosses her arms and stares at the ceiling. I throw up my hands and shake my head. Finally she gets up and huffs out of the room, mumbling just loud enough for me to hear, "I really wanted to watch *The Voice* tonight."

As soon as she's gone I slink back in my chair. There has to be a better way, I think. How can we have a happy family if every night we guarantee ourselves a bout of unhappiness?

LOVE IS IN THE EYES

Fighting. Every family does it. The ones who do it smarter are more likely to succeed.

All families have conflict. But twenty-five years of research shows that whom you fight with, what you fight about, and how often you fight matters far less to your family's health than how you fight. Studies have confirmed that there's no reason for fighting within a family to overwhelm positive interactions, as long as the distress is isolated, addressed, and used as a source of growth.

There are other encouraging signs. A major study on marital happiness from the University of Tennessee showed that couples who learn to negotiate are happier in their marriages and their jobs. So how can we become better negotiators? I picked up a few tips from my research that began to reshape how Linda and I quibbled at home.

First, there's when. Deborah Tannen points out in her book *I Only Say This Because I Love You* that fights within families often erupt when people are either coming together or saying good-bye. Getting kids out the door in the morning and coming together at the end of the day are particularly vulnerable times.

In the late 1980s, two psychologists in Chicago gave beepers to the moms, dads, and children in fifty families, pinged them at random times of the day, and asked them what they were doing and how happy they were. Their goal was to obtain an emotional photo album of the American family. They determined that the most highly charged time of the day was between 6:00 P.M. and 8:00 P.M. Men often claim they are stressed at this time, but according to these psychologists, these protests are really "theater," because men actually enjoy coming home to their families. Women, by contrast, really are stressed at this time, especially if they're coming from work. They see these hours as the brunt of their infamous "second shift" of housework and caretaking.

So 7:42 P.M. is the *worst possible time of day* for Linda and me to be having a difficult conversation.

Second is language. Turns out there's a huge body of knowledge about the words people use when talking to one another, and pronouns are the canary in the coal mine of conflict. James Pennebaker, a psychologist at the University of Texas and the author of *The Secret Life of Pronouns*, says if a couple uses first-person pronouns—*I* or *we*—it's a sign of a healthy relationship. *We* is a particularly good pronoun because the "we-ness" is a mark of high togetherness. The second-person singular—*you always say that* or *you never do this*—is a mark of unhappiness and poor problem-solving. The takeaway: One of the ways to stop fighting is to stop saying *you*.

Third is length. While everyone agrees some conflict is inevitable within families, fights shouldn't last too long. In fighting, all the good stuff comes out at the beginning. John Gottman of the University of Washington found that the most important points in any argument can be found in the opening minutes. After that, he says, people often just repeat themselves at higher and higher decibels. Think of a fight as a boxing match: The first three minutes set the tenor for the entire bout. After that, you might as well retreat to your own corners.

Fourth concerns the body. Boxing is also a good analogy for the physical part of quarreling. Everything—from how you sit to how you sway, from the way you bob your head to your facial expressions—plays a role in family disputes. Eyes were the biggest revelation to me. Researchers in Indiana spent years videotaping marital spats, carefully monitoring the twitching of noses, raising and lowering of eyebrows, and pursing of lips. They checked back with the couples four years later and determined that one gesture, above all, predicted marital tension: eye rolling. Rolling your eyes is a sign of contempt and a surefire predictor of trouble to come.

But eyes aren't the only thing that conveys disrespect: Shifting in your seat, sighing, and stiffening your neck do, too. By contrast, the best ways to ease a tense conversation are to lean forward, smile a lot, and nod your head. When all else fails, mimic the other person's positive gestures. Most people think they're right, so if you're doing what they're doing, they'll think you're right, too!

PIZZA V. PRETZELS

Since negotiation is considered the best model for how couples should navigate their relationship, I thought, Why not seek advice from the best negotiators in the world?

Two weeks later I was sitting in a ballroom at the Charles Hotel in Cambridge, Massachusetts. It was the start of a three-day seminar hosted by the Harvard Negotiation Project. These are the folks who get called in to handle the toughest disputes in the world—nuclear test ban treaties, Israeli-Palestinian peace talks, nationwide train strikes in Brazil. The group's cofounder, Bill Ury, stepped to the front of the room.

A wiry, affable man with thick black hair and widely gesticulating arms, Ury, along with Roger Fisher, pretty much invented the field of negotiation studies in the 1970s. Their book *Getting to Yes* was published in 1981 and has sold more than five million copies.

Ury looked out at the audience of around 150 people and asked what sorts of conflicts they were facing. One man described a border dispute between two countries in Latin America; a woman mentioned a $150 million deal with a Chinese manufacturer; another woman said a three-year deal with the Teamsters. I slowly raised my hand.

"My wife and I are fighting over whether we should serve pizza or pretzels at our daughters' sixth birthday party."

The audience erupted into applause.

"Perfect," Ury said. "You've all come to the right place."

Ury then asked everyone how much of the day they spend negotiating. The answers ranged from a half to three-quarters. "Let's say it's fifty percent," he said. "The point is, everyone negotiates all day every day. You discuss a raise with your boss. You strike a deal with a client. You negotiate with your spouse about where to go for dinner and with your child about when the lights go out.

"Now let me ask you another question," he continued. "How much time do you spend practicing negotiating?" Nobody spoke.

"Think about that!" he said. "Negotiating is something you do at least half of your life, yet you never work at it. I want you to practice negotiating like you practice a sport."

He then outlined his philosophy of "principled negotiation." While some of the techniques were clearly more suited to large-scale showdowns, most were applicable to the problems families face every day. Ury's philosophy is based on a five-step process:

- Isolate your emotions.
- Go to the balcony.
- Step to their side.
- Don't reject, reframe.
- Build them a golden bridge.

"The secret to negotiations is that it's very hard to get someone to change their mind," Ury began. There are two approaches: direct pressure, from the outside; or indirect pressure, from the inside. For families, indirect pressure is the only real option, since we don't have the option of never seeing the other party again.

Either way, the biggest hurdle we face is not the other person and their emotions, Ury said, it's ourselves and our emotions. He offered a simple way to prevent our emotions from getting in our way. It's called "Go to the balcony."

"When things are starting to go wrong in an encounter, imagine the negotiation taking place on a stage," Ury said. "Then allow your mind to go to the balcony overlooking that stage. From there you can see the macro view. From there you can start to calm down. From there you can exert some self-control."

As someone who occasionally loses control, I found this idea appealing. Ury recommended a number of ways of getting to the balcony. You can call for a five-minute break, you can say you need a cup of coffee or a trip to the bathroom, you can ask to reconvene in the morning.

"Remember, the point of a negotiation is not to reach an agreement," he said. "If that's your goal, you'll give in too early. The point is to serve your interests, and the only way to do that is to stay calm."

Once you've passed through this hurdle, you can go back to the stage and begin resetting the scene. Ury recommends switching things up a bit. Maybe a change of venue is a good idea, or a change of clothes. The most important thing is to begin looking at the other side's point of view.

"The ability to step to the other person's side is one of the best things you can do as a negotiator," Ury said. "Remember, you're trying to change their mind. How can you change their mind if you don't know where their mind is?" This doesn't mean making concessions. It just means putting yourself in their shoes—asking questions, trying to figure out where they're coming from.

"It sounds easy," he continued, "but it's not. The main thing it requires is listening."

The Harvard blueprint for negotiation can be divided into two halves. The first—go to the balcony, step to their side—is about removing the emotion from the situation. That part begins with another Ury classic: "Don't reject, reframe." The second half is moving toward a solution.

"One of the great powers you have in negotiations is the power to move the spotlight," Ury said. "You want to move it from the rigid positions both sides are starting with to new options you come up with together. The goal is to expand the pie before dividing it." He recommends asking open-ended questions. *Can you think of any alternative approaches?* Or *Do you have any other out-of-the-box ideas?*

Now you're finally ready to "build the golden bridge" to resolution. Ury recommends sitting side by side and writing down all the possible solutions, starring the most promising ones and eliminating others. "If you get stuck, go back to the list," he said.

Ury's last piece of advice went straight to couples.

"Remember, this isn't the last time you'll be negotiating with the other party," he said. "Your goal is not to leave either side embittered."

THE CASE OF THE FUZZY SOCKS

So would this technique actually work in families, either parents negotiating with each other or parents negotiating with kids? Let's start with the kids.

Two hours west of Cambridge is the small town of East Longmeadow, Massachusetts. This quaint village says it's the home of "a world-famous intersection, where seven streets intersect without a traffic light." It's also the home of Joshua Weiss, Adina Elfant, and their three daughters, Kayla (eleven), Aylee (nine), and Talya (five). Josh is the cofounder of Harvard's Global Negotiation Initiative and works closely with Bill Ury in the Middle East. Adina directs community learning at a nearby college. On the Saturday I arrived, they were confronting a negotiation crisis of their own. The source was not warheads, warlords, or warmongering. It was much more delicate.

Fuzzy socks.

Aylee's fuzzy socks had holes in them, so she asked Kayla if she could borrow hers for a week until she got new ones. Kayla said yes. Of course, at the end of the week, Aylee still didn't have new socks, so she asked for another night. Kayla agreed but five minutes later changed her mind. A fight erupted.

Luckily a peace negotiator was nearby. Talya stepped between her two older sisters. "Hold it!" she said. "Aylee, you go ahead and say your stuff. Then, Kayla, you say yours afterward. And don't interrupt."

Why did she do that?

"I don't know," she said. "My dad does it a lot when we get into fights, so I kind of picked it up from him."

On their first date years ago, Josh asked Adina how she dealt with conflict. "I never thought about it. I suppose I let things roll off my back," she said.

"In my experience, things don't roll," he said. "They just sit there, building up, until they become a crushing weight."

Josh said he preferred to deal with conflict head on by talking things through and to keep on talking until everyone was happy with the resolution. Eventually, when Adina and Josh started dating, the two of them had to reach a compromise about how to deal with disagreements. When issues arise, Adina gets to retreat and process her thoughts, and she returns when she's ready to talk.

Josh and Adina tried to let their daughters figure out their own way of doing this. Each of the girls had a slightly different way of responding to conflict. But their techniques all reflected what their parents had taught them from the world of negotiation studies.

Talya, the first grader, was the most straightforward. Beyond separating combatants, she was fond of rock-paper-scissors. "It's a start," Josh said.

Aylee, in fourth grade, had more tricks. She used a technique called Stop, Think, Control—a child's equivalent of going to the balcony, in which you get control of your feelings then return to the stage. She was also old enough to begin considering the other person's feelings. "There was this new girl last year who was being mean to me," she said. "I asked my mom and dad what to do, and they said, 'Think about it from her point of view. Maybe she doesn't have a lot of friends. Why not be nice to her?' I tried that one day, and it worked!"

Kayla, in sixth grade, had already mastered some sophisticated adult problem-solving tricks. For starters, she loved going to the balcony. "When I fight with my sisters," she explained, "I say, 'Look, I don't want to talk to you right now because I'm mad. Maybe we can talk later.' And I'll push away from the table and go to my room."

Even more striking was her response to a six-month standoff with her parents. In the spring, Kayla was invited to be on the traveling team for gymnastics, which required a commitment to two four-hour practices a week in a neighboring town. Her parents were concerned about her schoolwork, the logistical strain on the family, and her chores. They told her she first had to prove she could handle her responsibilities.

"When they first told me I couldn't do it," she said, "I got so mad I called my dad a 'dream crusher.' That's my nickname for him now whenever we get into fights."

"Great nickname!" I said. "So how long did you stay mad?"

"I found out in June, and I was still mad when school started. But I went to him beforehand and said 'Why?' and 'What can I do to join the team?' He told me if I got good grades and kept my room clean, I could join the team.

"At first I thought they were being mean," she continued, "but then I realized it was four hours at the gym, and I needed to figure out how to manage my gymnastics and my homework and stuff. There were certain classes I struggled with last year and I really had to work extra hard at them."

"In Bill Ury–speak," Josh said, "when she asked 'Why?' I thought that was terrific. She was stepping to our side, trying to understand our interests, which is a fundamental part of negotiation. We had explained our views before, but she was too mad to hear them. Now she was able to listen."

"Look, I was skeptical these techniques could work with the girls," Adina said. "I said, 'That's your work, Josh.' But I've noticed, as Kayla has gotten older, she has become a really good advocate for herself. Her teacher says she's a leader at school. And she's become especially good at addressing my concerns." Adina talked about a recent incident that involved Kayla asking for a cell phone. She knew her parents were concerned she would spend too much time texting with her friends, so she said she would let them check her phone every week.

Josh added, "If you ask me, as someone who's done negotiations for twenty years, I believe these strategies may be better suited for a family than a workplace. One of the things that happens in the world is that people try to avoid conflict. Whereas at home, you can't. You'll end up getting divorced or becoming estranged from your kids. Keep in mind, the hardest part of any negotiation is agreeing to start it. Once you've gotten past that emotional barrier, the solutions usually present themselves."

That's exactly what happened with Kayla and the traveling gymnastics team. "Six weeks into the school year, I went to my parents and said, 'Okay, I did my part, now you do yours.' Mom and Dad both e-mailed my teacher and asked them if I was doing good—"

"Doing well," her father interrupted.

"Doing well," she repeated, and everyone laughed. "And my teacher said I had good grades." A big smile crossed her face. "When my parents told me, I started jumping up and down and screaming. I think I did a cartwheel! And I joined the team."

CAMP DAVID FOR COUPLES

So what about couples? I asked Bill Ury how his techniques could help grown-ups negotiate with each other.

He pointed out that societies had always been top-down, with a paterfamilias making all the decisions. "But now we're in a period of transition," he said. "There's a spread of democracy in the world; organizations are becoming flatter. The same thing is happening with families, where more people want to participate in decisions that affect them. That means everything is negotiable. *Who does the dishes?* That wasn't a question a generation ago. Ours is the first generation where continuous negotiation is the norm."

"Does this mean I shouldn't be surprised I don't know the new rules?" I asked.

"No one knows the new rules! There's a lot more fluidity, agility, and reinvention going on. Focus on your 7:42 P.M. conversation with Linda and realize, first of all, that you're a pioneer. Once you do that, you'll be a little more forgiving."

"Linda will certainly like the sound of that," I said. "But what then?"

"Go to the balcony. You can do that individually, but better to do it with her. Go to your version of Camp David, take a little time to decompress. Then begin to design a constitution."

"A what?"

"A working plan. What you need is a decision-making system for your family. What are the rules that govern these conversations every night?" He recommended several.

- Anyone can call for a five-minute break at any time.
- When someone comes home, they get fifteen minutes by themselves.
- Pick alternate weeks in which one person gets to be right all the time.

(When I told that to Linda, she leapt at the idea. "You mean I get to be right twenty-six times a year?")

But what happens if we make all these rules, and we still disagree?

"You reframe," Ury said. "She's got a position: We should serve pizza. You've got a position: We should serve pretzels. That's two positions. So you begin asking problem-solving questions. *Help me understand why you want pizza.*"

We started ticking through Linda's reasons. Other families do it. She doesn't want to look thrifty. Ury pressed me to go deeper. She wants to appear generous. As a working mother, perhaps she wants to be perceived as an active parent?

"Now we're getting somewhere," Ury said. "She wants to be a mom. She wants to be a member of the community. These are real identity issues, and once you drill down to that level, she can start to relax. 'Okay, you're hearing me.' Then she can begin to negotiate."

"But what about my positions?"

"Yours have to do with identity, too. You don't want to be conventional. It offends you to go with the crowd, and pizza represents the crowd. When all that comes out, you begin to realize: That's why you're together as husband and wife. She's probably drawn to that part of you that's creative. You're probably drawn to that part of her that wants to be a good mom. Once you have that breakthrough, you can start solving the problem, and the first thing you're going to realize is: *It ain't so important. Look what we're putting ourselves through!*"

So there you have it. At the end of the day, Linda and I weren't arguing about pizza v. pretzels. We were arguing about who we were. Or, more precisely, we were arguing about trying to feel understood.

"Do you remember that question I asked at the beginning of the seminar?" Ury asked. "'How much time every day do you spend negotiating?' Everyone says it's more than fifty percent. If you're just using negotiation as a means to an end, you've just wasted fifty percent of your life. The point is: Negotiation is the stuff of life. We think of it as driving us apart, but if you engage in it correctly, it can actually bring us closer together."

TRASH TALKING

Back at home, Linda and I set out to apply what I had been learning. We got off to a promising start. We cut back on our 7:42 P.M. talks, choosing to move our logistics sessions later, to a time more compatible with our eating, exercising, and decompressing. For my part, I tried to de-escalate disputes more quickly and ask for a time-out when I felt myself about to lose it. I loved the idea that fights should take no longer than three minutes, so I tried saying everything up front, kind of like speed-dating, only for quarreling. But I found this hard. Linda has the tendency to bail out of fights quickly, but her peacemaking usually frustrates me. "Wait, I'm not done arguing yet," I want to say. "I've got seven more points to make!"

For her part, Linda said she was particularly chastened by all the reports about body language. I would often see her squirming as she struggled not to cross her arms or roll her eyes. I found it endearing, for the most part, as it reminded me of my daughters trying to hold in their pee.

But all this momentum didn't necessarily spill over to the rest of the day.

One morning I walked into the kitchen as Linda was preparing breakfast. She was searching in the fridge for some yogurt, when suddenly she went into a jag against all the food that had overstayed its welcome. She started madly purging, like one of those old Soviet dictators cleansing the politburo after a coup. She would pick up a container of cheese, chutney, or olives, glance at the date stamped on the package, and if the date was coming up in, say, the next few days, she'd summarily toss it in the trash.

"Wait a minute," I said. "That's still good. The kids will eat it. I'll eat it." I pointed out that I eat lunch at home every day.

"But haven't you seen all these stories in the news?" she said. "Food illnesses are everywhere." And besides, she added, "Stop being so cheap. I'm tired of scraping the bottom of the strawberry jelly jar."

Suddenly our 7:42 P.M. fight had been replaced by a 7:42 A.M. one!

This time, though, I was prepared. "Let's talk about this later," I said. After she left, I took the opportunity to have some balcony time. I scoured the Internet for facts to back up my case, and there was an abundance of them. The National Institutes of Health reported that Americans throw away nearly 40 percent of all the food the country produces. Watchdog groups noted that the vast bulk of the dates that appear on food packaging (excluding milk containers) were put there by manufacturers, who alone determine their rules. Just as I expected: Expiration dates are just a corporate ploy to get us to buy more food. Surely Linda would have to agree with me now.

That night, after dinner, we picked up the topic. I began by stepping to her side, as Ury instructed. "I know you do the bulk of the shopping," I said. "I know you work hard to get the girls to eat healthfully." Then I presented my brief, noting that if we kept food around longer, we could save money; she'd cut down on shopping time; and the kids would learn to be inventive with leftovers. As Ury had encouraged me, I was pointing out that we weren't just arguing about expiration dates, we were arguing about money, time, and creativity. I made an impressive case, I must say.

Linda, to her credit, also used some of Ury's tactics. As always, she was a master at stepping to my side. "I appreciate that you eat lunch at home every day." Then she reiterated her passion that a healthy home is the key to a healthy family.

Finally she asked for some time to think of a compromise. This seemed to fit Ury's model of "building a golden bridge," so instead of countering ("Did I tell you about the case of the 1.6 million bottles of salad dressing with fraudulent expiration dates?") I agreed. We parted; I was wary but optimistic.

The next morning I discovered her solution. When I opened the refrigerator, I instantly noticed the change. Linda had rearranged the entire thing, cleaned the shelves, and introduced a new system. Her food (kale, baba ghanouj) and the children's (string cheese, 2 percent milk) were carefully organized, date checked, and perky. Mine (pickled okra, four-day-old shrimp) was quarantined in a highly visible corner, blackballed, silently calling out, "You'll be having me for lunch today." I laughed. Sometimes you can win the negotiation, but still lose the fight.

5

THE BUCK STARTS HERE

The Warren Buffett Guide to Setting an Allowance

S UNDAY NIGHT IS money night in the Dwight household. As dusk falls in manicured Palo Alto, Selina, a biogenetics researcher, is watching the end of a San Jose Sharks hockey game. Bill, a software engineer, is barbecuing chicken in the backyard. Will, the seventeen-year-old, dressed in a Navy SEALs T-shirt, is just returning from the gym. His younger brothers, Peyton, the fifteen-year-old, and Quentin, the twelve-year-old, are upstairs playing video games. Two other siblings, Haley, a girl, and Taylor, a boy, are off at college. With so much testosterone, sports talk, muscle shirts, and grill mitts in the Dwight house, it almost seems like a clubhouse.

After dinner was served and grace shared, Bill turned to money talk. Bill grew up in Silicon Valley, the son of one of the area's earliest engineers. He's a tall, sandy-haired man with an all-American build and a genial but earnest manner that made him seem like the captain of the golf team. After high school, Bill went east to the university, married Selina, his college sweetheart, then returned to California, where he went to work at Oracle, the software company.

By 2005, his oldest children started bugging him about money, so he created an Excel spreadsheet to track how much allowance he gave them every week, when he fell behind for some reason, or when he spotted them a few bucks at the mall. Soon, though, he got tired of them nagging him all the time about their balances.

So one weekend he sat down and built a modest Web site where his kids could keep tabs on their own money. Now when his children badger him, "Dad, can you buy me an iPod?," he simply says, "No, but if you log in, you can see how long you have to save before you can buy one yourself." He also started docking the kids for misbehavior, everything from burping loudly at the dinner table to racking up overages on their cell phones.

"I grew up with means," he said, "and I always felt a little guilty about that. It robs you of the ability to be self-made. I wanted my children to understand the power of limitations."

When enough friends started asking to use his system with their kids, Bill quit his job and launched FamZoo, a Web site that helps parents teach kids how to manage money. The site lets parents set up a virtual bank to help them manage allowances, design budgets, and encourage charitable giving. Parents can also create artificially high interest rates—say, 5 percent a month—to encourage savings. Bill calls it financial training wheels, and of the handful of similar sites that have popped up on the Web in recent years, FamZoo is considered one of the more flexible and fun.

With five children, Bill understands the importance of being adaptable. One of his kids is a spendthrift, another a tightwad; one rides horses, another rides (and mangles) trick bikes; one splurges on online virtual reality games, another on clothes; and one was trying to talk his parents into letting him buy a firearm.

"Okay, everybody," Bill said cheerily when dinner was nearing completion. "Time to review our spending for the week." Jeers went up around the table as Dad pulled out his iPhone. "Oh, and I'm thinking the time has finally come to up the penalty for not making your bed. One dollar just isn't cutting it anymore." More groans. "So, who's going first?"

THE BANK OF MOM AND DAD

I grew up in a family business. From the time I was old enough to tie my own shoes, I was asked to get up on Saturday mornings, walk to my grandparents' house, eat scrambled eggs and fresh-cut french fries made by my grandmother, then head off to work with my grandfather. In a one-story, brick office in downtown Savannah, I learned how to type, file, fill out ledgers, and take small payments from the people who lived in the single-family homes built by my father and grandfather. My hands shook as I took the carefully folded bills, laid them on the counter, made change, and wrote out a receipt.

My grandfather stood over my shoulder. "This is my grandson," he boasted. I was paid a few dollars for a morning's work. To this day, Saturday mornings still feel like work time to me.

Given this background, I was looking forward to writing about families and money, but I was surprised to see how little scholarly writing there is about this subject. Sure, there are plenty of popular books, from *Rich Dad, Poor Dad* to *The Millionaire Next Door*. But I found only a limited number of papers on kids and money, couples and money, and families and money. For whatever reason, the family piggy bank is persona non grata in academia.

The few studies that have been done present a counterintuitive narrative. All experts agree that parents do a lame job of talking to their kids about money. A study of over 650 British parents found 43 percent taught their children very little about financial matters. Other studies have shown that children don't know what money is, don't know where it comes from, and don't know what to do with it once they have it. One report found that American kids can't properly make change until they are teenagers.

Although parents aren't talking directly to their kids about money, they are passing on their attitudes on the topic. Research shows that if kids see their parents feeling insecure about money, they internalize those fears. If kids see their parents being materialistic, they develop those same cravings. And if kids see their parents discussing financial matters responsibly and planning for the future, they follow those behaviors, too.

Of course, parents' first attempt to teach financial responsibility is to give an allowance. The custom started in the late nineteenth century when child labor laws made it illegal to hire children, and that restricted their access to money. These days, at least 75 percent of children get an allowance by the ninth grade. Most Western parents begin this when their kids are between six and seven, and start with about a dollar a week. Initially, two-thirds of that money is spent on candy and other sweets. As girls get older, they also tend to buy clothes, shoes, and magazines, while boys often buy more food and computer games.

Still, even some basic questions about how to handle allowances remained. I set out to answer them for Linda and me.

Question #1: Does an allowance actually teach children anything constructive?

An allowance is supposed to engender responsibility about money. The first major study of the matter, fifty years ago, supported that idea, finding that kids exposed to money early on do have more knowledge about how to manage it later. But a more recent study, in 1990, found that children did not view an allowance as an educational experience; they viewed it as an entitlement.

Getting an allowance does give kids practice with money, something they don't learn about in school. In 1991, researchers in Toronto gave six-, eight-, and ten-year-olds four dollars—either in the form of a credit card or in cash—to spend in an experimental toy store. They were allowed to take home any unspent money. Children who already got an allowance at home spent the same amount in the cash and credit card situations. Children who did not get an allowance spent much more with a credit card. Afterward, the children were asked to name the prices of the items they bought. Children who received an allowance scored higher on the test, leading the researchers to conclude that having an allowance does teach important financial skills.

After reading this, Linda and I tempered our expectations about what the girls might learn from having an allowance but decided to give them one anyway. We opted for another common practice: one dollar per week, per year of age. At six years old they would get six dollars a week, the next year seven dollars, and so on. That would give the girls a bigger pool to experiment with.

Question #2: Should the money be a handout or tied to chores around the house?

There's huge disagreement on this. Some parents feel they don't get free money, so why should their children? Plus, having children do chores for their allowance helps develop a work ethic. Others feel chores are part of day-to-day life and don't deserve compensation. "Sorry, you don't get to choose whether you set the table; it's part of being a member of our family."

No one's examined this question directly, but work in the larger field of behavioral economics does shed light. Daniel Pink, in his best-selling book *Drive*, concluded that contingent rewards—if you do this, then you'll get that—don't truly motivate people. He quoted a psychologist who reviewed 128 studies and found "tangible rewards tend to have a substantially negative effect on intrinsic motivation." In other words, people focus more on the reward—in this case, the money—than on why they should do the chore—in this case, because they are part of the family. As Pink noted, "That's why schoolchildren who are paid to solve problems typically choose easier problems and therefore learn less. The short-term prize crowds out the long-term learning."

For me, the most persuasive results came from Kathleen Vohs, a business professor at the University of Minnesota, whose work shows that thinking about money makes people work harder, but it also causes them to be less generous. As Vohs concluded, "When people are reminded of money, they don't behave pro-socially; they prefer to be alone rather than with others; and they're much more interested in an insulated orientation toward the world."

That was enough to scare us off from making money a daily argument in our house. Linda and I give our daughters chores to do every day, and we give them an allowance, but we don't link the two.

(One more insight I got from behavioral economics involved whether to bribe my kids. Is it acceptable to offer children money in return for special behavior, like letting your parents sleep late on Sunday morning or not throwing a tantrum at Grandma's house? Daniel Kahneman, in *Thinking Fast and Slow*, shattered conventional wisdom on this topic. He found that people are more driven to avoid losses than to achieve gains. In other words, the fear of *not* reaching a goal is stronger than the desire to achieve it. Golfers, for example, are much more successful at putting for par than for a birdie, no matter the distance, because they fear losing a stroke more than they desire picking up one.

At the time I read this, Linda and I were shamefully resorting to bribing our daughters to eat more vegetables. For years, we'd been trying to get them to at least try more vegetables, and finally we broke down and offered them a few extra dollars if they added three new vegetables a month. Kahneman's research persuaded us to change tacks. Instead of promising the payoff at the end, we gave it to them up front. "Here is five dollars. If you add three vegetables this month, you get to keep it. If you don't, you have to give it back." It worked! People I know have tried the same tactic with raking the leaves or curfew.)

Question #3: Should you force kids to do things with their money, like spend it, save it, give it away, or pay "taxes" on it?

Studies have shown that parents are very good at designing forced savings plans for their children's allowance, but fairly inept at following through with them. Journalist David Owen, in his charming book *The First National Bank of Dad*, described what happened when he did follow through with his scheme. He set up a fake bank account on Quicken to give his children an artificially high interest rate (70 percent a year!) to incentivize them to save.

"We save for selfish reasons," Owen wrote. The Bank of Dad turned his children into savers because it gave them a real reason to save. "If they deferred consumption for a while," he said, "they realized, they would eventually be able to consume more."

Other popular gestures include compelling kids to give money to charity or to a family kitty. Neale Godfrey, in her book *Money Doesn't Grow on Trees*, suggested telling kids they are a "citizen of the household" and requiring that 15 percent of their allowance go into a "tax" for the family.

Linda and I cobbled together a few of these techniques. We require our girls to divide their money into four pots:

1. *Spend.* They get to keep this cash in their piggy banks and spend it on whatever they choose, but we also require them to use their own money when buying gifts for us on our birthdays, Mother's Day, Father's Day, etc.
2. *Save.* I keep this money in an envelope in my office.
3. *Give away.* Linda, who works in philanthropy, takes charge of this and every few months brings the girls to donorschoose.org to pick their favorite charitable project to support.
4. *Share.* We also created a collective account for us to spend together as a family, usually on vacations. On our first joint shopping expedition, to a craft store in Santa Fe, Linda coached the girls on an important life skill: buying something that looked expensive but wasn't. Part of financial responsibility, she told them, is being a savvy shopper.

HOW MUCH IS THAT PROM DRESS IN THE WINDOW?

Bill Dwight tapped a few keystrokes into his iPhone and began looking at the credits and debits in his children's accounts. He started with his youngest child, Quentin, who was something of a hoarder. Beyond his weekly allowance ($3.96 following a 40 percent forced deduction for savings), he had a number of deposits:

$75.00—Christmas check from Grandma and Grandpa

$10.00—Feeding Shawn and John's fish over Christmas
vacation

$0.79—Change found in the car

$1.00—Found dollar bill

$0.41—Change found in the sofa

The first lesson everyone learned from this was to watch their wallets! The larger lesson is that Quentin was resourceful and willing to hustle for a few extra bucks. "You got ten bucks for feeding a lousy fish for three days?" his older brother, Will, asked. "Sweet!"

Quentin's only expense was $4.99 for an online video game. "I haven't played that in months," he said. "Why's it still there?" "We had to buy a year's subscription," his father responded. "Nice business model," Will added.

Peyton went next. His log had fewer inflows and more outflows, including gum, candy, half his monthly cell phone plan, and $18.99 for half a graphics card. The Dwights give their children loans for cell phones and computers, then ask them to pay for any add-ons. When Peyton's graphics card broke, Dad agreed to split the cost of a new one. Also, Peyton had purchased a new hairbrush and some hair care products at the drugstore. "He's got a girlfriend now," his little brother noted. "It gets expensive."

Will's issues were even more complex. For starters, when his father read his subtractions, they had a familiar ring to them.

$1.00—Did not make bed

$1.00—Did not make bed

$1.00—Did not make bed

$1.00—Did not make bed

$1.00—Did not make bed

"Ever since Will started making his own money lifeguarding last summer," his mother said, "he doesn't care about losing a dollar every now and then." "In one sense, I'm okay with it," Dad added. "I'm laying out less cash. But I think starting next month we're going to raise the penalty to five dollars. You're still part of our family."

Will's log also yielded several more interesting scenarios. The Dwights require their children to ask permission every time they spend their money—and they even make their kids write essays for major purchases. The children, naturally, resent this step. "I just wish Dad didn't ask me what the money is for," Peyton said. "He should have faith I won't be doing drugs or anything." But the parents find the practice cuts down on foolish expenditures. "We at least create the pressure that they have to ask us," Bill said.

In Will's case, he was approved for a purchase of Battlefield 2, a video game about a sniper, but turned down for an aerosol gun, which is used for paintball and other games. "We decided long ago we pay for passions," Dad explained, mentioning their daughter the equestrienne and their son the stunt cyclist. "And some of those are expensive. But we do have limits."

"In that case," Will said, "my passion is Ferraris!"

After dinner, I asked Bill what he had learned as the Mr. Rogers of money. Was he concerned, for instance, that giving kids an allowance was actually a way of teaching financial responsibility?

"For me it's not about that," he said. "For me it's about values. It's about wanting to have these conversations with my children. Do we really want to buy that air softener? Do we really need to go out to dinner tonight? It's about forcing conversations."

"So it's not really about financial literacy at all," I said. "It's about fatherhood."

"To me it is. In my mind, financial literacy is not, 'Do you know how a stock works'? It's about understanding the concept of constraints. I've done a lot of work advising startups over the years, and one reason they're so innovative is they're constrained."

He said his daughter, Haley, is very interested in clothing, so he taught her about limitations. The Dwights covered basic clothing expenses, but he gave her a supplementary budget, beyond her normal allowance, of $100 a month. "The name of her budget was 'Clothing Now,'" he noted, "so she was clearly interested!"

Turning to his computer, he called up her clothing purchases over the previous six years. "You can see how she managed the budget," he said. "At first she bought a couple of pairs of designer jeans. Then she figured out she could get stuff on eBay or get her jeans repaired. Creating constraints forced creativity."

When she got older, he continued, she wanted to buy a nice prom dress. The Dwights gave her some money toward the cost but told her she'd be responsible for anything above that. He showed me the account from May of her senior year, which shows these expenditures.

Prom shoes and earrings—$40.00
Neiman Marcus iridescent chiffon gown—$439.50

"That's almost half her annual budget!" I said.
"Yup. It's basically T-shirts for the rest of the year."
"How did she react to that?"
"She was fine with it. She had a wonderful night!"
"And how did you react to her spending so much money?"
"I'm cool with it, too. That's your allowance. You get to make the decisions."

I was impressed by his determination. Instead of allowing his kids to think only about the present, he was trying to prepare them for the future. Bill's attitude toward his kids' spending habits reminded me of something Eleanor Starr had said to me months earlier in Boise: "My whole goal is to make my children functioning adults."

Bill agreed.

"When Peyton says to me, 'I don't think purchasing insurance for my iPhone is the smartest thing,'" Bill said, "or Quentin says, 'I can't believe the World Wildlife Fund spends so much of my donation sending me mailings,' those are conversations adults are having. And when our older kids went off to college, I was astounded by the stories they told about how dysfunctional their friends were about money.

"I have a text I keep on my phone from Haley," he continued. "It says, "Thank you, Dad.' She had a friend who had a serious problem with her dad and then got into an abusive relationship with a boyfriend. She was just thanking me for being there for her." He paused to wipe a tear from his eye. "I'll tell you right now, it doesn't get any better than that."

TAKING OFF THE TRAINING WHEELS

Byron Trott is something of the banker to the stars. The stars, in this case, are not Hollywood stars; they are the richest families in America. Trott, a homecoming-handsome man who looks like a Hollywood leading actor from the 1950s, grew up on what he describes as "the wrong side of the tracks in an itty-bitty town in Missouri." He now lives in a twenty-eight-thousand-square-foot house on Lake Michigan. A former vice chairman of Goldman Sachs, he left to start his own firm, which advises the country's hundred wealthiest families. Warren Buffett called him "the only banker I trust."

Trott graciously agreed to meet me in a paneled boardroom in Manhattan. I figured his clients were uniquely skilled at passing down money values to their kids. Trott quickly quashed my naïveté. "I would say most are not very good at it at all," he said. "That's where I come in. I'm here to give them the skills to keep their families together."

His counsel was surprising.

1. *Show them the money.* Trott said most parents have an instinctive reluctance to be honest with their kids about money—how it's made, lost, invested, and spent. He said that 80 percent of college students have never had a conversation with their parents about managing money. Trott advises his clients to fling open the doors to the vault.

"I tell my clients that forcing their kids to have financial literacy is one of the most important things they can do," he said. He quoted statistics that say the more parents talk to their kids about debt, the less debt they rack up; the more they hear about savings, the more they sock away.

"What happens to a lot of families is they depend too much on osmosis," he continued. "I sat down with one of the richest women in America recently and told her she had to talk openly with her children. She said she didn't want to burden them with the truth, but burdening them with ignorance is really much worse."

2. *Take off the training wheels.* "One of the biggest problems I see in families," Trott said, "is a reluctance to let your kids make decisions for themselves." As an example, he cited the story of Jack Taylor, the founder of Enterprise Rent-A-Car, who with a net worth in excess of $9 billion has been ranked as high as the eighteenth richest American. When his son turned thirty-two, Taylor

handed him the company and never looked back. "Most parents meddle," Trott said.

He chided me for not letting our girls make enough decisions for themselves. For example, he said, Linda and I should not force our daughters to divide their money equally into the four pots. We should let them choose the percentages, even if that means one pot gets less. "You've got them on their training wheels, now take the training wheels off and let them ride by themselves."

"But if they ride into the ditch?" I said.

"It's a really good idea to bike into the ditch with a $6 allowance instead of $60,000 salary or a $6 million inheritance. Your six-year-old might be right if she doesn't give a nickel away, invests it Warren Buffett–style, compounds it into billions, before she gives it away. Had Warren been giving away $10 million along the way, instead of being worth $50 billion today, he'd be worth $10 billion. Then he couldn't give $40 billion to the Gates Foundation."

3. *Accept their passions, any passions.* Buffett is famous for not wanting to spoil his kids. Instead, after his wife gave each of their three kids $100 million, and the money didn't ruin them, Buffett gave each one a $1 billion foundation. Trott was privy to that decision, and I asked what he thought of it. Does money inherently spoil children?

"I don't think so," he said. "I've seen too many really rich kids who are great people. In my experience, great people are great because they find their passion. For some that's in business, but for others it's in philanthropy. One of Warren's sons is a farmer; another is a musician. Most families really don't let their kids follow their passions. They assume the parents' passion is the children's passion, and usually it's not. You should allow them to be outliers in their dreams."

4. *Put them to work.* There's a lot of vagueness in academic

circles about children and money, but the research is clear that part-time jobs are great for kids. The Youth Development Survey in St. Paul, Minnesota, followed a number of children from ninth grade through their midthirties to determine whether childhood should be the sanctuary of play and learning or if work can be a productive part of it. The study found that those who work don't lose interest in school and don't cut back on family, extracurricular activities, or volunteering. They even become better at time management.

As the survey's lead researcher, Jeylan Mortimer, observed: The more "planful" adolescents are about their future, the more successful and satisfied they are likely to be as adults.

Trott agreed. "The most successful adults I know were all involved in business at a young age," he said. "All of them. Warren believes it's the secret to success. Your kid has to be involved in business. Warren thinks I'm successful because I had a lawn mowing business, a clothing store, all these different businesses as a kid, so I understood money, even though I never studied economics. What he thinks is necessary for someone to be successful in business is early exposure to business. So if you really want your daughters to understand money, have them open a lemonade stand."

YOURS, MINE, AND OURS

Teaching kids financial responsibility is hard enough. Try doing the same with your spouse!

For starters, the old cliché that money is one of the most divisive issues in relationships turns out to be true. Researchers in Framingham, Massachusetts, asked four thousand men and women to rank their reasons for arguing with their spouse. Their top three answers were:

WOMEN	MEN
1. Children	1. Sex
2. Housework	2. Money
3. Money	3. Leisure

Money is the only issue both sides agree they disagree about.

Despite this combustibility, being in a family is actually good for your bottom line. Jay Zagorsky, a researcher at Ohio State, tracked the financial status of 9,055 married and unmarried people over fifteen years, beginning in their twenties. Those who remained single had a slow but gradual growth in wealth, accumulating an average of $11,000 over that period. Those who got married (and stayed so for ten years) gained an average of $43,000. Over a lifetime, getting married doubles a person's wealth, the study concluded, while getting divorced cuts a person's wealth by three-quarters.

Couples have a clear financial incentive to stick together. So what's the best way to arrange your financial affairs to make sure that happens? John Davis is a professor at Harvard Business School, the author of many books, and a guru on untangling families, wealth, and emotion. Two-thirds of the world's businesses are family owned, so he's got an endless stream of clients.

Dressed in a blue blazer and gray flannel slacks, Davis speaks crisply and authoritatively. "One of the basic rules of families," he told me, "is that 'structure is your friend.' Families are very good at avoiding money conversations; they're not very good at having them. You need a plan."

Davis has certain basic rules he tells couples:

- All couples should have quarterly meetings to discuss financial matters; more if you're having money troubles. (The same applies to extended families if they have shared financial interests.)
- Avoid talking about money at birthday parties, family dinners, or holidays; those occasions should be for fun.
- Have a third party or other neutral voice at the table; you'll sit up straighter, ask more questions, and avoid bringing up grudges.

But his more subtle advice had to do with bridging the differences between spendthrifts and tightwads, savers and splurgers. A handful of writers over the years have tried to analyze and label the different ways that people approach money, but none of these systems has really stuck. Whatever those inclinations, Davis says people tend to seek out partners who have the opposite inclination. Tension is the norm, perhaps for the better. To address that tension, Davis begins with a simple piece of advice: divide your money.

"When families get too collective, and everybody's business becomes everybody else's, it becomes confusing and overly emotional," he said. "Just as in your home you need private space that's just yours, in your budget you need private space, too. You need some chunk of cash where you can say, 'My money, my call.'" Regardless of who brings in the money, he said, a practical way of executing this vision is to divide your resources into three pots: yours, mine, and ours.

A similar approach works with children, he said. Each child in a family should be able to pursue his or her own interests, even if the costs are not even. This is the approach the Dwights took with their kids. But it's not as simple as it seems. "From the moment they come out of the womb," Davis said, "kids are on guard to be treated equally."

"As the father of identical twins, I surely know that!" I said.

"But that's not the right goal," he said. "The goal is not equality; the goal is fairness. Fairness is not necessarily equality, and equality is not necessarily fair."

He mentioned two examples. "Let's say one of your kids adores soccer," he said, "and the other digs art." You decide to send your child to soccer camp, but there is no comparable art camp in your area. What do you do? "Should you look at exactly how much you're spending on one kid? No, because you're trying to accommodate their interests, not make everything equal. If you focus on what they really need, not on how much you're spending, both kids will feel nurtured."

The second happened to a client of his. One child, a daughter, was a great student and landed in the Ivy League; the other, a son, was a great athlete and chose to go to a state school. The son came to his father and announced, "I did the math. You're going to invest $150,000 more on her education than mine. I'd like a check for that amount; I'll invest the money. Then we'll see where my sister and I end up."

"So what did your client do?" I asked.

"He said, 'Absolutely not. We're helping each of you pursue your own interests, and interests cost different amounts. You had a choice; you made it fair and square.'"

Davis's advice formed another stitch in a pattern that had been emerging in many of my conversations. Families that manage money successfully share the same things with families that manage time, space, conflict, and sex well: They talk a lot, hold regular get-togethers, find common ground, and keep some things private. Oh, and they remember to play. One of the proven benefits of money is that it allows you to buy gifts. As Davis mentioned, there's plenty of research showing that spending money on others brings us much greater happiness than spending it on ourselves.

I asked Davis what goals we should be trying to reach with our children. Getting a kid into college or paving the way for them to have healthy relationships seemed like tangible goals. What's the goal with money?

"I think what you're trying to do in a family is create responsible, self-reliant, creative people," he said. "Self-reliant, meaning they can take care of themselves. Responsible, meaning they're accountable for their own actions. And creative, meaning they come up with their own dreams and set out to achieve them. Having money is not the destination in any of these cases, but it is a means to those ends."

6

TALK ABOUT THE MARSHMALLOWS

How to Have Difficult Conversations

I HAD FLOWN FROM New York to Savannah many times before—to introduce Linda to my parents, to get married, to take our daughters for their first visit. But this was the first time I was flying for the express purpose of taking care of my aging parents.

My father, who suffers from Parkinson's, was recovering from back surgery. For weeks my mother nursed him through an elaborate ritual of bathing, feeding, and physical therapy. Then, just hours before he was going to have a follow-up procedure, my mother fell and dislocated her shoulder. Suddenly my father was on the way to one hospital, my mother to another.

My siblings and I, who all live in different states, huddled on the phone. Soon I was on my way.

Tensions were high when I arrived. My father was relieved to see me. He had a long list of small items he could no longer handle, from upgrading his cell phone to finding a place to rest his glasses. But he didn't want to burden my mom. He wept when I offered to clean out his desk.

My mother felt invaded. She had everything under control, she insisted, and didn't want me going through her house rearranging furniture. And besides, why did my sister keep calling her friends asking them to bring over dinner? What did we think they were, helpless?

I had been home less than an hour.

We were seated in the den as this talk unfolded. It was the place where pivotal conversations were usually held when I was growing up. Back then, my parents would usually summon one of us for a talk. Now, I was the one doing the summoning. Yet I hadn't fully planned what I was going to say. I took a breath.

"I was going to save this for later," I said, "but let's go ahead and have the conversation now."

TALK ABOUT THE MARSHMALLOWS

Difficult conversations. They're not just for unhappy families; happy families need to have them as well. So what have we learned in recent years about how to have them successfully?

Three of the more thoughtful people on this topic are the authors of *Difficult Conversations: How to Discuss What Matters Most*. If anybody could tell Grandpa he has to stop driving, insist that Mom cut back on the vodka tonics, or make sure Sis does not pick up the microphone at the rehearsal dinner, it's them. Sheila Heen and Doug Stone wrote the book (with Bruce Patton). The two of them invited me to dinner, along with John Richardson, Heen's husband and the father of their three children.

So why are these conversations so toxic in families? Where does all the hostility come from? Here's where.

When I arrived at Heen and Richardson's home in Concord, Massachusetts, their sons were having a quarrel. Nine-year-old

Ben had failed to buy twelve-year-old Pete a birthday present. "But you didn't buy me a present," Ben retorted. "Yes, I did," Pete responded. "You just didn't like it."

"When was your birthday?" I asked Pete, meaning, How long had this dispute been going on? "Five months and seven days ago," he said.

Their kids are not alone, of course. As I was leaving to come to this dinner, my girls were sitting down to cups of hot chocolate. Their grandmother carefully counted out fifteen mini-marshmallows for each child. But two of Eden's marshmallows were squashed together, so she promptly reached over and plucked one from her sister's cup. "You always take my things!" Tybee squealed. "You're always so perfect!" Eden shot back. Within seconds they were both in tears.

Before getting to the matter of adults, I was curious how Heen and Richardson, who also works in conflict resolution, handle these types of squabbles between their kids.

Disputes between sisters and brothers, brothers and brothers, and sisters and sisters are the most common conflicts families face. When siblings between the ages of three and seven are together, they clash an average of three and a half times per hour, studies show, with those fights lasting a total of ten minutes out of every sixty. Hildy Ross, of the University of Waterloo in Canada, found that only one of eight of these squabbles ends in compromise or reconciliation. The other seven wrap up when one child simply withdraws after being bullied or intimidated by the other.

The reason siblings fight so often is because they take each other for granted, and that's the same reason they fight when they grow up. Siblings know they're stuck with each other, no matter what happens. As Scottish sociologist Samantha Punch put it, "Sibship is a relationship in which the boundaries of social interaction can be pushed to the limit. Rage and irritation need not be suppressed, whilst politeness and toleration can be neglected."

Laurie Kramer, a professor of applied family studies at the University of Illinois, has devoted her career to studying siblings. She created a program called "More Fun with Sisters and Brothers" that gives siblings the words to handle their frustrations and the skills to rebuild frayed relations. She believes the conflicts between siblings when they are youngsters don't have to affect their long-term bond; it's absolutely possible to be close when you're grown. What matters is having enough fun together to balance out the bad. This "net-positive" is what predicts good relations as adults.

Kramer says parents can help by spending less time playing cop to bad behavior and more time playing midwife to good behavior. Some practical examples include:

- To reduce fights during mealtime, have siblings spend at least twenty minutes beforehand engaged in a joint activity that reaffirms their connection.
- To boost camaraderie, give siblings chores to do together to build trust and a sense of accomplishment.
- To increase confidence, spend ten minutes alone with each child every night doing something suited to that child— reading a book, reviewing ball scores, telling stories.

But Kramer's central piece of wisdom came as a shock to me: Get involved in your kids' disputes. This may seem obvious, but ever since my kids were young, I had often done the opposite. When one of my girls ran to me complaining about her sister having taken her toy, or stepped on her toe, or called her a name, my response was hands off: "I'm not a referee. Work it out yourselves." I thought this was an up-to-date parenting strategy. We should teach our kids to be independent and not hover over them like helicopters, rushing in to solve every problem.

"But we can't work it out!" the girls often complained.

Turns out they may have been right. Kramer says children under eight are "generally unable" to manage conflicts with their siblings on their own. "The research that I and others have done," she said, "has clearly shown that for children who don't already have those skills in conflict management, it *is* critical for parents to step in and help." She recommends helping children by giving them a tool kit for resolving difficult situations.

So what should be in that tool kit? Heen and Richardson had some advice. The first thing they shared with me is a kid-friendly version of the technique they've honed with adults. It has three steps.

1. *Think about yourself first.* "When one of my kids comes to me," Heen said, "they are usually wanting adjudication. Whether it's the birthday present or the marshmallows, they want to know who's right. John and I pretty consistently refuse to play that role."

The most immediate step is to get both parties to calm down, she said, or "go to the balcony," as Bill Ury would put it. Maybe they should spend a few minutes in their room, or read a book.

Then you can move on to getting each side to examine its role in what happened. "With kids," Richardson added, "it's usually a fight about who started it. I don't care who started it, I tell them. I care about what choice you each made to continue it."

"Even if one side is clearly at fault," Heen said, "I usually say to the other person, 'What were you doing right before?' That person gets very sheepish, then says, 'Oh, yeah. Well . . .'"

2. *Be curious about the other person.* Once a child pauses to consider their own responsibility, the next step is to get that child to explore the other side's motivation. "A good way is to invite curiosity about what's going on in the other person's head," Heen said.

"If you teach a child to think about the person they're in conflict with, it will serve them in good stead throughout their life."

3. *Apologize.* I've read different opinions about forcing kids to apologize. Some say it's a necessary step, while others feel it's just piling on. Heen believes in contrition. "Saying you're sorry really has two meanings," she said. "One is to describe how you actually feel; the other is to take responsibility for the impact you've had on somebody else. I'm really more interested in the second meaning—accepting accountability for your choices, even if you don't genuinely feel apologetic. Later, when you're less amped up on adrenaline, feeling sorry will come." Also, she noted, research has shown it's rare to see conflict after an apology.

"The key thing is to keep your eye on the big picture," Richardson said. "Your first instinct when kids are fighting is to think, 'I can hardly stand it! Marshmallows do not matter!'"

I nodded enthusiastically.

"But to them, they really do matter," he continued. "On the surface it's about marshmallows, but it's really about 'Am I being treated fairly in the world?' And they carry these issues with them their whole lives until one day they're no longer fighting about marshmallows, they're fighting about taking care of you."

The greatest lesson I took away from this exchange was *Have the conversation.* It won't resolve every conflict, but it will build grooves of conflict-solving behavior that will reap benefits later in life. This advice reminded me of what Byron Trott had said about money. You're better off having a child make a mistake with a $6 allowance than a $60,000 salary or a $6 million inheritance. The same applies to difficult conversations. Talk about the marshmallows today, or you'll be talking about them the rest of your life.

CREATE A THIRD STORY

Heen, Stone, and Richardson have a clubby, chummy way with one another, reminiscent of the years they spent as graduate students. Heen has shoulder-length brown hair and the kind of elegant smartness popular in old French movies. She's married to Richardson, a former lawyer turned professional negotiator who has a dark complexion and a sardonic smile. Heen founded a consulting firm with Stone, the taller and burlier of the two men. Professionally, Stone has defused crises from Cyprus to Ethiopia.

The central premise of Heen and Stone's book about difficult conversations is not to view them as isolated incidents, but to see them as parts of a larger narrative of the relationship. To do that, we need to take four steps.

1. *First, be curious about the other side's story.* This is the grown-up version of their advice for kids. Try to figure out what's motivating the other person. Difficult conversations are almost never about getting the facts right; they are about how people perceive those facts. Try first to understand the other person's point of view.

2. *Tell your own story second.* Once you know the other person's story, try to figure out the unspoken feelings behind your story. Then *tell the other side how you feel.* If you haven't told them how you really feel, you can't get mad at them for not listening to you.

3. *Create a third story together.* Once both stories are on the table, don't choose between them; embrace both. Since you're dealing with a difference of perception, both sides can be right. Once this "third story" emerges, you can begin scripting a compromise.

4. *Remember, this is not the last story you'll tell together.* Especially

in families, you will have many more of these conversations together. The story does not end here. Talk about ways to keep communication open in the future.

So how does this work in real life? Each of them gave me an example drawn from their own lives. (At their request, I've concealed some of the details.)

- A frail, eightysomething man with advanced Alzheimer's is admitted to the emergency room. Doctors say he needs invasive surgery that could extend his life by a few weeks. Three of his four children believe the time has come to say good-bye. But one, the youngest, is adamant, saying, "We have to do everything to save Dad's life."
- A man in his forties has a confession that might rend his family apart. He and his wife have become estranged. They haven't had sex in years; the torment and shame have been relentless. Yet everyone thinks they're the perfect couple, and no one in his family has ever been divorced. He fears his upstanding parents may disown him, and his siblings will turn their backs on him. On Thanksgiving Day he flees to the beach for five hours to avoid telling everyone the truth.
- A still-sharp hundred-year-old woman lives by herself in the home where she raised her two children. One day she takes a fall in her beloved backyard garden. Her son, who lives in another state, thinks it's time for her to move in with her daughter, who lives nearby. But the daughter refuses. The grandchildren are concerned the standoff is putting a chill on their family.

What happened next in these situations reveals how misplaced expectations often derail these conversations before they get started.

The hundred-year-old woman living by herself embodies Lesson #1, *First, be curious about the other side's story*. The woman's children were in a standoff about whether she should stay in her home or move in with her daughter. For years, no one had budged. Finally, one of the grandchildren couldn't stand the awkwardness and decided to inject herself. She telephoned her aunt. But instead of confronting her aunt, she led with curiosity. "I'm interested in understanding why you don't want to take Grandma in?"

"Because Mama lives for her garden," her aunt said. "She's tended it daily since the 1940s, even in the middle of winter. If I take her away from it, I'm worried she'll lose her will to live."

"The answer was so persuasive," Stone said, "it instantly changed their entire dynamic. 'Now I get it!' the granddaughter thought. This is a reminder that you must genuinely be open to the possibility that you might not have all the information."

Even better, once the topic of where Grandma should live was out in the open, the rest of the decisions were much less painful. Grandma stayed where she was for several years, and today, at 104, she lives happily with her daughter.

The second story, the fortysomething man who was afraid to tell his family he was getting divorced, turned out to embody both Lesson #1 and Lesson #2. The day he fled to the beach he had no choice but to tell his parents his marriage was ending. He braced for their condemnation. "You're a failure," he expected to hear.

Instead his mother said this: "Son, I'm so sorry for you." His father was equally sympathetic.

"He just misread the rules," Heen explained. "He hadn't cheated on his wife. They didn't have kids. Being a loyal husband was important, but it had limitations."

His mistake was not fully understanding what really mattered to the other party, his family. That falls under Lesson #1: He wasn't curious about the other side; he just assumed he knew what they felt. "Sometimes the story you're telling yourself is wrong," Heen said.

But he also made another mistake, not clearly expressing the pain he was in. That's Lesson #2: He wasn't self-reflective.

After his confession, the family rallied. He was invited to move in with one of his siblings during the transition. His parents called to ask how he was doing. Instead of feeling burdened by his family, he felt protected by them.

The siblings who disagreed about their father's surgery illustrate Lesson #3, *Create a third story together.* After the blowup in the emergency room in which the siblings disagreed about whether to green light invasive surgery, the situation spiraled downward. The holdout son started calling his siblings and berating them.

"We can't do this to Dad," he said.

His sister returned fire. "You're losing your mind," she said. "Let him go."

Finally a third sibling went to see his brother. "I want to understand what you're feeling," he said. That made his brother start crying. "I don't want to see him die," he said. "I think we can bring him back. Dad can't speak for himself, so somebody has to speak for him." The conversation continued for over an hour.

By the end, the holdout son felt respected and was sure he had stood up for Dad. His brother reaffirmed what everyone else agreed should happen next, and together they reached a decision.

"The conversation totally solved the problem," Richardson said. "But more important, it made a lifelong difference to the ongoing relationships. Everyone was at peace with the decision. No one felt shut out. Instead of being ripped apart, the family was pulled closer together."

The next day, all four children gathered to be with their father when he died.

THE LAW OF TWO WOMEN

These three examples all grew out of crises. And no wonder. John DeFrain, a psychologist in Nebraska, has interviewed scores of what he calls "strong families." A quarter of them cited serious illness or surgery as the most difficult crisis they had faced in the last five years; another 20 percent said it was a death in the family.

But these kinds of crises are not the only way difficult conversations can start. Sometimes it's just a long-simmering dilemma, a financial decision, or any multilayered life choice that impacts lots of people. Heen and Stone present one way of going about these conversations, but theirs is not the only approach. How complex teams make tough decisions is one of the more active arenas in contemporary social science. Here are four suggestions that have emerged from this research that might be applicable to families:

1. *Too few cooks spoil the broth.* A lot of attention has been focused in recent years on the power of groups to make better decisions than individuals. *The Wisdom of Crowds* by James Surowiecki is the defining book on this subject. Surowiecki opens the book with the story of British scientist Francis Galton, who in 1906 attended a regional livestock fair. Galton came upon a demonstration in which visitors were asked to guess the weight of a fat ox. Eight hundred people tried to come up with the right answer.

Galton was skeptical that an "average person" could determine the answer correctly, and he thought this gave him the perfect vehicle to prove "the stupidity and wrongheadedness of many men and women." After the competition, he calculated the mean of all the answers. Collectively, the crowd had guessed that the ox, after it was slaughtered, would weigh 1,197 pounds. It actually weighed 1,198 pounds. The crowd, in other words, had been perfect. As Surowiecki wrote, "What Francis Galton had stumbled upon that day in Plymouth was the simple, but powerful truth: under the right circumstances, groups are remarkably intelligent, and are often smarter than the smartest people in them."

Considerable evidence has been gathered to support this. Brian Uzzi, a sociologist at Northwestern, collected data on twenty-one million scientific papers published worldwide between 1945 and 2005. He found that team efforts were judged to be higher quality than individual efforts. What kinds of teams are most effective? Uzzi analyzed 321 Broadway musicals and found that teams of people who had never met did not work well together and produced more flops. Meanwhile, groups that had collaborated before were also not that successful, because they tended to rehash ideas and not come up with fresh concepts. The sweet spot was a mix of strong and weak ties, where trust existed but new ideas could flow.

Extended families, with their mix of parents, siblings, in-laws, senior citizens, twentysomethings, and the occasional ne'er-do-well, are a near perfect mix for drawing on the heterogeneous advantages of groups.

2. *Vote first, talk later.* I was shocked to learn that groups are better at making decisions if participants express their views at the start of a meeting *before they've had a chance to listen to anybody else.* Countless studies have shown that once the discussion begins, the people who speak first tend to persuade others of their position, even when their positions are wrong.

Daniel Kahneman offered a helpful blueprint. "A simple rule can help: before an issue is discussed, all members should be asked to write a very brief summary of their position." This procedure ensures that the group takes advantage of the wide range of knowledge and opinion among its members. "The standard practice of open discussion gives too much weight to the opinions of those who speak early and assertively, causing others to line up behind them," Kahneman added.

Once everyone's views are out in the open, the discussion will be much more productive.

3. *Hold a premortem.* As the conversation reaches a climax, it's important to encourage people to express their true opinions, especially if they disagree with the group. One way to do that is to conduct what psychologist Gary Klein calls a "premortem." When teams engage in prospective hindsight—imagining that an event has already occurred—they increase their ability to correctly identify what might possibly go wrong. A premortem makes that process easier. When the group has almost come to an important decision but not committed itself officially yet, one member says, "Let's imagine it's a year from now. We're following this plan, and it hasn't worked out. Let's write down what we think would have gone wrong."

Klein says the main value of a premortem is to legitimize doubts and let skeptics voice their concerns. As he wrote, "In the end, a premortem may be the best way to circumvent any need for a painful postmortem."

4. *The Law of Two Women.* My favorite tip for improving difficult conversations within families is what I call "The Law of Two Women." One night I was having dinner with an executive at Google, and I asked him to tell me the most significant change he's seen in how his company runs meetings. Without hesitating, he told me they always make sure there is more than one woman in the room. He then told me about the study that led to this principle.

In 2010, a group of researchers from Carnegie Mellon, MIT,

and Union College published a study in *Science* called "Evidence for a Collective Intelligence Factor in the Performance of Human Groups." The scientists scrupulously analyzed 699 people, working in groups of two or five, and tried to determine whether "collective intelligence" exists, and if so, what causes it. After finding that the groups did make better decisions than the individuals, the researchers moved on to the second question, and their results surprised even themselves.

Two factors mattered most, they found. First, groups in which a few people dominated discussions were much less effective than groups where everyone spoke up. Second, groups that had a higher proportion of females were more effective. These groups were more sensitive to input from everyone, more capable of reaching compromise, and more efficient at making decisions.

These researchers are not alone. A growing body of evidence from an eclectic cross section of disciplines has shown that having more women on teams makes the teams work better. In 2006, researchers at Wellesley conducted extensive research on women on the boards of Fortune 1000 companies. Their report, entitled "Critical Mass on Corporate Boards: Why Three or More Women Enhance Governance," found that a lone woman on a board can make a substantial contribution, but two are better than one. Reaching the threshold of three, meanwhile, makes it more likely the women are heard. Why? As lead researcher Sumur Erkut summed up the findings, "Women bring a collaborative leadership style that benefits boardroom dynamics by increasing listening, social support and win-win problem solving."

Similar results have been shown in the legal profession among judges. A study out of the University of California, Berkeley, found that the presence of at least one woman on a three-member panel of federal judges breaks the polarizing instinct of the men and makes the body more deliberative; when two women are seated on the panel, the effect was even greater.

These studies might be dismissed as isolated examples, but they are consistent with a large body of research in recent decades that shows women are wired to be more cooperative, more sensitive to other people's emotions, and more interested in building consensus—all skills that are extremely handy in difficult conversations involving extended families. If you're making a complex decision, the more women you have in the conversation, the easier time you'll likely have in reaching a final decision that makes everyone happy.

BRINGING DOWN PARENTS

The situation when both my parents faced medical crises at the same time occurred just a few days after my visit with Heen, Richardson, and Stone. The crisis forced me to test everything I had been learning about difficult conversations.

Sitting in my parents' den, I was nervous. I'd had little experience guiding conversations like this in which I was the one taking care of them more than they were taking care of me. My father, who watched his own mother struggle with Alzheimer's, once captured this challenge well. "Bringing down parents is much harder than bringing up kids," he said.

I began slowly. Since I had already heard their feelings—my father's fear; my mother's sense that we were intruding—I felt as if I had met my obligation to "be curious about the other side." Now I had to tell my side of the story, or in this case, that of my siblings and me. We felt sad we didn't live closer, I said. We had no desire to take over their lives and couldn't even if we wanted to. We were only trying to be supportive, the way they taught us when we were growing up. Surely there's some way we could be helpful. "Our bodies are far away, but you can still rent our minds," I said. "Let us handle things that can be outsourced."

The conversation was a breakthrough, and that weekend was the most affirming time I had spent with my parents in years. But there was one nagging issue. My mother was considering purchasing long-term care insurance to help care for her in the event of a debilitating disease. My father would be unable to take care of her, she rightly reasoned, and all of us were far away. But it was expensive.

Like many people who care for aging parents, my siblings and I had become increasingly involved in our parents' finances, from going through their bills to monitoring their expenses. After years of managing their money themselves, they didn't always welcome our intrusion.

But now was different. When I took my dad to replace his cell phone, for example, I quickly discovered he was being charged $200 a month under a ten-year-old plan. A few moments later I had lowered his bill to less than $40 a month. That experience led me to go one by one through my parents' bills—electricity, water, cable, insurance. The good news was that I saved them thousands of dollars a year. The bad news was that it led to some awkward exchanges as I had to quiz them about their expenses and gently make the case that they no longer needed certain items.

Some experts have recommended a "financial driver's license" for older Americans to prove their competence. If my experience is any indication, a learner's permit also seems like a good analogy in some cases: You're allowed to drive your own decisions, Mom and Dad, but please ensure one of your kids is in the car.

To her credit, my mother understood she shouldn't make the

decision about whether to purchase insurance alone, so she asked me to wade through the options. When it came time to make the decision, I suggested we hold a family-wide conference call. No one agreed. My father said the topic was too emotional for him. My sister said she knew nothing about insurance. My brother said he was too busy with other family matters.

I pushed back. We need every voice, I said, including emotional ones and ill-informed ones. Reluctantly everyone agreed. Once on the call, I asked everyone to state their opinion up front: Two of us were against the plan (including me); three were for it; one was agnostic. Then my mother started to cry. "I don't want to be a burden on my children," she said. My sister leapt in to offer support. I was impressed. I would have been much more impatient. Instead, with Mom feeling heard (by the second woman, no less!), we moved on to considering the proposals.

We discussed the various pros and cons. Eventually my father joined in with some thoughtful questions. I could feel the momentum shifting. Finally I made an attempt at a premortem: If we bought the insurance and regretted it, what would be the reasons? A waste of money, everyone agreed. If we didn't buy it, what would we regret? Mom got sick, and we couldn't afford the care she wanted.

Finally, we took a vote. It was unanimously in favor of buying the insurance.

Our difficult conversation had one crucial thing in common with the ones Heen, Richardson, and Stone outlined: They all involved family members of multiple generations, with conflicting agendas and unspoken emotions, trying to navigate a delicate situation. And they highlighted one overlooked feature of families: power dynamics are constantly shifting.

Parents expect to care for their children when they're young, but those same children are often surprised when they're called on to care for their parents when they're old. Siblings often battle when they're children, but those same siblings are often obliged to work together when they're adults.

We think of families as being entrenched in old habits. We think of our roles in those families as being fixed. Both of those notions are wrong. One thing you learn from having difficult conversations is that families are fluid. The difficulties can come from any quarter—and so can the solutions. The person who steals your marshmallows one day may be the same one who brings you hot chocolate the next.

7

LESSONS FROM THE SEX MOM

What Your Mother Never Told You About Sex (but Should Have)

"HERE IT COMES!" one of the girls squealed. "The sex talk! Everybody, come, you've got to hear this."

It was a Sunday evening in early September, and two dozen teenage girls from a high school swim team in northwestern Connecticut were having a cookout at Kate and Brad Eggleston's white-clapboard home. There were spaghetti and hot dogs, a few soft drinks, salad, and brownies. And in about fifteen seconds, the girls were going to hear a speech about fellatio, Trojans, and how to say "no."

Kate Eggleston calls herself the Sex Mom. She is a proud suburban housewife. She carpools; she cooks meatless chili and apple crisp; she goes to every game her three teenage daughters and twelve-year-old son play. And she likes to drink a glass of wine with her balding-yet-still-handsome husband at the end of a long day with the bedroom door closed. She also likes to talk to her kids and their friends about sex.

This all started one day when her oldest daughter, Brady, came home from fifth grade and said "blow job." Kate nearly swallowed her duster. "What's a blow job?" Kate asked. "Oral sex," Brady answered. "Everybody does it." "Really?" Kate said. "What do you mean?" "Well, *oral* means talking," her ten-year-old said, "so it means talking about sex."

Kate smiled. "Now, in some ways, that's a very intelligent response," she told me. "And when I explained exactly what it is—a penis in your mouth—Brady was like, 'Oh my God!! It's not!!' She was totally mortified. This language is being thrown around so commonly these days, but the kids have no idea what it means. That's when I realized they need to have information."

She started slowly at first, then with more confidence, adjusting her words to the ages of the kids. She would corner a group of girls after dinner; she would badger teenage boys when they called to speak to her daughter. She did a lot of talking during carpools, which she found particularly effective, because no one could flee. She even put a box of condoms on the kitchen counter, being careful to remove a few so no one could keep track of who took one. Everyone started calling her "Sex Mom," the aproned crusader keeping the neighborhood safe from ignorance.

Did any parents ask her to back off?

"No," she said. "Quite the opposite. They asked for help. I have this one friend, who came up to me every day and said, 'I can't do it! I can't do it! I can't have the sex talk with my son.' I said, 'You have to.' Then one day she walked in like Rocky and said, 'I did it! I had the talk!' I looked at her. 'Did you get the penis in the vagina?' She slumped away, only to return the next day. 'It's done!' I said, 'Really? What did your son say?' 'He said, "I don't believe you. I'm calling Dad."'"

With all this buildup, no one on the swim team was surprised when Mrs. Eggleston walked over to the table that night, hardly broke stride, and gave her little talk. It had four rules.

1. *Blow jobs are sex, too.* ("You can't imagine how many of these girls think oral sex doesn't count.")
2. *Always use a condom.* ("I usually give a quick demonstration on my finger. The school nurse is not allowed to.")
3. *If you're not mature enough to buy a condom yourself, you're not mature enough to have sex.* ("I tell the kids, until your brain catches up with your bodies you really should hold off.")
4. *Only have sex when you have nothing left to share.* ("If you can pick your nose in front of him, if you can share any thought with him, if you can tell him 'no,' then you're beginning to understand.")

And what do the girls think of these little talks?

"Why don't you ask them yourself?" she said. "Have you ever been in a room with teenage girls? You're in for quite an earful."

WHO'S AFRAID OF THE BIRDS AND THE BEES?

It's time to talk about the pink-and-blue elephant in the room. Sex. For most families, it's the one subject they find most difficult to do well. Thinking about sex in families—from how to talk about it with kids to how to get enough of it for adults—was the single most challenging topic I considered.

Sexuality was just not openly discussed in my home when I was growing up, and that has left me somewhat tongue-tied on the topic. It also seemed impossible to figure out what families who've navigated this successfully have done. Finally, as soon as

I started digging into the topic, I realized that Linda and I had already made a lot of rookie mistakes.

Let's begin with the research, which itself is myth shattering. The first thing is that adolescents are far more chaste than you might think. They fool around on the bases, if you will, but they don't reach home all that often. The Guttmacher Institute, the most respected authority on teen sexuality, reports that only 13 percent of teens have had sexual intercourse by age fifteen. Most have sex for the first time around seventeen. More noteworthy, those figures are largely unchanged over the last sixty years; they've even ticked downward in recent years. The most common reason teens give for not having sex is that it's against their religion or morals; the next reason, at least for girls, is they "don't want to get pregnant" and "haven't found the right person." So for starters, we can all pull our fingers off the panic button. There's much more sex on the TV your kids are watching than on the sofa where they're sitting.

That's the heartening news; now the disheartening. Parents are wimps when it comes to talking to kids about sex. Adolescents who are experimenting—hands, mouths, genitals, you know the drill—are doing so without much information. When they do reach the point of going all the way, 40 percent do so without first talking with their parents about birth control or sexually transmitted diseases. For boys, the numbers are particularly worrisome. A study out of New York University found that 85 percent of girls get talked to by their parents, but only half of boys do. Researchers at UCLA found nearly 70 percent of boys had not discussed how to use a condom or other birth control before having intercourse.

Even parents who do talk to their kids are bailing out before they get to the hard stuff, like coercion or how to say "no." If you think this doesn't make a difference, consider that in Europe, where research shows sex is more openly discussed within families, teenagers engage in intercourse an average of two years later, and the rate of teen pregnancy is eight times lower.

One more thing is clear from the research: Families make an enormous difference not only in what their kids know about sex, but also in how early they engage in it. Numerous studies have shown that children who live with both biological parents have their first sexual experience later than those who do not. In addition, how warm parents are to their children, and how attached those children feel to their parents, all delay the onset of sex.

Mothers are especially influential. Jessica Benjamin of New York University has found that girls assume their gender coding in the first two years of life by identifying with their mothers. As girls grow, if mothers denigrate their own bodies, constantly talk about dieting and not feeling desirous, and generally devalue their sexuality, their daughters will do the same. Also, the more supportive mothers are of their daughters, the later they have sex. The same is true for sons. Mothers are so important as a gateway to sexuality that a study by the Girl Scout Institute found 61 percent of children turn to their moms for these conversations, as opposed to just 3 percent for fathers.

But dads are still critical. The landmark Add Health study of ninety thousand adolescents showed that girls who have a close relationship with their fathers were more likely to delay sexual activity. Dad-involvement also produces greater confidence in daughters and sons, increased sociability, and more self-assurance. Father-absence had a host of negative side effects, from premature menarche in girls (the technical term for first period) to increased aggression in boys. The message from all this data is consistent with other areas of my research. Sex, like so many aspects of life, is a family affair.

"I WISH MY PARENTS WOULD HAVE TOLD ME"

I first realized that Linda and I were off to a hapless start with our girls when I read Joyce McFadden's *Your Daughter's Bedroom*. McFadden was a mild-mannered psychoanalyst and new mom in New York City when the 9/11 attacks occurred. Anxious for her safety, she moved her family to Long Island. But she soon felt cut off from her friends, so McFadden came up with a novel way to reach out to other women by having them express their innermost feelings on the Internet. She wrote sixty-three open-ended questions covering everything from grief to childbirth to beauty. She posted these online under the title "The Women's Realities Study" and invited women to answer however many they wanted.

In no time, three thousand questionnaires were completed, and the results flabbergasted her. The three most popular questions were all about sex, and not just any aspect of sex. The topics women most wanted to discuss were ones they hadn't discussed in their families while growing up: menstruation, masturbation, and their mothers' romantic lives. McFadden wrote about these things in her book, surveying all the research and interviewing scholars and lay women alike.

We met for coffee one day, and she told me what she thought were the most effective ways to approach sexuality with boys and girls.

Lesson #1: *It's never too early to start.* I have a confession. When I gave my daughters a bath or sat with them while they were being potty trained, I never named their genitals. I was too embarrassed, or afraid. "Wash your privates," I would say, or "Clean where the pee-pee comes from." Apparently I'm not alone. Research shows that half of all two-and-a-half-year-old girls know the correct name for boys' genitals, but not for their own. In our culture, boys have penises; girls have "down there."

McFadden was outraged by this. "How can we give our daughters confidence in their bodies if they can't even name the parts of their body?" she said. "When my daughter had a diaper rash, I would say, 'Is your labia sore?' or "Do you want some cream on your vulva?' I didn't say, 'Does your hee-ha hurt?'

"We are so afraid of saying the wrong thing," she continued, "or that they'll ask us about our sexuality, [that] we don't tell them anything. To me this is about language: Nose. Lamp. Chair. Nipple. We don't change the names of people's ears, their scalp, their fingernails. Why change their genitalia?"

The American Academy of Pediatrics agrees. In a 2009 report, the group recommended speaking to children as young as eighteen months old about sexuality. At that age, "It is important to teach your child the proper names for body parts. Making up names for body parts may give the idea that there is something bad about the proper name." When your kid eventually starts asking questions, the report recommended a careful response:

- Don't laugh or giggle, even if the question is cute. Your child shouldn't be made to feel ashamed for her curiosity.
- Be brief. Your four-year-old doesn't need to know the details of intercourse.
- See if your child wants or needs to know more. Follow up with, "Does that answer your question?"

Lesson #2: *It's easier to talk with a nine-year-old than a thirteen-year-old.* The stories about menstruation in *Your Daughter's Bedroom* are heartbreaking. Girls feeling horror, shame, guilt, disgust. Some women said their mothers insulted them when they first got their periods; others were sad their fathers withdrew and never hugged them again. McFadden's book contains memorable thoughts from such women.

> *I wish my parents would have told me all the details before it happened rather than afterwards.*
>
> *I wish my mother had been more comfortable in her body and been able to instill that in me.*
>
> *I wish it had been taught to me in a way that made me excited and proud rather than anxious.*

McFadden said these responses told her that it's important to start talking about menstruation when girls are in their latency period, around seven or eight. "We do it backward," she said. "We wait until they're teenagers, when they withdraw from us, then we try to talk to them. If you start when they're younger, they're still sponges and happy to learn."

I reported all of this to Linda, and she apparently took it to heart. A few weeks later, I was giving the girls a bath. Trying to find the courage to follow this advice, I said to Tybee, "Wash your v-v-vagina." "Oh, yes," she answered enthusiastically. "It's a little red right now. But don't worry, Daddy. Soon, I'll get my period and it will be very red."

Lesson #3: *A little bit goes a long way.* If I tell my eight-year-old daughter that a baby is made by inserting a penis into a vagina, what happens when she discovers that's not the only reason penises are inserted into vaginas? The whole subject seems such a slippery slope.

"But we don't have that problem with other things," McFadden said. "When we sign up our kids for Little League, we don't say, 'Now when you're playing in the majors' or 'We need to talk about steroids.' It's no different than when you tell your child 'This is an *a.* Then later, 'Here it is in the word *apple.*' Then, 'Here's a book about apples.' Just because you tell your daughter about *a* doesn't mean you have to tell her about *Anna Karenina.*"

IT'S NOT A "TALK"; IT'S A CONVERSATION

So what do kids think about their parents yakking away at them about sex? I put that question to the girls from the swim team at Kate and Brad Eggleston's house. All three of their daughters were there: Brady (nineteen), now a sophomore at college; Zoe (sixteen); and Eliza (fourteen). Their younger brother peeked around the corner, but he was hurried off to bed. The girls wanted free rein to school me.

Most of the girls had gotten their first lesson around third or fourth grade. "I was probably eight," Eliza said. "I overheard Mom talking to my sister about the penis being inserted into the vagina, and I rushed into the room and said, 'What are you talking about?!'" Her mother explained everything to both girls, and that night, as the news sunk in, Eliza lay in bed, calling out to her sisters, "The Johnsons, nine kids! Oooooh! The Coffees, five kids! Ooooooh." Then she started in on teachers. "Mr. Bircher. Oooooooh!" The next day she called her grandparents. "'Grandma, did you have sex?' 'Yes, Eliza, I had sex.'

"'Ooooooooh!'"

Did any of the girls think there was an age when they were too young to learn about sex?

"I don't think so," said one. "We learned about body parts in the bathtub because that was natural. And by fourth grade it's natural to start hearing expressions like 'humping,' because that's how boys talk."

"The thing to understand," Brady said, "is it's no longer 'The Talk.' It's a series of talks. It's a conversation. There's one when you're one age, another when you're older. You have to get over this idea it's one and you're done. When you're a kid, this stuff comes up every day!"

Next up: "Do you really want to hear this information from your parents?"

"You get a very distorted view if you hear things from your friends," said one of the girls. "Or even on the Internet. If it's coming from your parents, at least you know it's true."

"Sometimes I'm confused," said another. "I have to pretend, 'Yeah, I know what that is,' but I have no clue. With my mom, I know she won't make fun of me."

"But do you actually ask your parents," I said, "or do you secretly want them to bring it up?"

"I'm happy I didn't have to bring it up," Zoe said. "To me it's like this." She put her fingers in her ears, then pulled them halfway out. "I pretend I don't want to hear, but secretly I'm listening."

Next I told them I wanted to talk about menstruation. "As a guy, I'm not comfortable talking about this," I said, "but as a dad, I'm realizing I have to."

"First of all," Zoe said, "don't call it menstruation. Call it 'period.'"

"The technical term for the first one is menarche," I said.

"If you call it that, you'll get your ass kicked."

First periods are often accompanied by ignorance, crying, and trauma, they said. But they also mentioned something I'd never heard before: jubilation. That's what McFadden had told me is how successful families handle this.

"I was incredibly excited," Brady said. "My mother had promised I could get my ears pierced. She took me out to dinner with my great-aunt to this fancy restaurant. I got a cappuccino. I put about ten pounds of sugar in it, and it still tasted disgusting."

Kate Eggleston calls this a "period party," and she's had one for each of her daughters. She even put together a period care package with tampons, chocolate, something salty, and a CD with appropriate songs like "I Am Woman" by Helen Reddy. She handed them out to all the girls in the neighborhood. Sex Mom had become Period Mom.

Finally, I wondered if these girls had any tips for dads about talking to their children of either gender about issues around sexuality. They were fairly blunt.

- *Be open.* "You love your dad and stuff," one girl said, "so you don't want to keep things from him. But your dad can't be judgmental when you bring something up."
- *Don't gross out.* "My dad hates it when the garbage cans fill up with tampons," someone added. "He gets so awkward. Once he wouldn't even buy me tampons from the drugstore. Even if you are embarrassed, pretend you're not, and your kids will feel more comfortable."
- *Never get mad.* "I told my dad, 'I promise not to do anything big and stupid sexually if you promise not to yell at me for doing something small and stupid.'"
- *Relax.* "Talking to kids about sex doesn't mean you're laying out the red carpet," Brady said. "We know the difference, and you should, too."

THE FORMULA FOR MARITAL HAPPINESS

Building a healthy dialogue with kids about sexuality is only one issue. For the parents there's the even dicier issue of maintaining a healthy relationship themselves. And I thought the first topic made me uncomfortable!

Again, let's start with recent research—most of which is surprisingly upbeat. There is lots of evidence that sex is a boon to families. Sex improves our health, brightens our moods, and deepens our connection to our partners (as long as they're the ones we're having it with). Men are particularly fortunate. A study in England found that men who have three or more orgasms a week are 50 percent less likely to die from heart disease. Researchers in Australia discovered that frequent ejaculation reduces the risk of prostate cancer. And scientists in Belfast tracked a thousand middle-aged men for a decade, and those who reported the highest frequency of orgasm enjoyed a death rate half that of the laggards. Unzip, men, your life depends on it!

Women benefit, too. Female orgasms boost your immune system, help you sleep better, calm your cravings for junk food and cigarettes, even reduce depression. A 2002 study from the State University of New York found that women whose male partners did not use condoms were less subject to depression. Researchers speculated the hormone prostaglandin, found in semen, may act as an antidepressant.

Even more significant is that monogamy, for all its flaws, appears to be a fairly reliable institution. In any given year, 90 percent of married couples say they are faithful, according to the General Social Survey at the University of Chicago. Over a lifetime, 28 percent of men admit to cheating, as do 15 percent of women.

All this news about sexuality makes the facts about marital

sexuality even harder to hear: Married people simply have less and less sex over time. Researchers at the University of Georgia studied more than ninety thousand women on four continents and concluded "the longer a couple is married, the less often they have sex." Couples have sex fifty-two fewer times in their second year of marriage than their first; they lose another twelve times in year three, and it drops off even more after that.

Marriage even seems to diminish the quality of sex. A survey of nine thousand people by David Schnarch, head of the Marriage & Family Health Center in Colorado, found half of couples said their sex was friendly but predictable. Another 17 percent went further, saying their sex was passionless, mechanical, and nonerotic.

These views can have an effect on the quality of family life. In an elegant study, behavioral scientist Robyn Dawes examined marital satisfaction and devised a simple, undeniable formula:

Marital happiness = the frequency of lovemaking − the frequency of quarreling

So what's a couple experiencing bed death to do? For years, the standard advice was to try to draw closer to your partner. Everything from therapy sessions to morning chat shows tells couples to fix the relationship, and you'll fix the sex. This idea grew out of attachment theory, the notion that however successful you were at bonding to your parents as a child predicts how successful you will be in relationships as an adult. The idea is that we try to find in our lovers the same kind of security and nurturing we craved from our parents. Without that intimacy, sex cannot flourish. This is where we got such advice as: have date night, schedule alone time with your partner, do something to meet your lover's needs—and presto libido, sparks will fly.

But this standard advice just didn't work for many people, and so it came under attack in recent years. A group of psychologists led by David Shnarch, the author of *Passionate Marriage*, and Stephen Mitchell, the author of *Can Love Last?*, devised a new approach. Their radical idea was that intimacy is the last thing couples need. All that living together, sharing a bathroom, and hearing about each other's lives all day gives couples a surfeit of togetherness. What couples need is more separation. Too much familiarity quashes desire, these authors said, while sex thrives on mystery and adventure. If you want more sex in your marriage, you don't need more cuddling, you need more creativity and escapism.

BREAK THE TYRANNY OF 11:00 P.M.

So how does this theory play out in the bedroom? To answer that question, I met one of the leading voices of this "new sex" movement. Esther Perel is smart, attractive, and occasionally blunt. A native of Belgium, she speaks nine languages, and she speaks them all with a tone that's both sexy and stern. (She's also married to someone from Tybee Island, Georgia.) Perel is the author of the international best seller *Mating in Captivity*, which is the bible of this new movement. I asked her to help me understand how couples in high-functioning families maintain the fire.

"They know what sex means to them," she said. "Sex isn't something you do. It's a place you go. The people who are good at it know what they want to express in that space. Is it a place for escape? A place for rebellion? A place to be safely aggressive? The key is to remember it's about pleasure. The killer of sex is obligation.

"I am the child of Holocaust survivors," Perel continued. "There are two groups in my community. Those who didn't die and those who came back to life." Those who didn't die, she explained, remained tethered to the past. They don't take risks anymore. They don't play. They are the couples who've been married for years and have sex without feeling anything.

"The people who came back to life are the ones who reclaimed the capacity to dream. To imagine. To live. They are the couples who are constantly discovering new things with their partners."

When couples complain about the listlessness of their sex lives, Perel said, they sometimes want more sex, but they always want better sex. "And the kind of sex they're talking about is about renewal; it's about playfulness; it's about connection. It's sex as an antidote to death."

There are a myriad of ways of renewing that connection, she said. What works for some might not work for others. Still, she gave me a few suggestions, which I gathered along with ones from other people into the following tip sheet for sex in long-term relationships.

WHERE

- *Curse the bed.* It has failure written all over it. Find other surfaces in the house.

WHEN

- *Break the tyranny of 11:00 P.M.*
- *Be spontaneous.* Cancel lunch with a friend and meet in the middle of the day. Wake up early before the kids get up. Anything that feels a little transgressive.

HOW

- *Talk dirty.* Set up private e-mail accounts where you can send each other secret messages. iChat, Skype, or text in advance of a big night to build up anticipation.
- *Have sex with the lights on or with your eyes open.* Try to see "behind the eyes" of your partner.
- *Be selfish.* First take care of yourself, then take care of your partner.
- *Moan.* Researchers have highlighted the importance of "female copulatory vocalization." One scholar identified 550 copulation calls from female baboons alone. Even the Kama Sutra endorses moaning, recommending a woman choose among the "cries of the dove, cuckoo, green pigeon, parrot, bee, nightingale, goose, duck, and partridge."

I was struck by how much Perel's ideas mirrored those I had been hearing in other parts of my research into happy families. Sex, like negotiating, is something we have to practice and get better at. Sex, like life, can't just follow the same routine. It needs to be agile.

During our visit, Perel asked me to play a short game. Each of us had to finish the sentence, "I turn myself off when _____."

She went first. "I turn myself off when I look at my e-mail before going to bed."

Me. "I turn myself off when I take forever to brush my teeth, take my medicine, and get ready for bed."

She. "I turn myself off when I haven't had time to go to the gym."

Me. "I turn myself off when I have to take twenty pillows off the bed."

"As you can see," Perel said, "ninety percent of the answers have nothing to do with sex per se. They have to do with feeling deadened inside. Now let's flip it," she said. "I turn myself on when I go dancing."

"I turn myself on when I say what I want."

"I turn myself on when I take time in nature, when I see friends, when we have time to go out."

"The point is," she continued, "each of us is responsible for our own desire. For being shut down or being turned on. I have asked people in twenty-two countries the same question, 'What draws you to your partner?' And the answers are universal. First, when he's away, when she comes back, when we are separate and reunite. Second, when I see the other at work, on the stage, surfing, singing; when I see my partner doing something he's passionate about. And third, when he makes me laugh, when he surprises me, when she dresses differently, when she introduces an element of the unknown."

This is the closest thing we have to a universal truth about happy couples, Perel said: They combine the familiar and the unfamiliar into a workable tension. "The couples that have successful sex lives," she said, "turns out they like it. They enjoy what happens there. And they do everything they can to keep reinventing what happens in that place."

There's one more thing couples can do, she said, that can help both their sex lives and the sex lives of their children in the future. "Be sexual in front of the kids." This doesn't mean French kissing, petting, or anything explicit, she added. Parental discretion is advised. But you want to give your children a positive, healthy example of sexuality in a loving family. When you censor yourself, she said, you pass on this censorship to the next generation. When you keep your desire hidden away, you teach them to do the same with theirs.

"At first they'll go 'oooh' when you start getting flirty in front of them," Perel said. "Then, when they get older, they'll say 'Can you do this in your room?' Then, when they're teenagers, they'll feel comfortable enough to hold hands with their boyfriend or girlfriend in front of you. That's when you know you have a healthy sexual attitude in your family."

Because if you can make sexuality an open, integrated part of your family, she said, then all that talk when they're young isn't wasted. It's well spent.

8

WHAT'S LOVE GOT TO DO WITH IT

The Simple Test That Saved Millions of Families

S USANNE ROMO WAS finally happy. She and her husband, Ernie, lived in a sunny home near the Pacific Ocean in Chula Vista, California, outside San Diego. They had a spacious backyard for their dog, Maggie, whom they adopted from the pound. They sold Farmers Insurance together and reached the level of platinum elite. They volunteered in the local schools. After a difficult childhood, Susanne, who was in her midthirties and had a cheerful face, a big smile, and an amber bob, at last had the life she always wanted.

Except for her marriage.

"I had the seven-year itch," she said. "I told my husband it wasn't that I didn't love him anymore, it's just that I didn't feel connected to him anymore.

"Ernie loves to watch TV. I mean loves it," she continued. "He has a 'man cave' filled with hundreds of DVDs, a fifty-two-inch flat-screen television, and surround sound." After dinner,

Ernie would retreat to his lair and watch sports or political shows. Susanne would often follow him so the two could spend time together. But she quickly grew bored and resentful.

"In the early years of our marriage, we would do things—take a walk on the beach, have a glass of wine, even run errands together," she said. "There were these amazingly beautiful things he used to do in our relationship. Now all we do is sit on the couch."

Eventually she fled to the backyard in the evenings and played with the dog.

Then one day she attended a financial conference. "The speaker talked about her marriage, how strong it had been, how happy. But they were starting to slide into a rut. It sounded so familiar," she said.

The woman recommended a book called *The Five Love Languages*, by Dr. Gary Chapman. Susanne wasn't used to getting marriage advice at an insurance conference, so she was intrigued. She ordered a copy of the book.

"And suddenly the axis of my life tilted," she said. "Not just my marriage, but my entire family life. It unlocked for me what I needed in order to feel loved—and to love others."

She finished the book in one evening and afterward went running to the man cave.

"Honey, there's something I want you to see," she said. "I think it can help our marriage."

LOVE AND MARRIAGE

Marriage. It's the foundation for many families. Whether it's a first marriage, a second marriage, an arranged marriage, a common-law marriage, or just a committed relationship in which to raise children, a partnership between adults is at the heart of most families. Yet it's among the hardest things to get right in families.

So what's the latest thinking about the best way to do that?

Marriage has been the subject of a wave of recent scholarship, much of it encouraging. Despite what you may have heard (or felt), marriage is one of life's most proven routes to happiness. Some of this may be a reverse correlation. As Jonathan Haidt noted in *The Happiness Hypothesis*, "Happy people marry sooner and stay married longer than people with a lower happiness setpoint."

But as Haidt and others have shown, marriage actually promotes a number of changes that make people happier. Married people smoke and drink less, get fewer colds, sleep more regular hours, and eat more regular meals. (This last fact also has a downside, as married people do get fatter, as anyone who's attended a high school reunion can attest.) The result of all these health benefits: Married people simply live longer. It's no wonder that a survey of 59,169 people in forty-two nations determined that married people have greater life satisfaction than nonmarried people.

Marriage is also a far more successful institution than most people think. The oft-quoted statistic that half of all marriages end in divorce is appallingly misleading. Marriage went through enormous changes in the 1960s and 1970s as a result of the women's movement and sexual revolution. The divorce rate for those unlucky enough to get married before those changes set in does appear to be around 50 percent.

But the rate has been plummeting ever since. Divorce is now at a thirty-year low in America, down a third since its peak in 1979. A primary reason is that people have been getting hitched later. The biggest single risk factor for divorce is getting married before you turn twenty-four; the biggest predictor of marital success is graduating from college. In her book *For Better*, Tara Parker-Pope showed that the ten-year divorce rate for female college graduates married in the 1990s was a mere 16 percent.

All that is a boon to families. The happier people are in their marriages, the happier their families tend to be. But it does raise a high-stakes question: Since marriage is so important to families, how do I get more happiness out of the one I'm in?

Americans have been asking that question for more than a century, ever since marriage shifted from being an institution based primarily on economics and child rearing to one based on personal fulfillment and "finding your soul mate." The results have been mixed. As Rebecca Davis chronicled in her book *More Perfect Unions*, the marital enrichment business has gone through many fads, from Freudian analysis to hypnosis to Tantric sex retreats.

Recently many of the traditional routes for marital assistance have come under attack. Couples therapy has been rocked by internal criticism. In 2011, the editor of the industry's leading trade publication wrote a cover story about growing frustration in the field. Practitioners often feel "confused, at odds with at least one of [their] patients, out of control," he wrote.

More popular approaches, meanwhile, from going to the movies to lighting candles to making time for each other, also seem shopworn. Other ideas, like listening actively, repeating what your spouse says, and responding in an even tone, come across as idealistic, irritating, or both. (One friend of mine, fresh from a lesson in active listening, was walking on the beach with his wife, dutifully echoing back what she said. "So you're not happy with how I reacted?" "You were disappointed in my behavior." Finally she turned to him. "For God's sake, why do you keep repeating everything I say!?")

So what's a couple to do? Aren't there any fresh ideas out there? Yes, but they come from quarters you might not expect.

LOVE POTION NUMBER 5

At just after 9:00 A.M. on a picnic-perfect morning in late August, Gary Chapman took the stage of the Brentwood Hills Church of Christ outside of Nashville. It was the start of a six-hour seminar called "The Marriage You Always Wanted." The event was inspired by Dr. Chapman's book, *The Five Love Languages,* which has sold eight million copies in the United States and has been translated into forty languages.

Nearly a thousand people crowded the pews. Some men wore blazers, others T-shirts and jeans. The women wore sundresses or bright-colored blouses. A few couples held hands; others crossed their arms as if to say, "I'm being dragged here against my will."

"It looks like Noah's ark," Linda whispered. "Everyone's in twos."

At seventy-three years old, Dr. Chapman is an unlikely guru. He wears khaki trousers and a sweater vest. He looks like Senate Minority Leader Mitch McConnell and sounds like Gomer Pyle.

But his appeal is his direct, avuncular style. "My goal for today is that your marriage will get better," he said. "Marriages either get better, or they get worse. They never stand still. And I certainly hope your marriage will not get worse because I came here." A warm chuckle filled the room.

"The key to a successful marriage is one word, *love,*" he went on. "But we are not lovers by nature. We are self-centered. I want to show you love is not simply a feeling. It's a way of thinking, a way of behaving. This might require a change of heart for some of you, but I believe you can do it. Now, let's get started."

Gary Chapman did not set out to become a marriage expert. He was born in China Grove, North Carolina (population 2,000). His father, a high school dropout, ran a Shell gasoline station. Dr.

Chapman was the first member of his family to go to college and attended Moody Bible Institute in Chicago. "As a senior in high school, I had a strong sense that God wanted me in some kind of ministry," he told me the night before the seminar in a rare interview. "There were only two things I knew in a Christian framework that I could do. One would be the pastor of a church; the other would be a missionary. I didn't particularly like snakes, so I decided I should probably be a pastor."

Back in North Carolina after his ordination, he began offering part-time classes on marriage and family, and was stunned by the number of couples who asked if they could stop by his office to chat. He also became captivated by all the new research on attachment theory, specifically the experience of being "in love." Divorce was becoming widespread, and a host of scholars were trying to figure out how love could come on so suddenly in people and dissipate even more quickly. In 1977, psychologist Dorothy Tennoy coined the term "limerance" to describe the compulsive feeling of being romantically attracted to someone and obsessively craving their reciprocation. That infatuation lasts no more than two years, she concluded.

As Dr. Chapman described the idea to the audience in Nashville, "You can't get anything done when you're in looooooooooove. Being in love is next door to being insane. I call it the tingles. But nobody told us the tingles go away, so when we come down off our high, our differences emerge. We start arguing. We meet somebody at work. We get a tingle with them. Before long, we're obsessed with them and start thinking, 'I can't stay in this marriage. I don't love you. I don't know if I ever loved you.'" He paused. "We've got to stop this cycle in this country, and I want to show you how."

In the 1980s, Dr. Chapman began combing through more than

a decade of his notes in an attempt to identify different ways that individuals express love. "Adults all have a love tank," he said. "If you feel loved by your spouse, the whole world is right. If the love tank is empty, the whole world can begin to look dark." Challenges arise because individuals have different ways of filling their tanks.

To illustrate, he told us about a couple who came to see him. The man was dumbfounded. He cooked dinner every night for his wife; afterward he washed the dishes and took out the trash; every Saturday he mowed the grass and washed the car. "I don't know what else to do," the man said. "But she still tells me she doesn't feel loved."

The woman agreed. "He does all those things," she said. Then she burst into tears. "But Dr. Chapman, we never talk. We haven't talked in thirty years." In Dr. Chapman's analysis, each one spoke a different love language: He liked to perform acts of service for his wife, while she was seeking quality time from him.

"Each of us has a primary love language," Dr. Chapman explained, though we also often have secondary or tertiary ones. He said the way to identify your language is to focus on the way you express love. What you give is often what you crave. "In a marriage, almost never do a husband and wife have the same language," he said. "The key is learning to speak the language of the other person."

Dr. Chapman calls these different styles of expressing and receiving affection "the five love languages."

1. *Words of affirmation.* Using compliments and expressions of appreciation, like "You are the best husband in the world" or "I admire your optimism."
2. *Gifts.* Bringing flowers, leaving love notes, or buying tokens of affection.

3. *Acts of service.* Doing something for your partner you know
he or she would like you to do, like washing dishes, walking
the dog, or changing a diaper.

4. *Quality time.* Giving your partner your undivided attention
by turning off the television, sharing a meal, or taking a
walk.

5. *Physical touch.* Holding hands, putting your arm around
your partner, or tussling your partner's hair.

He describes these ideas in *The 5 Love Languages: How to Express Heartfelt Commitment to Your Mate*, which Moody published in 1992. It sold 8,500 copies the first year, quadrupling the publisher's expectation. The following year it sold 17,000; two years later 137,000. In a rare feat of publishing history, every year (except one) for the next twenty years it outsold its previous number. (Dr. Chapman eventually published spin-offs, including *The 5 Love Languages of Children.*)

A friend in Georgia gave the book to me when Linda and I got married. The cover photograph of lovers walking hand in hand on a sunset beach made me think it came free with a fruitcake at a truck stop. I stuffed it unread on a bookshelf. A few years later, I opened it and was flabbergasted. It nailed a particular knot in our relationship with uncanny accuracy.

I work alone all day, so I look forward to sitting down with Linda at night and discussing many subjects. But Linda works in a busy office all day, serving other people, and she wants nothing more than to be alone. If I let her sleep late one morning or run her clothes to the dry cleaner, I am (however briefly) the Greatest Husband on Earth. She's acts of service. When she gives me her full attention and devotes time just to talking with me, I feel special. I'm quality time.

A similar revelation happened to the Romos in San Diego. Susanne learned that her primary love language was quality time. At first her husband didn't understand. "We spend lots of time together!" Ernie said. "We work together. We eat together. We watch TV together."

"It's not the same," she said. "It's time, but it's not quality time." Then she showed him the book.

"Then I got it," he told me. "Finally I understood where she was coming from

Ernie's primary language was physical touch. "At first this bothered me," Susanne said. "I had never had that type of physically loving relationship that didn't mean sex, sex, sex, demands, demands, demands."

But they adjusted, slowly. "I learned to touch Ernie all day long," she said. "Give him a hug." He learned to prepare her when an important game was coming up and schedule more walks on the beach. "Now when she says, 'Hey, there's some outdoor event going on in Little Italy, would you like to go?,' instead of saying, 'Nah, I'd rather stay home,' I'll say, 'Is it important that I go with you?'" If she says yes, he gives up his game. If she says no, he gets to stay home.

Susanne smiled. "Little things, incremental things," she said, "that can skyrocket love back to the stratosphere." And it worked. The couple recently celebrated their twentieth anniversary.

Inevitably, Dr. Chapman's book was criticized. Some say it has a preachy tone; others say it's too simplistic. But one reason the book resonates is Dr. Chapman's honesty about his own failings. His marriage, to a fellow parishioner, Karolyn, at age twenty-three, was so troubled in its early years he turned to God in desperation. "If I hadn't made a covenant," he told me, "I would have left."

I met Karolyn a few months after the seminar when she visited

New York and invited Linda and me for coffee. She is the opposite of her straitlaced husband. She is flamboyant, loves leopard print blouses and zebra-stripe pants, and has mile-high Texas hair, a five-foot-tall firecracker cheering loudly on the sidelines. No wonder her husband's contribution to the world is to explain that lovers speak different languages!

When they were first married, Karolyn, whom he later realized was an acts of service person, expected her husband to clean toilets and vacuum floors. He, who is a words of affirmation person, needed to be told how wonderful he was. Fifty years later, neither has changed. Recently, he told the crowd, he and Karolyn were sitting around the house one morning when she said, "The blinds are getting dusty." "Yeah, they are," he said. Two mornings later, at 6:30 A.M., he started vacuuming the blinds. Karolyn walked in. "Honey, what are you doing?" He turned to her and said, "I'm making love!" A big smile came over her face. "You have got to be the greatest husband in the world." Dr. Chapman gave her an even bigger smile. "Tell me one more time, baby. Tell me one more time!"

TAKE THE FIGHT OUT OF THE NIGHT

In one way, Dr. Chapman's success is not a surprise. Religion has long been inextricably tied to family life in America. One truth that appears repeatedly in scientific studies is the persistent correlation between religiosity and happy families. Research on this is all but unanimous over the last fifty years. The more committed families are to a religious or spiritual tradition, the happier they are. Recent surveys have confirmed the correlation. A study from the University of Virginia in 2011 showed that mothers who attend religious services weekly are happier than those who do not. A study in 2008 showed that men who regularly attend religious services have happier marriages and are more likely to be involved with their children.

The most comprehensive study ever done on this topic, in 2010, gives some clues about why this might be. After examining studies of more than three thousand adults, Chaeyoon Lin and Robert Putnam found that what religion you practice or however close you feel to God makes no difference in your overall life satisfaction. What matters is the number of friends you have in your religious community. Ten is the magic number; if you have that many, you'll be happier. Religious people, in other words, are happier because they feel connected to a community of like-minded people.

But religion brings something else to communities. A hallmark of religion for millennia has been helping people mark life cycle events, both happy and sad. Most of these happen within families. I asked Dr. Chapman what we can learn from religion to improve our family life. He mentioned three things.

First, joy. Shelly Gable, of the University of California, has highlighted the importance of taking joy in your partner's success. In a wonderfully titled study, "Will You Be There for Me When Things Go Right?," she asked partners to share good news with their spouses. Those who said merely "Good job, honey" failed. Those who performed best didn't just toast their partner's achievements, but they also attributed them to their spouse's unique self. "You got that raise only because someone with your guts and ingenuity could have won that big account."

Religion cultivates that sense of generosity. As Dr. Chapman said, it magnifies joyous occasions to large-scale celebrations and gives people practice glorifying "the other" in their lives. Even those who aren't observant can take note. As Gable's study concluded, if you want more happiness at home, make more of the positive moments. This turns out to be more important than being supportive during the negative ones.

Second, forgiveness. "In human relationships, none of us is perfect," Dr. Chapman said. "We all hurt people we love the most from time to time. And if we don't deal with that, it's a barrier between us and the other person."

Extensive research confirms this. From the home to the workplace, scholars have shown that apologies deepen empathy, stabilize crises, and improve long-lasting relationships. For those like me who find this hard to swallow, there is at least some upside: Apologizing can save you money. Researchers at the Nottingham School of Economics found that customers were twice as likely to forgive a company that apologized instead of giving them cash. As the study's coauthor said, "Talk really is cheaper." Forget roses, guys. A mea culpa serves just as well.

Finally, resilience. As the dean of social scientists, Erving Goffman, once said, "corrective rituals" are vital to successful relationships. Religion has perfected redemption. In tradition after tradition, the language of faith continually reminds people they can recover from suffering.

The most memorable thing Dr. Chapman said in the seminar I attended was that people often get trapped in painful places, but those in successful relationships find a way to recover. One of them "takes the fight out of the night," he said. I love that line, and I love even more his advice on how to accomplish it. "Guys, I'm going to give you a sentence and encourage you to write it in your notebook," he said. "I guarantee it will change your life forever: *Honey, what you're saying makes a whole lot of sense.* You say that, you are no longer her enemy. You are her friend who understands her."

CHASING BUTTERFLIES

The marriage enrichment business has built up a vast library, and I decided to wade into it. Linda would go off to work in her business clothes; I would sit home in my pajamas and read about rearranging our pillows or who should do the ironing. This made us oddballs at school events. Men would come to her for investment tips; women would come to me for marriage tips.

Much of what I read completely bored me. But every now and then I encountered a wow idea. A notion so counterintuitive and smart I instantly wanted to try it out. I began collecting a small grab bag of these ideas. Though each item is based on science, my list is not intended to be rigorous. Its sole criterion was "An Idea So Interesting I Wanted to Tell Linda at the End of the Day." I don't think you can get a Nobel Prize for this standard, but I do know you can get a night or two of better sex.

1. *Put yourself first.* The cliché position is that good marriages are all about "we"; but new research shows that successful relationships have a lot of "me" in them. Psychologists Arthur Aron and Gary Lewandowski studied how individuals use their relationships to better themselves. They learn new things from their partners, meet new people, try new experiences.

When couples are first falling in love, for example, each person uses a wider variety of words to describe themselves. The new relationship literally broadens their self-conception. Over time, each partner slowly adopts the traits of the other, growing individually as they grow together. As Dr. Lewandowski concluded, "People have a fundamental motivation to improve the self. If your partner is helping you become a better person, you become happier and more satisfied in the relationship."

2. *Rethink date night.* A common piece of advice for couples is

to schedule regular one-on-one time. "Date night" is the default answer to most problems in modern marriages. And research backs this up. A study from the National Marriage Project in 2012 showed that couples who have weekly time to themselves are 3.5 times more likely to be happy, including sexually happy.

But not just any date will do. A growing body of research says that simply going to dinner and a movie has little impact on a relationship. If you want to improve your relationship, try something novel with your partner. Helen Fisher, of Rutgers, has observed that couples who participate in unusual or different activities, from taking an art class to driving to a new part of town to cooking a new recipe, flood their systems with the same chemicals as do couples just falling in love.

3. *Double-date.* One surprising way to score some of those novelty points is go on a date with another couple. Richard Slatcher of Wayne State University did a fascinating study called "When Harry and Sally Met Dick and Jane." He divided sixty couples into two groups and had each couple spend time with another couple. One group was given highly revealing questions; the other, small talk. The results were dramatic. Couples who disclosed more about themselves felt closer to the other couples—and to each other. Slatcher said the experience of being intimate with another couple was sufficiently novel to trigger the same chemical reaction as the exotic date night.

4. *Have family night.* The widely held view among scholars and laypeople is that married people with kids are less happy than their childless peers. There is ample evidence to support this view, and even more ample chatter, much of it fed by a *New York* magazine cover story in 2010 called "All Joy and No Fun: Why Parents Hate Parenting."

Inspired by that article, the Institute for American Values commissioned a comprehensive study, "When Baby Makes Three," to examine the question. The results were eye-opening. The transition to parenthood is, indeed, so stressful it does make first-time parents less happy, and it does so overnight. (Or overnight, after overnight, after overnight, as the case may be.) But childless couples also experience a decline in happiness; theirs just happens over time. "By the time both groups have been married an average of eight years," the report concluded, "their marital quality is not that different."

The report uncovered even more intriguing news. Married parents clearly outperform their childless peers in one important category: meaning. Both moms and dads—but especially moms—are more likely to say, "My life has an important purpose."

This captures the paradox of parenting: In the short term it often leaves parents exhausted, short on money, and starving for stimulation; but in the long term it gives them a deeper sense of purpose. As every parent knows, sometimes the most satisfying moments in a marriage come when you look up from that board game on Friday night and catch the eye of your spouse, walk in on them putting cookie dough on a child's nose, or reach over and take their hand when you tuck in a sleeping child. It's like what those explorers of old must have felt upon enduring the perilous slog through the jungle and finally coming upon Shangri-la. Maybe that's why the authors of "When Baby Makes Three" were most startled to find that parents who have the most children (four or more) were actually the happiest of all.

Sometimes the best way to get the marriage you've always wanted is to just stay home and play with the kids.

9

THE CARE AND FEEDING
OF GRANDPARENTS

How to Avoid Throwing Granny from the Train

THIS IS WHAT Debbie Rottenberg does on Mondays. She goes to the supermarket near her home in Waban, Massachusetts, and picks up supplies. These include her grandson's two favorite kinds of pasta, "squiggly" and "bow tie"; his two favorite vegetables, string beans and carrots; his two favorite fruits, cantaloupe and grapes; and his two favorite flavors of ice cream, Oreo and vanilla. She also buys fresh hot dog buns, along with some potato chips, which she hides in the coat closet so her husband won't eat them.

"It's a problem," she said. "Sometimes I'll go to the cupboard and Alan has demolished the chips! Then what am I supposed to give Nate for lunch? He always asks for his 'regular.'"

The next morning Debbie sleeps late to rest up for her weekly date babysitting, chauffering, and playing with Nate, who's the eldest of her five grandchildren. By noon, she gets into her station wagon and makes the ten-minute drive to the elementary school in Newton Centre, where Nate is a first grader.

"I like to get there early, so I can get a good parking space," she said.

Once in place, Debbie removes her own audiobook and cues up one more suited to Nate. Then she walks to the front of the school.

At sixty-five, Debbie is fit and fashionable, favoring khaki Capris and long-sleeved white T-shirts. She's often mistaken for one of the class moms. She exchanges a few words with the actual moms, then peers excitedly at the door, as she must have done for her junior high school sweetheart near her home in Woonsocket, Rhode Island. She married him when she turned twenty-one, and forty-five years later they've barely spent a night apart.

"I like coming to school," Debbie said. "I get to say hello to Nate's beautiful teacher and to see all his friends. I feel like an insider."

Finally, Nate emerges and scans the crowd. He has straight brown hair and his grandmother's expressive brown eyes. He's also got a splint on his arm from a tumble he took off the sofa. He sees his grandmother and comes sprinting to her side.

"Hi, DeDe!" he says, squeezing her legs.

"Hi, sweetheart," she says. "How was school today?"

He steps back and grins, ignoring the question. "App alert! App alert!"

"I know," she says, chuckling. "You want to play with my iPad. Come on, I'll give you some lunch."

The two proceed hand in hand toward her car. Nate beams like the luckiest boy in the world; Debbie has a similar expression. Another week when he hasn't outgrown me, she thinks.

"DeDe, can I have my regular today?" he asks.

"Let's hope Papa hasn't eaten your chips!"

THE GRANDMOTHER EFFECT

Grandparents. They are often considered second tier in families, but there's a striking new body of research that says they're a primary reason humans were able to live in families. As Sarah Blaffer Hrdy, an evolutionary anthropologist and the architect of much of this thinking, told me, grandparents are the "ace in the hole" of humanity.

So what's behind this thinking? And what does it mean for those of us who love it when Grandma and Grandpa come to babysit—even though we bristle when they take this time as an opportunity to criticize us?

Let's begin with the research. The belief for the last five hundred years in Western culture has been that the power of the individual drives society. The single-minded focus on individualism came primarily from several sources. One was the Protestant Reformation, which stressed personal responsibility and salvation. Another was the Enlightenment, which celebrated individual freedom. Perhaps the signature statement of this worldview came from English philosopher Thomas Hobbes, who in 1651 wrote that life in its natural state was "solitary, poor, nasty, brutish, and short."

Three hundred and fifty years later, the biggest intellectual breakthroughs of the early twenty-first century point to a different understanding of human nature. "Hobbes was not wrong in asserting that our ancestors could be brutish," John Cacioppo wrote in *Loneliness*, "but he was certainly off base when he described their existence as solitary." Cacioppo, the director of the Center for Cognitive Neuroscience at the University of Chicago, offered a more communal vision of human beings. "The driving force of our advance as a species has not been our tendency to be brutally self-interested, but our ability to be socially cooperative." We crave other people, he said.

One reason why humans love being together so much is we have something virtually unique in the animal kingdom: caretakers who are not biological parents who help raise us. The official term for such individuals is "alloparent." Anybody can be an alloparent—a babysitter, an older sibling, an aunt—but throughout history the primary alloparents have been grandmothers. Without them, Hrdy said, "There never would have been a human species."

Grandmothers in other species hardly play a role in caring for their children's children because the females do not live for decades beyond their reproductive years, whereas human females do. While men (including old men) were hunting and women were foraging, grandmothers and other alloparents were taking care of the young. Their influence was so central to humanity's ability to evolve it's been labeled "the grandmother effect."

But the impact of grandmothers wasn't just limited to early humans; it continues today. Countless studies have shown the extraordinary benefits grandmothers have on contemporary families. A meta-analysis of sixty-six studies completed in 1992 found that mothers who have more support from grandmothers have less stress and more well-adjusted children. The more involved the grandmothers are, the more involved dads are, too.

Now you see why Hrdy called grandmothers humanity's "secret benefactors."

So what are these grandmothers actually doing? They're teaching children core social skills like how to cooperate, how to be compassionate, how to be considerate. Researchers at Brigham Young University in Utah interviewed 408 adolescents about their relationship with their grandparents. When grandparents are involved, the study found, the children are more social, more involved in school, and more likely to show concern for others. Also, as lead scientist Jeremey Yorgason said, parents take the lead in disciplining negative behavior, leaving grandparents free to encourage positive behaviors.

Oh, and there's one more thing grandmothers do for grandkids: They indulge them. Just ask Nate Rottenberg.

TUESDAYS WITH DEDE

Once they're back in Waban, Nate immediately runs into Grandma DeDe's house and hunts for her iPad. While he plays with his favorite apps, Debbie makes him lunch—one hot dog in the bun, one hot dog out of the bun, chips, carrots, and grapes. She retrieves a child's wooden chair from the basement and places it behind the coffee table in the den, facing the television. The whole setup reminds me of a throne. Over lunch, Debbie gives Nate the option of watching pretaped episodes of *Dino Dan*, *Toot and Puddle*, or *Magic School Bus*.

"The shows are educational," she said. "Plus, they give me something to have a conversation with him about."

For dessert, Debbie used to give Nate two packages of Disney gummi bears, but his father complained they were getting stuck in his teeth. For a while she hid the gummi bears in the coat closet (along with the potato chips), "but then Dan really put his foot down, so now I give him a piece of gum."

After lunch Debbie takes Nate to a math class nearby, plays a baseball game with him on her computer, then gives him a bath and dinner. In many ways, Debbie is part of a larger movement. In 2004, the National Survey of Families and Households found that half of all grandparents provide some type of regular child care. While some give only a few hours a week, others give as many as forty. And that doesn't include the five million children who live with their grandparents full-time. As BYU's Yorgason said, "Grandparents are like the National Guard." They're ready to step in as needed, but otherwise they're mostly used for week-end stints.

There are clear benefits to this type of relationship. In the case of the Rottenbergs, Nate gets one afternoon a week where "I'm wrapped around his little finger," as Debbie put it. Plus, Nate's parents get to save a few bucks on child care. But there are challenges, too. Debbie feels that her strength as a grandmother comes from listening to her grandchildren, then giving them what they want. Nate likes apple juice, so she gives him apple juice. But Nate's mother, Elissa, is antijuice. For years they had a standoff about this, culminating with Debbie sneaking a bottle of Mott's into Nate's house against his parents' wishes. Though she lost that battle, Debbie still sneaks Nate a glass of watered-down juice every now and then.

I know these tensions well. Debbie has six grandchildren, and Tybee and Eden Feiler are two of them. Linda and I have benefit-ted endlessly from Debbie's single-minded commitment to being an active grandmother. But we have stress points, too. You know that plucky, natural inclination teenagers have to rebel against their parents' rules? Debbie takes that attitude toward the way we run our home, from our morning list to our bedtime routine. No wonder her grandkids love her so much. She's constantly aiding and abetting their rebellions against their parents!

And that's just the way she likes it. "I do set some boundaries," she said. "I try to be respectful of the limitations Elissa and Dan or you and Linda have for your children. But at the same time, I like the kids to know that with me they can have a stress-free situation. It makes me relaxed, and it makes them relaxed as well."

By 7:00 P.M., Dan comes to retrieve Nate, who's been bathed, fed, and dressed in his pajamas. Debbie gathers his belongings, gives him a kiss on the cheek, and waves as he scampers out the door. Then she goes upstairs and collapses.

"I'm working much harder at being a grandmother than I ever did in the twenty years since my last child left home," she said. "And in some ways it's harder than being a parent. When you're raising kids, it's your whole life, so you're multitasking. When I'm with the grandkids, I have to stop my own life and just be with them. For those hours, it's my job."

And does she ever think about adding more days with Nate?

"Oh, no," she says without hesitation. "That would be too much!"

Her answer reminded me of my favorite line about grandparenting, which I once overheard on a plane. "I love it when the headlights come," one grandmother said to another. "I love it even more when the taillights go."

WHY GRANDPARENTS ARE HAPPIER

But is Debbie right? Is unconditional love, a few hours without tension, and a contraband glass of apple juice what grandparents ought to be providing their grandchildren? To answer that, I called on one of the country's foremost experts on aging.

Laura Carstensen is the director of the Stanford Center on Longevity and a grandmother herself. With a wide smile, friendly face, and dramatic streak of white locks coming out of her straight black hair, she comes across as the grandmother any parent would want. Carstensen is best known for one of those big insights that forever changes how society looks at one segment of its population. Her idea: Older people are happier.

Between 1993 and 2005, Carstensen and several colleagues tracked 180 Americans between the ages of eighteen and ninety-four. Every five years, participants carried pagers for a week. Whenever those pagers buzzed, participants were asked to respond to a series of questions about how happy, sad, or frustrated they were.

The results were dramatic. As they aged, these people reported having fewer negative emotions and more positive. The study found a number of factors that contribute to this increased happiness. First, older people phase out people they're friendly with but not particularly close to (like the parents of their kids' friends) and concentrate on the people they actually care about, like family. This reduced circle is usually 5 individuals, Carstensen found, a far cry from the 150 people Robin Dunbar found is the maximum number a person can maintain social relations with.

"When we're young, we tend to make choices that will expand our horizons," Carstensen told me. "We go to parties; we join clubs; we accept blind dates. As we age, we have less tolerance for hassles. Older people don't go on blind dates!"

The second major reason older people are happier, she found, is that while younger adults experience more anxiety and disappointment over their career goals, finding a soul mate, and making money, older people have typically made peace with their accomplishments and failures. This lets them take more enjoyment out of life.

"As we get older, we're more aware of mortality," Carstensen said. "So when we experience wonderful things, they often come with the realization that life is fragile and will come to an end. The tear in the eye while you're watching the grandchild play with the puppy outside. You know this is not going to go on forever. You know that little girl is going to be an old woman. You know you probably won't see her become an old woman. All these influences come into that experience, making it richer and more complex."

Carstensen believes this population of more emotionally balanced older people is an extraordinary, untapped resource. "In modern society we've never had extended families before," she said. "We have this image that back on the family farm, you had your grandparents, your great-grandparents. But that's not true. They were dead. Only a hundred years ago, life expectancy was so short people didn't even have both biological parents. Twenty percent of kids had been orphaned by eighteen. Orphaned!"

Today, by contrast, grandparents and great-grandparents are becoming increasingly common. She noted that even with some parents having children when they are older, in their mid- or late thirties, demographers predict that by 2030 the vast majority of American children will have not only both biological parents present, but the full complement of grandparents and great-grandparents. "Now that's a spectacular family!" she said. "*If* we can create a culture that includes grandparents and great-grandparents in the family."

So how can these older, happy family members help make the families around them even happier? Carstensen gave me three suggestions.

1. *Offload siblings.* A friend of mine was the editor of Grandparents.com, and he shared with me a memorable detail about their readership: Parents are more interested in Web sites that cater to the problems of newborns up to three-year-olds, while grandparents are more interested in issues related to five- to nine-year-olds. Carstensen's research backs this up. "What happens," she said, "is when the first child is born, grandparents don't

have a lot to do. Sure they can help around the margins, but the parents still take the brunt. It's when the second child arrives, you see a spike in their involvement."

Carstensen has an eight-year-old grandson, Evan, and a five-year-old granddaughter, Jane. "I remember when Jane was born," she said. "I just felt this incredible connection to Evan. I was worried about him. Here he's been the total attention of his family, now there is this interloper. I felt my role was to protect him and show him that he was still loved. One way my husband and I did that was to offload him from his parents when things got stressful."

2. *Be an escape valve.* All families have difficult times, and it's during those times that older people can be especially helpful, Carstensen said. "There have been times when my son and his wife are fighting," she said, "and Evan or Jane would slide up to me on the sofa and say, 'Sometimes my daddy yells,' or 'Mommy is sad.' And I say, 'Yes, sometimes mommies and daddies fight' or 'Yes, we all get sad.' And that's all I have to say. They squeeze close to me, and it's okay.

"What I'm getting at," she continued, "is it would be really great for families if grandparents could provide the stability that sometimes parents can't. It's just too hard to be a parent. You can't always be calm. You can't never fight. But grandparents have almost conflict-free relationships with kids. I said to Evan recently, 'Do daddies get angry?' He said, 'Yes!' 'Does your mommy ever get angry?' 'Yeah!' 'Does Grandma ever get angry?' He stopped and went, 'Noooo!' What a joke. Grandma would never get angry."

3. *Hover.* Parents these days are told not to hover, especially as their children grow older. But grandparents should hover, Carstensen said. "There's a lot of research that predicts how well teenagers do if there's an adult in their life, aside from their par-

ents, who is crazy about them," she said. "I think questions like 'Did you do your homework?' 'Did you get a report card?' 'Are you being responsible?' help to show you care."

Parents may not always like grandparents to be so involved. "There's going to come a moment," Carstensen said, "when you want to say, 'Keep your hands off my kid!' But you have to take the perspective that there are many ways to raise children. There are lots of ways to be a family. And the upside of having grandparents around far outweighs the downside."

THE BEST DEFENSE AGAINST NAGGING

All this talk about how grandparents make their children and grandchildren happier does raise a question: What happens when those same grandparents drive their children crazy by needling, badgering, or just plain criticizing them all the time? Has anybody figured out how to combat nagging?

Nagging is not a particularly well-understood phenomenon. Diana Boxer, a linguist at the University of Florida, did one of the few comprehensive studies on the subject and found that nagging is prevalent in families because members don't think they have to be as polite as they would be with friends or colleagues. Nearly half of all nagging involves chores and errands, she found; a quarter involves asking someone to do (or not do) something; the others involve requests to contact someone. Women accounted for two-thirds of all nags.

"I think there's a stereotype of a nag as a wrinkled, unhappy, older woman," Boxer said. "But when men do it, it's not considered nagging; it's hounding. And when children do it, it's considered something else entirely—pestering."

I wanted to figure out some guidelines for how to handle pesky grandparents. First I called some friends whom I knew had challenging relationships with their mothers-in-law. I got three "bite your tongues," two "do an extra load of laundry when she visits," and one "install a separate thermostat in the guest room." One person advised giving Grandma a long list of to-dos when she arrives that matches her interests. One person quoted Dr. Phil: "Good fences make good neighbors. You need to set up a really good fence."

The one thing everyone agreed on: When a problem does arise, it's the blood relative who has to confront the offending mother.

Next I called Cliff Nass, an old pal who's a leading authority on talking machines. From your GPS to your phone to that automated voice that answers when you call your bank, Nass, a professor at Stanford, likely had a hand in teaching it how to speak. His job is to create computerized voices that don't make humans feel like they're being nagged. Did he have any advice for how to handle a real, live human who's failing that test?

The challenge, Nass said, is that the human brain is not designed to process constructive criticism. "The criticism part always trumps the constructive part," he said. As soon as we hear something critical, our brain is designed to do something. We either fight back or flee. "But that's exactly the wrong thing to do with your mother-in-law," he said.

To counteract these impulses, Nass advises trying to slow down the instinctive parts of our brain and reengage the thoughtful part. "Say to your mother-in-law, 'My mind is racing right now. Before we talk about your criticism, do you have anything positive to say about our parenting?'

"Now she will struggle to do that," he continued. "You might interpret that to mean she thinks you suck as a parent." But what's really happening, he said, is she's enlisting the thinking part of her brain, which takes a little time. "Once that happens, you can ask her to explain the reason behind her criticism. And who knows? There may be an insight embedded in her comment, which at that point you can engage."

GRANNY RULES

Finally, Linda and I sat down to make our own rules. We were in the distinctive position that Debbie is more indulgent as a mother and grandmother and found us to be too strict as parents; my mother is stricter and found us too lenient. No matter the situation, we invariably got diametrically opposed criticisms. We ultimately settled on one set of guidelines we applied to both mothers.

1. *Your house, your rules; our house, our rules.* When we come to your house for the weekend, you get to set the standards. If you come to our house to help out, please don't disrupt our routine.
2. *You're allowed to say what you want, as long as you're not offended if we don't take your advice.* My mother and mother-in-law have at least one thing in common: They're not very good actresses. The old "Oh, I'm keeping my opinion to myself" routine doesn't work. Let's not pretend. We told them: Tell us what you think; we'll happily listen; but we get to make the final decision.
3. *Grandparent our children; don't parent them.* When you criticize us for what our girls are eating, what time they go to bed, or what kind of manners they display, you may think you're merely commenting on our children. But you're really

commenting on our marriage. As parents, we often disagree
on these matters, and suddenly we find you in the middle
of our relationship. No matter how much we love you, we
certainly don't want you there.

Despite these rules, every now and then the stars will cross,
rare winds will blow, and our mothers will agree we're doing something horribly wrong with our children. In the last instance, at
least, Linda and I know that we're finally doing something right.

Still, the lesson for harried parents is that grandparents offer
so many dividends that setting the proper rules and building the
proper fences is worth the investment (and occasional bruised feelings). Grandparents have been humanity's ace in the hole since the
dawn of humanity itself. But the only way to fully benefit from that
ace is to use it to your advantage.

10

THE RIGHT STUFF

How Rearranging Your Furniture Can Improve Your Family

IT SEEMED LIKE such a good idea. I had invited a snooper to our house—and not just any snooper, the Thomas Edison of snooping. Sam Gosling is a mild-mannered native of England, who has the slender frame of a teenage skateboarder, a bushy Victorian mustache, and the crunchy wardrobe of an alt-country fiddle player in Austin, where Gosling is now a professor of psychology.

Snoopology, as Gosling dubbed his field, is the science of nosing around people's homes and other personal spaces in order to figure out how people and their environments influence each other. I wanted to get Gosling's take on our home because living under the same roof is one of the most difficult things families do. The chore wars are among the knottiest problems in marriages. Messy rooms are among the biggest lightning rods between parents and children. If I could crack the code of how smart families share space, I'd really be able to improve my family life.

Of course, after endorsing my idea, Linda spent the week before frantically purging her piles and shoveling unpacked dry cleaning into closets—a sort of Botox and tummy tuck on our actual life. She had good reason to worry because Gosling was no more than two steps into our entryway when he started to snoop! He began by commenting on the two six-foot-tall Burmese drums we have there.

"They're clearly an identity," he said, slowly, quizzically. "Having lots of cultural artifacts is generally an indicator of high openness. But I have this feeling that if I moved this drum a little bit, it would be moved back. Rather quickly. That would be conscientiousness, verging on the neurotic."

I hadn't even shut the door!

He stepped to his right, where we have a shelf filled with books written by friends.

"The fact that you have this here suggests you're trying to send a message," Gosling said. "You're a writer, but you're also connected to all these people. Plus, there's a diversity of books, not six hundred volumes on chemistry. That's a sign of extroversion."

Of the five major personality traits, three—openness, conscientiousness, and extroversion—clearly come out in people's spaces, he said. The other two, agreeableness and neuroticism, are more internal.

"We often assume people are trying to fool us and be something they're not," Gosling said. "The truth is, people want to be known. That's why places are so informative. I can learn more about you and your family by looking at your home than I can by talking to you."

Just then Linda appeared, and I invited Gosling into the living room.

"But wait," he said. "I'm not done here. Sometimes the most

revealing places are the ones people don't want you to see." He turned toward our closets. "I haven't looked in here yet. . . ." I heard Linda suck in her breath. I tensed my shoulders. He opened the doors.

"Oh, my!" he said. "Now we're seeing the true you."

Guess who's coming to lunch, dear? The Sigmund Freud of snooping.

A HAPPIER HOME

I find it impossible to separate family from place. My father was a builder, which meant when I was a child, we never walked past a house under construction without "checking the dirt," as he would say. My mother was an art teacher and artist. That meant we were constantly doing wacky things around our home like painting the doors different colors, making tables out of lobster pots, or gluing Monopoly houses, toy soldiers, and dice onto a stuffed swordfish.

Linda grew up outside Boston in a much more traditional house, with lacy window dressings, paisley wallpaper, and upright, Yankee furniture. My mom had a mortar and pestle on our living room table filled with pistachios. Linda's mom had a crystal candy dish with pastel mints. It was something of a shock when Linda and I got married and realized we had to make a home together. When she gave birth to our daughters, and our Brooklyn brownstone apartment filled with cribs, bouncy seats, and throw-up stains, the challenge became even greater.

So how do you take people with different senses of place and combine them into a single home? How do you integrate kids into that home and teach them to respect? What can I do to make my home a happier place for my family?

Larry Wente is one of the most thoughtful people I know who has tackled that question. An architect in Manhattan who's designed everything from churches to hospitals, Larry helped us renovate our place before we moved in. At the start of that process, he sent us a questionnaire. He told us to concentrate on three questions:

1. Describe your image of your new home using ten adjectives.
2. What is your favorite building? Why?
3. Is there a memorable characteristic or important living space from your past?

The first step to building a home together, Larry explained, is identifying the types of spaces where each person feels most comfortable—your place personality, if you will. "We all have a fundamental desire to organize and create our own environment," he said when I asked him about it recently. "It's who we are." And those ideas begin in childhood. Questions like where did you play, where did you hide from your parents, and where were your strongest memories help us articulate where we are most ourselves. "If we can tap into those memories," Larry said, "we can unlock the types of spaces we envision for ourselves."

Linda and I uncovered some significant differences. She rarely set foot in her living room as a child. Her family gathered in the open kitchen, making it the center of her sense of safety and intimacy. I viewed the kitchen as merely a place to prepare food. My family gathered in the dining room or living room. It's in those spaces where I felt most myself.

So what happens once you identify these differences?

"You begin to compromise," Larry said. "You try to determine who does more of the cooking, and build that space around them.

Who likes to watch more TV and needs an enclave there? Who prefers to sit and read? The key is to give everybody ownership over certain spaces."

Larry's approach was inspired by an influential designer of the 1970s named Christopher Alexander. In 1977, Alexander, a professor at Berkeley, published (with several colleagues) a quirky book called *A Pattern Language*, which identified 253 "patterns" that all effective spaces share. The list for private residences includes indoor sunlight, staircases as a stage, a tapestry of light and dark, a farmhouse kitchen, an area for couples, a children's realm, alcoves, ceiling height variety, open shelves, a sequence of sitting places. It sounds like a fantasy!

But there are many practical applications to this approach that can improve the homes of people of all budgets, Larry said. He helped me identify a few:

Privacy

Alexander helped define the idea that successful homes all have three types of spaces:

1. *Individual.* Space that belongs to each person alone.
2. *Shared.* Space that belongs to a subgroup, like parents or children.
3. *Public.* Space that belongs to everyone.

If, like us, you live in a place that doesn't have unlimited space, Alexander advocated creating tiny hideaways within larger spaces. Women prefer nesting areas, research shows, while men like perches or wide-open spaces. Most homes are designed by men, which explains all those lofted ceilings, two-story entryways, and "great rooms" that feel cavernous and impersonal to many women. (A great room is a space that combines two or more functions, such as the kitchen and the family room.)

The solution: Break up those big spaces. Use bookshelves, plants, or screens to create a computer corner or workstation. Take two easy chairs and create a private nook overlooking a window. Find the quirkiest corner in the house, throw down some pillows and a lamp, and create an "adult fort."

Kids, especially, need their own spaces. They love to create "secret" hideouts like clubhouses, dungeons, or tree houses. Just think of the classics of children's literature, from *The Lion, the Witch, and the Wardrobe* to *The Secret Garden* to *The Magic Tree House*. They all have mysterious enclaves. If, like our girls, your kids sleep together in one room, you can use area rugs, individual reading lamps, or personalized pillows to give each kid control over their own half.

Color

There's a vast literature on color focusing on how hue, tint, and saturation can affect people's moods. All around the world, among every age, gender, and income bracket, blue is people's favorite color. Blue reminds people of the ocean and the sky and is considered limitless, calm, and serene. Green, red, black, and brown also rate highly, while yellow is much less popular. Gray, the color of rainy days, regularly scores the ugliest. (Orange, my favorite color, strikes people as so alarmist that fast-food companies make their trays that color so you'll inhale your food more quickly and leave, making room for more customers.)

So how can color improve your family?

- *Use bright colors in the kids' rooms.* Among children especially, lighter, more saturated colors are associated with positive emotions, while darker colors trigger negative emotions.
- *Use a single color in adult rooms.* Rooms that incorporate several intensities of the same color are relaxing. Avoid white, though, which reminds people of sickness, and red, which reminds people of teachers' marking pens and leads them to give up on tasks too quickly.
- *Use warm shades in the kitchen.* If, like Linda, you want people to hang around the kitchen and have family time, use warmer shades—tomato reds, Granny Smith greens, pumpkin oranges (finally!). But be warned, these colors are appetite enhancers. The price of togetherness may be flabbier waistlines.

Light

Finally, dim the lights. Research going back to the 1950s shows subdued lighting encourages social interaction. The "father of lighting psychology," John Flynn, found dim lighting makes people feel more relaxed and safe, allowing them to talk more intimately and be more revealing. Whether you're confronting your sibling about her addiction, trying to help your spouse get over a bad day, or soothing an adolescent through a breakup, atmospherics matter. The lower the light, the more loving the conversation is likely to be.

A BIG, FAT MESS

That's how you design a place. Now how do you live in it? That's what we wanted Sam Gosling to tell us.

Here's what Gosling found in our closets:

Linda looked at this and saw heaps of the girls' old clothes on the floor, the jumble of wooden masks at the top, and lots of mismatched hangers. She was embarrassed. But Gosling had the opposite reaction. "This is among the top end of most organized closets I've ever seen!" he said.

Linda was shocked.

"There's a place for umbrellas," he continued, "and the umbrellas are in there. There's a place for trays. All the back-to-school gear is ready to go. But there's one thing I've never seen before: a box of extra water bottles. Getting stuff before it runs out is a classic sign of conscientiousness."

"But I thought this closet made us look disorganized," Linda said.

"We see this all the time," he said. "People cannot judge their own homes. You say, 'Don't come in! My place is a terrible mess.' But what you mean is the vase isn't centered on the table or a chair is out of place. Many people would die to have things this organized."

He pointed to a piece of Japanese calligraphy and a collection of country music and salsa CDs, carefully stored in our closet. (The country was mine; the Latin Linda's.) They were hidden behind other things, he said, suggesting they weren't used very often. He was right. Both date from our twenties and thirties.

"All these are part of your personality," Gosling said, "but they've literally been displaced by new priorities. Getting your kids to school on time is more important to you now than listening to music."

I was stunned by how much he could tell about our lives just by looking in our closet. Were we that transparent? Psychologists are trained to look at people's personalities, he explained, but families have personalities, too. Understanding how our homes affect that personality can help us improve how we live in that space.

One simple way we do that is through what Gosling calls "feeling regulators." These are items we place around our home, like the watercolor from our honeymoon or our children's art, that remind us of happy times we shared together. These cues become the visual equivalent of comfort food, a blanket of soothing images that make us feel secure.

The most powerful of these are photographs, he said. Brain research suggests when we see an image of a person, our minds unconsciously register "friend" or "foe." If it's "foe," our instinct is to flee; if it's "friend," we relax. Snapshots of family members are particularly potent. For moms of newborns, even seeing a photograph of their baby can cause them to generate oxytocin, the so-called cuddle hormone, and to let down milk. Gosling says people place photos around the house for what he calls "social snacking," bite-size encounters that soften the pain of separation. Eighty-five percent of adults have photographs of loved ones on their desks, in their wallets, or on their cell phones.

When Gosling reached our living room, the first thing he commented on was photographs. The space is decorated with a sofa and chairs, two bookcases, a Bedouin carpet, a coffee table made from a Moroccan door, and a painting my mom made of Tybee Island. But there are no photographs.

"I rarely see that," he said. "I'm beginning to think you're not as extroverted as you seem."

Extroverts, he explained, tend to surround themselves with photos that have prominent faces in them. They also prefer music with vocals, and we have no visible sound system in our living room either. (It's tucked away, and rarely used.)

"Of course you have chairs," he continued, "but they're not really arranged to accommodate a lot of people. I would say you're extroverted when you go out into the world, but when you come home, you both like to be by yourselves, maybe spend time reading or chatting with one another. This room is used for 'down-regulating.'"

Gosling's observations made me look at our home in a new light. For all the symbols of the outside world it contains, our home really is a place for us. It's designed for family, not for friends. If anything, his comments made us want to make it more focused on our family. Maybe we should print out more photographs of our relatives—not just our immediate family, but thinking of Marshall Duke's "What do you know?" game, more photos of our parents and grandparents. Maybe we should make a more conscious effort to display art from the kids. And maybe we should balance out the mementos from trips we took before the girls with a few more from trips we took with them.

In Gosling's eyes, those sorts of objects make us feel positively toward one another. But what about the ones that make us want to kill one another? I'm speaking, of course, of mess. For that conversation, we moved upstairs.

Mess is one of the most divisive things in families. Eric Abrahamson, a professor at Columbia University and the author of *A Perfect Mess*, found that 80 percent of couples say that their different views about mess is a source of tension in their marriage. One in twelve named that very tension as a factor in their breakup or divorce.

Part of this tension may be rooted in gender. Studies show that men and women care about different things in the home. Men tend to favor areas that celebrate hard work and mastery. That's why they love spaces with computers, stereo equipment, or hunting gear. The "man cave" is real. Women have a more social view of the home, so they lavish attention on things that encourage interaction, like bowls of snacks or fluffy throw pillows that entice you to sit down and chat. A woman's idea of respite is not a place where she would do something for others (compared to a man's tool area, say); it's where she doesn't have to do anything for anybody—the tub, or "mom spa," if you will.

But the real culprit appears to have nothing to do with gender: it's self-aggrandizement. Daniel Kahneman found that both members of a couple overemphasize their role in cleaning the house. In *Thinking, Fast and Slow* Kahneman cites a study in which spouses were asked to estimate how much time they spend keeping the place tidy, taking out the trash, or doing other chores. In every case, both men and women said their contribution was higher than it actually was. This information was so powerful, Kahneman said, that when couples learned about it, it often defused marital spats. Remember, he said, even though you may think you're doing more than your fair share, your partner is thinking the exact same thing.

Could this information help us?

As we headed upstairs, I pointed out to Gosling all of Linda's mounds of stuff. There were piles of work papers by her computer on the dining room table and piles of mail on the stairs. In our bedroom, while my side was more orderly (though certainly not perfect), Linda's had a skyline of piles. One pile was for unperused magazines, another for unread books, another for unpaid bills. Obviously, living with all these heaping mounds was proof I was a long-suffering husband, right?

Not exactly. Gosling was struck not by the volume of the piles but by their orderliness. "I've seen mess," he said. "This is not mess! You have a system for your piles. The books are all ones you want to read. The bills are clipped together, then wrapped in a rubber band. There's a difference between those who are messy and reconciled to it, and those who are messy and aspire to be orderly. You are clearly in the latter camp."

Linda beamed, and I felt the air coming out of my nightly rants. "Exactly!" she gloated. "My piles are aspirational. I'm going to read those books someday! I'm going to pay those bills by the end of the weekend! I just bite off more than I can chew."

Gosling nodded, and Linda pounced. "But what about him!" she said. "I know I like my piles, but for someone who likes clean surfaces, he never puts the milk back in the fridge."

We were back where we started.

"This is part of the art of living together," Gosling said diplomatically. "You guys are both pretty organized, but there's still a discrepancy. The challenge of sharing space is finding a compromise where you both meet your psychological needs. As we've found, it's a lot easier to change your space than your partner."

In the end, this notion of focusing on the space instead of the person is the main idea I took away from Gosling's visit. Now, instead of criticizing Linda for her tendency to create piles, I criticize the piles themselves. "Dear, could you take at least some of your carefully organized piles and push them more toward your side of the bed?"

As for me and the kitchen, I've been forced to concede that since she spends more time there, she gets to set the rules. I've tried to use this to my advantage on occasion. "Sorry, I can't do the dishes tonight. It would infringe on your space." But that didn't work. There's only so many times you can cite a snoopologist to get out of taking out the trash.

SIT UNTO OTHERS AS THEY SIT UNTO YOU

But can we take this one step further? Are there specific, no-cost things you can do around your home to draw your family closer together?

Sally Augustin calls herself a place coach. One of one hundred practicing environmental psychologists in the world, she's the founder of Chicago-based Design with Science and a popular consultant to corporations. She's also six foot two and sharply dressed, and has orange hair.

"When I go into spaces, I do a human spirits audit," she said. "I try to evaluate whether your environment is meeting your needs. Then I suggest changes."

Augustin is often asked to design spaces where people can be more productive at work. She urges employers to use lots of natural materials, maximize daylight, and allow people to personalize their environment. In our homes, our goals are slightly different, she said. "We need privacy to sort through what happened to us during the day. But we're also social animals, even the most introverted of us, so we need to socialize in order to live."

So what changes can I make in my home to promote family interaction? Augustin offered these recommendations:

1. *Circle the sofas.* In 1957, a Canadian doctor named Humphrey Osmond began noticing patients in a mental hospital in Saskatchewan were friendlier to one another when they were facing one another. By contrast, when furniture was lined along the wall or arranged in rows, people were less friendly. He called the first arrangement "sociopetal" (radial) and the second "sociofugal" (gridlike). His terms continue to be used today. Want to have more successful family gatherings? Sit in an O, not a U, an L, or a V.

2. *Sit like Mona Lisa.* When we renovated our home, Larry Wente told us we were putting our living room furniture too far apart. I ignored him. I was wrong. Research shows Americans don't like to sit closer than eighteen inches or farther apart than five and a half feet. That five-and-a-half-foot gap is called the "portrait" distance, because it's the one Leonardo da Vinci, Rembrandt, and other painters used to depict subjects. At that distance, the eye can comfortably take in the torso, along with micro-movements of the face and hands. Closer together, the other person's head will seem too big, and you're more likely to be distracted by the other person's odors. Farther apart, your eyes and ears will have to strain, and you're more likely to be distracted by the environment.

3. *Eat like a Parisian.* Scientists seated individuals at rectangular tables, then evaluated their conversations with people sitting across from, alongside, and catty-cornered to them. Those sitting across from each other split into two camps: Half chatted with each other, half confronted each other. Those sitting at right angles

were more likely to talk, while those sitting next to each other, as in a Parisian café, were more likely to collaborate. If you're having an important conversation, sit next to the other person.

4. *Lean unto others as they lean unto you.* Your mother was right: posture matters. In my 7:42 P.M. fight with Linda, I was usually seated upright at my desk, while she was six inches lower in a swivel chair from Ikea. "Oh, so bad!" Augustin said. "The higher person is clearly in the power position." Other power poses include putting your feet up, looming over a table, lacing your fingertips behind your neck, or holding something rigid, like a clipboard.

Studies have shown that people in power positions have elevated testosterone, reduced cortisol, and increased feelings of superiority, she explained, while people in low-power poses (sitting lower, slumping, crossing your arms) are defensive and resentful. Her advice: Everybody in a meaningful conversation should sit at the same level, with the same posture. It doesn't matter if you're seated upright or stretched out, as long as everyone's doing the same thing.

5. *Cushion your blows.* When I told Augustin we held our family meetings at our breakfast table, where the seats are padded, she was thrilled. People are more accommodating when seated on cushioned surfaces, she said. A fascinating study published in 2010 by professors at MIT, Harvard, and Yale showed that when people sit on a "hard wooden chair," they are more rigid, strict, and inflexible. When they sit on a "soft cushioned chair" they are more flexible, accommodating, and generous.

"If you want to talk to your daughters about curfew," Augustin said, "I would want to have that conversation on cushioned chairs, because no one will be as doctrinaire, you'll be more open to the opinions of others, and you'll have a more conciliatory conversation, or at least less contentious."

* * *

The upshot of all this advice was that we made some major changes around our home. Linda and I agreed we would no longer hold major conversations in my office and would instead go to the living room or our bedroom. To reduce the idea that one chair was the seat of power, we started rotating who sits where in our family meeting. And I finally listened to Larry and moved all my living room furniture into a tighter circle. The net cost of all these improvements: $0.00.

AWESOME STUFF

We also did something else Larry recommended: We brought our children into the conversation about how to improve our home. Larry said children as young as seven years old have filled out his questionnaire about what types of spaces they're most comfortable in. "It's remarkable how strong their memories can be," he said. "Plus, it gives them a sense of ownership over their environment."

One day we took the girls out to lunch and distributed a kid-friendly version of Larry's three questions. The first was *Describe your image of your ideal home using ten words/phrases.* These were their answers:

EDEN

Big pool	Art studio
Colorful	Ice cream parlor
Always clean	Fluffy pillows
Bunk beds	Library
Heart-shaped room	Tybee living there

TYBEE

Lots of books	Board games
Swimming pool	Clean
Feel welcome	Pillows
Warm in winter/cool in	Overlooking water
summer	Eden lives there
Lots of candy	

I was struck by how vibrant their fantasies were. Heart-shaped room! Ice cream parlor! Fluffy pillows! It sounded like a Vegas honeymoon suite. More notable was how similar their answers were. They both wanted a swimming pool and a library, and each wanted to live with her sister. When we cross-referenced their lists with the ones Linda and I created, which also included color, light, and books (along with some more adult fantasies like Linda's "Japanese spalike bathroom" and "large, open Tuscan kitchen") certain patterns began to emerge.

"That sounds like our house!" Tybee said of the common words.

"Except the big swimming pool," Linda added.

"But that's what we wanted the most!" Eden said.

Next we moved on to *What is your favorite building, and why?"* Linda said La Sagrada Familia, the unfinished Gaudí cathedral in Barcelona. I said St. Catherine's Monastery in the Sinai peninsula, at the base of the mountain where Moses is said to have received the Ten Commandments. Tybee said a seaside hotel near her grandparents' house on Cape Cod. "They have two pools and a beach, and you can do anything you want!" she said. Eden said a hotel in Italy we once stayed in. "We all slept in the same room," she said, "and it had giant windows and a white curtain you could see through."

I immediately thought of our family mission statement: *May our first word be* adventure *and our last word* love. Our sense of exploration shone through every answer.

But it was the third question, *Is there a memorable place from your life you especially love?*, that produced the most revealing answers. I said Tybee Island. Linda said her family's Cape house overlooking the harbor. Tybee said the farm of friends we often visit in Vermont. Eden said the playground near our home. "I went there every year I was alive," she said. "It reminds me of when I was a baby."

All four spaces were nurturing, protective, warm.

Having reinforced this idea that places are critical to our well-being, Linda then moved on to the main reason for our gathering. "Now we know what our fantasy home is like," she said. "It's time to talk about the reality." We all have to live together in our actual home, she said. And in order to do that, we all have to play a role in keeping it nice.

We then unveiled a new plan for them to take more responsibility around the house. We created two lists, thirty-minute jobs and fifteen-minute jobs, and assigned them to complete a certain number every week. The longer jobs included: sweep front porch/steps, fold laundry, make weekly grocery list. The shorter jobs included: empty trash cans in all bathrooms, distribute extra toilet paper, empty dishwasher. Because they both mentioned they liked pillows so much, we added "fluff pillows" to the fifteen-minute list.

Linda and I braced for tears and complaints, but none came. That was a surprise. The only change they requested was that they hated the word *chores*. "It sounds like boring work," they said. They proposed the phrase "awesome stuff," as in "Things we do to make our house more awesome."

We then asked what changes they wanted around the house. They wanted more pillows, a place to put their gymnastics mat, some extra drawer space for dress-up clothes, and a private shelf for each to keep her own books. All those seemed reasonable. We even agreed to spend our shared money from allowance on pillows they could pick out.

One of the central lessons I took away from trying to build a happy home is you need to have three types of spaces—individual, shared, and public. While that's difficult enough for couples to pull off, it's even more difficult to include children in the process. Yet it's critical, especially as they get older. As children clamor for more and more private space, it becomes increasingly important to keep them as connected as possible to the family spaces. One way to do that is to give them a greater voice in shaping them.

The place questionnaire is a way for children to begin mapping out their own sense of place. Linda compared it to our family mission statement. In the former you articulate your best possible self; in the latter you identify your best possible home. Sure, they're both ideals. We harbored no illusions that our eye-opening lunch meant they would always clean their room. But at least we had written proof they both *wanted* a clean home.

The challenge for us was to give them the independence they wanted in our home while getting from them a commitment to help keep that home running smoothly. This idea was tested a few weeks later when they sat us down at breakfast one morning. "We held a meeting," they said. "We don't want our room to be yellow anymore. We want it to be green."

I was reminded of Randy Pausch's memorable line from his "last lecture." After showing photos of his childhood bedroom, which was covered in mathematical notations, he said, "If your kids want to paint their bedrooms, as a favor to me, let 'em do it." The next time a snoopologist comes to visit our home, he'll find that our daughters' bedroom is the color of mint chocolate chip ice cream. And he'll know exactly who chose it.

PART THREE

GO OUT AND PLAY

11

THE FAMILY VACATION CHECKLIST

How to Make Travel More Fun

IT WAS THE night of our annual Valentine's week double date, and our friends Campbell and Dan sat down at the table and didn't look at each other. We had certain unspoken rules for these evenings. We didn't talk about our kids. We didn't talk (too long) about our politics. We did talk about our marriages.

But tonight they weren't talking, so the marriage talk was going to be somewhat challenging.

A week earlier, they had taken their first family ski trip to the mountains. "I grew up being a ski bum," Campbell said, "so I really want my boys to love to ski." As this was her terrain, she had made all the arrangements, bought special equipment, loaded up the suitcases. All Dan had to do was wake up on time, pack himself, and get all of the luggage into the car. But he'd flunked the first task, was late completing the second, and for the third, well, as soon as they reached their destination, Campbell realized the bag she had carefully packed with newly purchased ski supplies for their three- and four-year-old sons was still sitting in their bed-room in Manhattan.

"She handed me the phone," Dan said, "and I didn't know if she wanted me to call the doorman or the divorce lawyer."

Family vacations—they help families break harried routines, reboot fraying relationships, and return enjoyment to our lives. The backbones of highly functioning families are enhanced by the time together, connectedness, and fun of a long weekend away or the annual trip to the beach. For generations of families, the Kodak moment was the manifestation of happiness.

But if my family is any indication (the one I grew up in and the one I have with Linda), family vacations are where the most fertile, ferocious fights imaginable can happen. Money. Planning. Navigation. "You only want to go shopping." "Do we have to go to another museum?" Add in canceled planes, lost luggage, bad traffic, and one kid who always has a nose buried in some electronic device, and it's a marvel anyone is speaking by the second day.

Even the Kodak moment isn't what it used to be. The minute someone snaps a photo, everyone has to stop for ten minutes while the photographer Photoshops Mom's hair, Instagrams in a special effect, then Facebooks it back to Grandma.

There must be a better way, I thought, so I decided to give a go at improving family vacations. I focused on three areas: getting out of the house more effectively, improving long car rides, and making lasting memories once you're at your destination.

INTRODUCING THE FAMILY VACATION CHECKLIST

Peter Pronovost is the recipient of a MacArthur "genius" award. He has been the subject of one best-selling book and the author of another. And he is personally responsible for saving millions of lives. He achieved these milestones because he devised a seemingly simple tool that has transformed the way medicine is practiced around the world.

Pronovost's miracle invention was not a drug, a device, or a procedure. It wasn't revolutionary at all. It's one of the oldest, most mundane things on earth. It's a checklist.

As a critical care specialist at Johns Hopkins Hospital in Baltimore, Pronovost came up with the idea that emergency rooms should use a checklist modeled on the one airplane pilots use—fuel tank filled, check; engine on, check. By adding such preposterously basic items as "wash hands with soap" and "clean patient's skin with antiseptic," and by empowering even the lowliest person in the room to speak up, Pronovost saved lives, saved time, and saved money. Soon hospitals around the world were adopting his lists.

I was interested in applying his technique to the problems families face when leaving home for a trip. He gave me a number of recommendations.

1. *Create different lists for different times in the processs.* "Checklists have to be linked in time and space," Pronovost said. "So I have a checklist for ICU admissions, and another for blood transfusions. You should have a checklist for one week before the trip. Then two days before you'll likely need another. Then one more for when you're walking out the door. But you always need time to recover, so if you have one for when you're at the airport, it's too late."

2. *Make it specific.* "A checklist should take less than a minute to complete," he said. "Each item should be a very specific behavior. Avoid vague language."

3. *Killer items only.* "Target your checklist on things that

commonly go wrong," he told me. "If you put down things you don't fail at, you'll drive people crazy. This has been borne out in aviation, where accidents have been caused by checklist fatigue."

4. *The rule of seven.* "I have a rule that checklists can be only seven items," Pronovost said. "It's the same reason our telephone numbers are seven digits. Otherwise, people will take shortcuts and items will get missed."

5. *Include the kids.* "I would sit down with them and say, 'Hey, girls, I'm trying to improve how we travel, so I made a checklist. Does this make sense to you? What else can you add?'"

Armed with this advice I made a master list of our family's common travel mistakes. There were the things we often forget: sunscreen, cell phone chargers, stuffed animals. There were the things we forget to do: turn off the air-conditioning, shut the curtains, empty the trash. There were the things we assumed others were doing: pack snacks, print out directions, cancel the newspaper. Linda added her own favorites: set the DVR, make sure the kids go to the bathroom. The kids threw in a few of their own: bring enough books, charge the iPad!

I passed our list around to friends and got some pretty serious blowback. Some people found the whole thing too programmatic; others found it too rigid. A few said it seemed unnecessary. "I just put a pad by my bed," one person wrote. "I never forget anything." I didn't know whether to think my friends are lax, perfect, or just blunt, but I chalked it up to a failed experiment and stuffed the whole thing into the drawer of rejected ideas, along with carving our family mission statement into the mantel and asking my parents about their sex life.

A month or so later, we took a trip. Sure enough we forgot the stuffed animals, left behind the girls' socks, and didn't pack the tennis rackets. Tybee, crying and unable to sleep in the backseat of the car, said, "We should have used the checklist!"

I went back to the drawer. Our family vacation checklist may not be for everyone, but it helped us. And it worked even better after a few trips when we assigned our daughters the task of being list monitors, which gave them the rare chance to be disciplinarians when Linda and I slipped up. Ultimately, when I was satisfied we had a workable version of the list (see opposite page), I sent it to Campbell and Dan.

A few weeks later, Campbell sent this reply:

Very helpful with everything—except perpetually late husband.

Be warned: The checklist can help you remember what to do, but it can't wake you up to do it.

BEYOND TWENTY QUESTIONS

Stepping into the headquarters of Zynga is like entering a pinball machine. Nicknamed the "dog house," the seven-story building in a trendy neighborhood of San Francisco is filled with neon-lit tunnels, arcade games, foosball tables, and food carts that dole out free gourmet treats to employees. The atmosphere, a mix of childhood tree house and frat house basement, belies one of the most intense gaming factories ever created.

Since its founding in 2007 by Mark Pincus, Zynga (the name of his bulldog) has become the fastest growing social gaming company in history. Two hundred and fifty million people play

FAMILY VACATION CHECKLIST

ONE WEEK BEFORE DEPARTURE	ONE DAY BEFORE DEPARTURE	ONE HOUR BEFORE DEPARTURE
☐ Identify special packing items (car seats, Pack 'N Plays, bikes, sporting equipment)	☐ Ready electronics (GPS, camera, video camera, charge batteries); program DVR.	☐ Did we remember stuffed animals, blankies, and other kid necessities?
☐ Verify logistics (reservations, tickets, directions).	☐ Assemble tickets, directions, passports, cash.	☐ Snacks, food, drinks?
☐ Make list of gifts to purchase/ bring.	☐ Pick up dry cleaning, fill up the car.	☐ Do we have enough books, games, CDs, devices?
☐ Cancel newspaper delivery.	☐ Get luggage from storage.	☐ Chargers! Cell phones! Tablets!
☐ Do you have photocopies of your passports/driver's licenses?	☐ Lay out clothes, shoes, etc.	☐ Did we turn off oven, AC, lights? Take out trash? Close curtains? Lock doors? Water plants?
☐ Need to refill any prescriptions? Get traveler's checks?	☐ Gather prescriptions, toiletries, sunscreen, etc.	☐ Did everyone use the bathroom?
☐ Have you arranged for pet care?	☐ Pack children's carry-ons.	☐ Who's making the last run through the house? Count the pieces of luggage to verify at future stops.

one of its online games every month. These include collective, community-building games like FarmVille and CityVille and online versions of familiar tabletop games like Zynga Poker and Words With Friends (a knockoff of Scrabble). The company's revenues top $1 billion a year.

I wanted to see if the folks at Zynga could help me resolve the nagging problem of engaging kids on long car rides, getting through extended layovers, or spicing up a restless afternoon in an unfamiliar city. In short, could Zynga make my vacation as much fun as one of their games?

On a foggy morning, a dozen of the company's top designers, all parents with young children, gathered over bagels and fruit salad in an attempt to outline for me a Zynga playbook for the ideal vacation. They started with a crash course in why games work.

Good games, they said, have four things in common:

1. *A clear goal.* Players know what they're trying to achieve.
2. *Rules.* Limitations that force creativity and strategic thinking.
3. *Feedback.* Points, levels, scores, or something that lets players know how close they are to the goal and gives them motivation to keep playing.
4. *Voluntary participation.* Only if players choose to play will the game be fun.

Games make us happy because we work toward goals. By mastering obstacles, we feel a sense of accomplishment. With that success, our bodies release a wave of chemicals, from adrenaline to dopamine, that make us feel exhilarated and resilient. The effects are even more powerful when we play those games in groups. By achieving goals with others, our bodies generate additional chemicals, including oxytocin, the so-called cuddle drug, that deepen our connection to those we're playing with.

Zynga pioneered a new kind of online game that allows people in different places to play the same game together, which can be particularly effective for busy families. One player makes a move in the morning; another responds later that day. Pincus famously said he wants gamers to play for "five minutes, five times a day." As one designer said over breakfast, "These bite-size chunks fit my busy life as a working parent. And it fits into my kids' lives, too. They don't want to sit there and play games all day with their parents, but they will as long as it's a two-minute round."

For families, the Zynga way of playing mirrors what scholars are finding about family dinner: You can take many of the benefits of concentrated family time and parcel them out in small chunks throughout the day. Zynga and other social game creators make this easier by adding chat features alongside their playing areas. Screens fill with, "Has your leg healed?" "What do you want for your birthday?" "Your stepdad says hello."

"We do a lot of player profiles," Zynga's head of marketing told me. "One that I love involves a mother who lives in North America and her daughter who lives in Australia. Every day they play Words With Friends back and forth. Sometimes it's only a word a day. Just knowing her daughter is okay means everything to the mom, she told us. 'Even when I'm losing, I still have a chance to say, "I love you."'"

These benefits are even greater with games like FarmVille and CityVille, which oblige players to cooperate. In 2009, researchers from eight universities in the United States and Asia studied the effects of games that require "helpful behavior." In three different studies, they looked at children under thirteen, teenagers, and college students. All three studies concluded that the more time young people spend helping others in games, the more time they spent helping friends and family members in real life. The project's coauthors called this the "upward spiral" of gaming. Families that play together stay together.

I gave the Zynga team three scenarios and asked them to help with some analog solutions.

Over the Mountains and Through the Woods

The first case involved a long drive. We've eaten all our snacks. We've exhausted the scratchy CDs. We're bored with "Twenty Questions," a game that was popular in the 1940s. Can't we come up with something new?

I'm Thinking of a Time When

The designers told me keep it simple. "With kids it's short-attention-span theater," one designer said. "Start with what they already know. It will give them a sense of mastery quickly. Then modify it with all sorts of back doors and sidebars."

They recommended a homemade version of Twenty Questions. "Kids have all this memory of things they've done with you," one designer said. "Throw out a statement, 'I'm thinking of a time when we went to a place . . . All you can ask is yes or no questions. Go!'" Suddenly the kids become actors in their own game. "'What's Mom thinking about?' 'Where did we go?'"

Another advantage of this game is that the kids are on the same side. "With young kids especially, if one kid keeps score against another, it ends up being a disaster," one designer added. "So it's a joint scoring system. They work together for a while, then they compete. By mixing it up, they get along better." The winner chooses the next place.

Let's Tell a Story

Zynga has found that people play games for one of three reasons:

- "Achievers" play because they want to win.
- "Maxers" play because they want to build the biggest or amass the most.
- "Decorators" play because they like to create a world, fill it with things they design, then share it with others.

This last category surprised me. "Decorators" tend to be female, and it's one of the secrets of Zynga's success, as they've been able to tap into that market better than most.

"The key is to give people what they want in a game," one designer said. "So if you're a decorator, I want to give you houses to furnish, haunted forests to imagine, or magical lands to populate. The game becomes about embellishing."

For our car trip, they recommended that we create a new world with the family. One person offers a few sentences of a story, then passes them to the next person, then the next person. If you need to add a scoring component to keep people interested, dole out points based on whether each passage makes sense given what came before. If the entire story makes sense at the end, the whole team gets a reward. As one dad said, "I've noticed a thread with my children. The games they're really excited about have this immersive, environmental aspect. They get to inhabit a different world. That's when kids lose track of the miles and want to keep going."

Not Leaving on a Jet Plane

Okay, we're at an airport; it's raining out; our flight has been canceled. We can move around, but only in a confined space. Now what?

Mission Impossible

Ever since my girls were young, we've played a game called "missions." In waiting areas, I would send them on errands to find letters on billboards; at the pool, I would have them count chairs. Because they were shy, I often asked them to find out someone's name or hometown. In every instance, they had to make a presentation when they returned: "My name is Eden. There are nine storm clouds overhead."

Many of the Zynga designers play a similar game with their kids, but they were much better at it. First, they mix up items more creatively: I need two luggage tags from United Airlines, then three stirrers from Starbucks, and I need you to find out what time the next flight for Amsterdam leaves. Next they generously sprinkle in rewards: If you introduce yourself to five people and bring me three business cards, I'll take you to get frozen yogurt. Finally they escalate: How many baby steps does it take to get to Gate 16? Now how many dinosaur steps? If you can cut that number in half, I'll give you three bonus points.

"For many children, leveling up is their main goal when playing a game," one designer said. "It taps into a basic human need to achieve. The guys in karate figured this out ages ago. The only reason there's a black belt is it's mysteriously better than a white belt."

Tell Me About Her

Continuing the pattern of giving me an active game and a more imaginative game, the moms in our group recommended taking advantage of the other passengers. Point to a person, then take turns making up stories about who they are, where they came from, and where they're going.

"I play this with my kids," one mother said, "and they've gotten smarter at looking at people, hearing them, trying to figure out what they're wearing and why. My son now knows where all of the airlines fly, which ones fly to yucky places or cool, and using that information to guess what people might be doing there. It gives them practice telling these elaborate stories, which I love."

The Amazing Race

After breakfast, Steve Parkis, a baby-faced midwesterner who's the vice president in charge of CityVille, gave me a tour. Though he's in his early forties, he still looks like he could slip undetected into a game of peewee baseball. It was midmorning by now, but the cubicles and conference rooms were still empty. "It's kind of early for us," he said apologetically. "If you were here at two in the morning, it would be humming."

I wanted Parkis's help with my third scenario: Every parent wants to make lasting memories with their kids, especially on vacations, which are precious and hard-earned. How can I make sure I get the most out of a trip, especially something like a week in a new place?

"I worked at Disney for ten years," Parkis said, "and I think a good game is a combination of Pixar and Jerry Bruckheimer." Pixar's philosophy is that story trumps all, he explained. You want to build a game that can last multiple days, so you need a narrative, with a beginning, a middle, and an end.

"But you also want what all Jerry Bruckheimer movies have," he continued, "ordinary people in extraordinary circumstances.

How many chances does a kid have to go to the top of the Empire State Building or stand where Martin Luther King Jr. stood on the steps of the Lincoln Memorial?"

So what does that game look like? "*The Amazing Race*," he said.

"We're about to take our kids to Mexico for vacation," he continued, "and I'm already planning an 'Amazing Race' for our entire family." Modeled on the television reality show (produced by Bruckheimer), the game has a unifying structure: Who can score the most points over the entire week. It has a rhythm—minor task, minor task, major task; minor task, minor task, major task. It has different stunts designed for different people. If you're athletic, you get points for swimming with sea turtles; if you're a helper, you get points for toting bags.

Does he map out the game in advance?

"Quite the opposite," he said. "Sometimes I'll arbitrarily give one kid extra points just to keep it close. 'Matt's in the lead!' 'Hey, how did Matt get in the lead?' 'Oh, you didn't see what he did back there? Better catch up!' "

He also switches up alliances. "In Hawaii last year, I couldn't get one of my kids to swim under a waterfall," he said, "so I made his brother his partner. 'If you can get your brother under the waterfall, you get three bonus points.' Suddenly it's not just Dad trying to pressure my son; he's doing it for his team. This year, I'm going to give the boys an epic reward if they can get Mom to ride the zipline."

And what if somebody doesn't want to participate in one of these games?

"The juice has to be worth the squeeze," he said. "In a game, if you succeed every time, it's boring. If you fail every time, it's boring. The trick is to mix easy and hard. Plus, it's your job to make sure the reward is worth it."

Steve Parkis's "Amazing Race" had an immediate—and lasting—impact on our family. The next day, I took our daughters on a four-hour "Amazing Race" through Golden Gate Park. Their challenges included building a human replica of the Transamerica building, jumping off a cannon, and guessing how many steps it took us to walk across the Golden Gate Bridge. My "Amazing Race" was the first way I found to get our kids excited to spend more than fifteen minutes in an art museum. Count the number of Georgia O'Keeffe paintings with skulls; come up with new names for the colors in a Matisse collage; tell us which sculpture is your favorite and give us three reasons why. Get ten points by the end, you get $10 to spend in the gift shop.

I found some of Parkis's tips particularly challenging, especially his insistence that I let the girls fail regularly. "It's not like getting a D on a report card," he said. "In gaming, selective failure is one of the most proven routes to success. It builds persistence and makes you more optimistic."

But I stuck to his model, and a year later, on a trip to London, we pulled off our first weeklong game. The girls got five points for counting a hundred double-decker buses; three points for mustering up the courage to ask a bobby the official address of the prime minister's residence; and a bonus for getting over their fear of animals and touching a horse at the queen's parade ground. They officially reached the "winning" total by leading the entire family through four stations and two transfers on the London Tube. This "Amazing Race" had provided up to six hours a day of pleasure, distraction, and mind-expanding adventure. And what extravagant prize did the girls claim with all their winnings?

Ice cream.

And I relearned a lesson I had been picking up over and over during my research. The latest thinking about families consistently shows that some chaos, disorder, and tension are perfectly normal. You will bicker every now and then over where to eat on a trip. You will forget a piece of luggage. But with a little ingenuity, some agile adjustment, and a checklist or two, you can reduce the stress and recover more quickly from your stumbles.

Far more important to the success of your trip, or any other aspect of family life, is to worry less about eliminating the negatives and focus more on maximizing the positives. One easy way to do that: put away your phone, get down on your kids' level, and play. As Steve Parkis told me at the end of my visit to Zynga, "I realized over time that I don't have a lot in common with my children. They're eight and nine. We don't share that much life experience. But I do play games, and that gives us something we can do together on a pure, peer level.

"I didn't have a good relationship with my dad," he went on. "So my goal was to not have that happen with my kids. My inspiration has always been theme parks. You know how it goes: The family argues the entire car ride down. When they get back home, nothing is perfect. But during the time they're in that theme park, everybody just gets along."

That's what games like the 'Amazing Race' can do," Parkis said. "They can be that pause moment in your year, when everybody just lets the world go and shares an experience that's delightful. 'Oh, I actually do care about you.' 'Yes, now I remember, we're a family.'"

12

SHUT UP AND CHEER!

What Successful Coaches Know About Successful Families

S TEVEN MAIL WAS having trouble. It was an early Saturday afternoon in January, and the forty-seven-year-old was standing on the side of a soccer field in Apopka, Florida, not far from Disney World. His ten-year-old daughter, Zoe, was starting at left midfield for the North Florida Fury in the opening game of a preseason classic. Her team was favored to win. She had her uniform all together, but her mother was at a family event, leaving her father to be soccer dad. And even though Steven is the president of Zoe's soccer club, he still didn't know how to make a ponytail.

"I know so many dads who are superinvolved in their daughters' teams," he said. "But we all struggle with the hair. We miss the moms when it comes to making ponytails."

Steven grew up in working-class Glasgow, Scotland, and is a brawny, former childhood boxer with a strong accent. He married a sparkling, dark-haired honor student from Dallas, and the two settled in Jacksonville, Florida, a place that was safely removed from both of their families. Steven trades stocks and complains about Americans; his wife raises their three daughters and tries to fit in with the local culture. They were considering moving, but then something unexpected happened.

One day Zoe came home and announced she was quitting soccer. Naturally shy and artistic, she wasn't instinctively drawn to competition. But Steven, who grew up following underdog soccer teams in the UK, was heartbroken. "I said to her, 'If I take over the team, will you try your hardest?'"

Suddenly Steven found his calling. Zoe's team hadn't won a single game in the previous season, but Steven taught the girls how to strike and pass. He showed them how to change direction and use their alternate foot. He showed them how to be aggressive. "We had lots of library girls on the team," he said. "And Zoe was the worst. She's creative, she's sweet, and she's soft. But I grew up in a tough neighborhood, and I was taught if somebody pushed you, you have to push them back. In a more civilized fashion, that's what I taught the girls."

And it worked. The next year the team went undefeated— Northeast Florida had its own "Bad News Bears." Soon Steven was coaching his other daughters. He recruited star players to join their team. And several years later, he decided to step down from day-to-day coaching and run for president of the club, an unpaid, nearly full-time job. In a contentious election against a well-funded opponent, he was elected by a narrow margin.

"My pitch to families to join our club was simple," he said. "As parents, our goal is to create happy, successful adults. So what are the secrets to success? It's not the kids who are most intelligent who are going to be the most successful. It's the ones who have the ability to be happy and get along with others. It's the ones who have determination and perseverance.

"In soccer you learn those skills," he continued. "You learn that when you get knocked down you get up again. You learn that if you're down two-nil, you can still win the game."

On this morning, the girls would need those skills. Rusty after a long winter break, the Fury came out flat. Within minutes, they were down 0-2. Coach Robin Mott, an active-duty Air National Guardsman, called out adjustments. "Amelia, pass the ball!" "Madeline, you've got backside."

But the real frustration, even hostility at times, came from the parents of Fury players on the opposite sideline. Huddled on blankets or seated on beach chairs, the dozen moms and handful of dads were coiled with so much nervous tension they looked like they were watching their children tiptoe across a swamp filled with alligators. Their comments were more scolding than encouraging. "Olivia, you're out of place." "Shoot the ball, Emily! You're not thinking." It was the pure expression of ambition and need.

And it perfectly captured the roiling passions of youth sports. Viewed from one angle, these under-ten girls were frolicking on fields that would mold their character, hone their confidence, and burnish skills that would serve them in everything from schoolwork to dating. Viewed from a different angle, these fields showed the most destructive tendencies of modern parents—the relentless pressure they put on children to work too hard, succeed too mightily, and specialize too quickly. These two fields combine to make kids' athletics one of the most fraught arenas for modern families.

So what are the new rules for parents and play? How do happy families cope with sports?

"Oh, no. Zoe! Are you okay?"

Just then, Zoe took a ball to the head and fell to the ground. Her father suddenly went limp and stared blankly at the field. He knew parents are never supposed to step on the field, so he showed remarkable restraint in remaining on the sideline. The ref ran to Zoe's side. The other players kneeled down. Time stopped. And suddenly all the vulnerability of children and games was laid out onto the grass. Was Zoe an injured athlete at this moment? Or was she a distressed daughter?

FOLLOW THE MONEY

Team sports is the number one out-of-school activity for American children between the ages of seven and ten. Team sports are more popular than band/chorus, religious groups, even individual sports. The most respected research on this topic, done annually by the Sporting Goods Manufacturing Association, shows that fifty million boys and girls ages six to seventeen participate in at least one team sport, with another ten million participating in a nonteam sport. That's about 70 percent of American children. Basketball is the most popular sport, followed by soccer, baseball, softball, and lacrosse. Football is the most popular sport among high school boys.

As the organization's president put it, "The U.S. is truly a team sports–driven society."

This wasn't always the case. Sports is a relatively new phenomenon for families to deal with. Until the late 1800s, religion was the dominant force in most children's lives and working alongside parents was the main activity. Team sports really began with the rise of industrial society as an attempt to provide organized recreation to an increasingly urbanized population. Teddy Roosevelt, a childhood asthmatic who found meaning in boxing, pushed sports as a way for boys to avoid becoming "sissies," a term coined at the time to reflect the fear that city life was making boys weak. Roosevelt's support of athletics was followed by the growth of playgrounds, phys ed, the YMCA, and Little League, as well as the modern Olympic Games. Sports was becoming a central part of childhood.

And with good reason. Countless studies have shown the benefits of athletics for young people. Participation in sports results in an increase in self-confidence, time management skills, and positive body image, as well as a decrease in depression, teen pregnancy, and smoking. A 2005 study by the U.S. government found that athletes are more likely than nonathletes to attend college and graduate. A survey of senior executives in Fortune 500 companies found that 95 percent had played high school sports, compared with half who were in student government and less than that in the National Honor Society. No wonder the Duke of Wellington famously claimed, "The battle of Waterloo was won on the playing fields of Eton."

Perhaps nothing better illustrates Americans' obsession with sports than one statistic I encountered: Up to two-thirds of couples using artificial insemination prioritize athletic genes, instead of intellectual traits like SAT scores or college performance. For high school study grinds like me, this is a bit tough to take: Even when they're just flipping through dirty magazines in a windowless room, the jocks still get the girls!

But the disadvantages of childhood sports are equally pronounced—and getting more so. The heart of the problem, according to every possible metric, is parents who don't understand how children develop; don't understand why children play; and don't realize how much pressure they're putting on kids. Add to that the booming business of youth sports—from televised coverage of the Little League World Series to all those pricey preseason classics, custom jerseys, private coaches, and summer camps—and the result is a warped reality.

Consider just a few statistics: NCAA colleges give out more

than $1.5 billion in athletic scholarships every year. Because Title IX requires that money be divided equally between men's and women's sports, women have particularly benefitted. As one mom of a Fury player told me, "If you get to the level where these girls are playing, you're going to get a scholarship. Guaranteed." You heard that right: Even though these girls are nine or ten years old, their parents are already working angles to get them a free ride to college.

On the one hand, who can blame them? If schools are giving out free money, why not take it? On the other hand, there are consequences to this new world of childhood moneyball. First, specialization. Gone are the days when children routinely play seasonal sports—soccer in the fall, volleyball in the winter, baseball in the spring. Now kids are increasingly forced to pick a sport and commit to it. Most nine- and ten-year-old girls on the Fury, for example, play soccer for three seasons and attend some sort of soccer camp in the summer. The mom who told me her daughter was guaranteed a soccer scholarship had hired a private soccer tutor to guarantee that guarantee. And she wasn't the only one to do this.

The chief problem with specialization is that kids are choosing a sport before their bodies have fully matured, which can lead to injuries and other problems. Here's a simple chart of the ages at which 60 percent of children are able to perform basic athletic skills:

	BOYS	GIRLS
Throwing	5½	8½
Kicking	7½	8½
Jumping	9½	11

How can you commit to a sport at age seven, eight, or nine if you can't even execute all the skills it requires?

All this intensity leads inevitably to misconduct, and not from the players. Everyone's heard stories about abusive parents at sporting events.

- In Maryland, a group of parents of U-14 girls (under fourteen) threatened a sixteen-year-old referee and followed her to her car after a game.
- A California U-14 boys' soccer game was disrupted by a brawl involving thirty adults.
- In Wisconsin, a father knocked a U-10 boy to the ground because he believed the boy had tripped his son.

It is tempting to think these incidents are isolated, but the numbers say otherwise. The National Alliance for Youth Sports reports that 15 percent of games involve a confrontation between parents and coaches, parents and officials, or parents and other parents. Steven Mail said he sees at least one incident every few weeks and has had to ask the parents to leave his club.

But the biggest source of stress comes from the expectations parents place on their children. Again, the research is disturbing. A study of wrestlers ages nine to fourteen showed that their biggest prematch worries were related to how their parents would respond if they didn't perform well. A study of thirteen-year-old skiers found that athletes who feared their parents' "disappointment or disapproval" performed worse in competition, while those who saw their parents as "supportive and positive" performed better.

The anecdotal evidence is even more wrenching. The president of the American Youth Soccer Organization spoke about a boy who had always played soccer, then one year refused to try out. He chose snowboarding instead. "Why?" he was asked. "My dad doesn't know anything about snowboarding," he said. "And, you know, it's cold on the slopes, so he doesn't come and watch me. So I get to snowboard without someone yelling at me all the time."

SHOWDOWN ON FIELD #6B

What role does this play in families? In the course of the preseason classic in Apopka, I saw many of these tensions between parents and children surge to the surface.

The first game was tough on the Fury. Zoe recovered from her injury. She took a sip of water, had a short walk, and decided to stay in the game. Her teammates, opponents, and both sets of parents applauded when it was clear she was not seriously hurt. The sportsmanship was impressive. A moment of concern became a shared lesson in resilience.

But the Fury lost 4–2, and the defeat meant the team would probably not make the tournament finals. But the girls didn't seem bothered by this. All through the game, in the brief meeting that followed, and at lunch afterward, the girls just chitchatted about school, their hair, their favorite movies and books, as if they were at a weekend-long sleepover.

The parents, however, couldn't let the defeat go. They replayed key moments as they walked to their cars. At lunch, they talked about missed calls from the ref, the heat, the grass being different than it was at home. By the time the second game started, they were on the warpath.

I had stood on the players' sideline during the first game, but for the second game, I moved to the parents' side. I was amazed by the difference. Though it was mostly moms, there seemed to be more testosterone here than at my local gym. "Go for the goal!" "Attack." "Get in there, fight!" And the Fury was winning this game! What stood out most was that the parents were all talking about individual achievement: Does my child need better equipment? Should I get her more lessons? Is she shooting enough? The coach, meanwhile, who did not have a child on the Fury but was a former college standout hired to coach the squad, was more focused on the team.

I wasn't the only one who noticed. By the third game, on Sunday morning, the children were so fed up with their parents yelling all the time they asked their coach to intervene. In a slow walk as ominous as any Gary Cooper took in *High Noon*, he headed across the field during a water break to scold the parents into silence. "It's okay to cheer for the girls," he said. "But stop telling them what to do. I'm telling them to run a play. You're yelling at them to shoot. You're confusing them."

Afterward I asked him why parents go so bonkers at sporting events. You don't see this kind of behavior at the school play or a piano recital.

"First of all, parents are unrealistic about their children," Robin Mott said. A former all-state high school soccer player and the father of three, Mott has been around youth soccer for four decades. "Parents don't understand where their children are skill-wise," he said.

He talked about children developing athletic skills in phases. In the 1980s, psychologist Benjamin Bloom analyzed world-class performers in six fields—concert pianists, Olympic swimmers, sculptors, tennis players, mathematicians, and neurologists. Bloom interviewed the high achievers, along with their parents, teachers, and coaches. As he wrote in *Developing Talent in Young People*, he found one overarching commonality. "The child who 'made it' was not always the one who was considered to be the most 'talented.'" Many parents said another one of their children had more "natural ability." So what distinguished the high achiever from the under-achieving sibling? "A willingness to work and a desire to excel," Bloom wrote. The most common words used were *persistence*, *determination*, and *eagerness*.

Bloom said children go through three stages of developing talent:

- *Romantic* (ages six to thirteen). The field entices them. They are drawn in, explore, and discover it. They learn basic skills in an atmosphere of fun. They work for praise, applause, and approval. Enjoyment is critical.
- *Technical (ages thirteen to sixteen).* An instructor or coach begins working with a child, focusing on technique and discipline. This transition is fraught with peril because something that was once enjoyable becomes work; for some the joy goes out of the experience. Many drop out. Involvement in youth sports peaks around age eleven, then drops off precipitously by age fourteen.
- *Mature (ages sixteen and up).* Participants move toward mastery. They go beyond rules to develop their own style and interpretation. Practice is intrinsically motivated.

Of course, these phases are flexible, but Bloom's larger point is what matters: "One of the most startling discoveries of our study has been that it takes a while to recognize talent." In sports, he said, fewer than 10 percent of children could confidently be identified as gifted by age twelve. Coach Mott agreed. I asked him whether he could predict which of his U-10 girls would be a successful athlete at sixteen. He gave a resounding "no." "Some people grow," he said. "Some people don't. Some people never develop the technical skills, others get really motivated and suddenly spurt forward."

I asked him whether he could predict which of the players would be successful at life. "You can certainly tell who's better at adapting to situations," he said. His own seventeen-year-old daughter is only five feet tall and has juvenile rheumatoid arthritis, he said, but she has a passion for soccer, developed great technical skills, and has a grasp of the game. "She's not the biggest, she's not the fastest, she's never going to win the ball in the air, but she's smart, she can track the ball, and she knows where to pass it." She's started every game in high school.

Parents have to know they are not a talent scout. If they're driving their preadolescent kid to excel in a particular sport, odds are that kid will drop out before they even have the chance to get good. The most important thing for children under twelve is to enjoy the game. Nothing more.

After the tournament, I asked the ten girls on the Fury what was the best thing about being on this team.

"Being with all your friends," they said.

"Meeting new people."

"Hanging out in the hotel and playing games together."

"Having a bond with people who go to different schools."

I asked them what they saw as the difference between playing an individual sport and a team sport.

"With individual sports you may have a friend there, but when you're playing with a group, you're, like, together."

"Team sports are funner."

"*Funner* is not a word," a teammate added.

"More fun."

"If you make a mistake in an individual sport, it's just you. If you're a team, everyone hugs each other."

"What do you not want your parents to do on the sideline?" I asked.

"When they encourage you, it's fine, but when they tell you to move out of your position, you have to ignore them, even if they get mad at you."

"Like when they say, 'Go to the ball! You can do it! Keep your chin up!' It just makes you go 'Bleeccch! Ugh! Gag!'"

"Sometimes they say, 'Come here and say hi to so-and-so, she came to watch you.' I hate that!"

I asked, "So what should parents do?"

"Shut up and cheer!" they said in unison.

YOU'RE THE KIND OF PERSON WHO . . .

Fair enough. I was getting a clear sense of what parents should not do at this point, but I still wasn't clear about what they should do. I quickly discovered one parent who's thought about that question more than any other.

Jim Thompson looks more like a sports dad than a sports star. With his soft, friendly face and reddish, Scandinavian complexion, he reminded me of a small-town pastor. In 1998, Thompson started the Positive Coaching Alliance, which is dedicated to transforming youth sports into a happy experience for both parents and kids. The organization has trained two hundred thousand coaches affecting more than three million children. Their board includes Phil Jackson, Bill Bradley, Dean Smith, Kerri Strug, and Nadia Comaneci.

"My first job was working with emotionally disturbed kids in

Minnesota," Thompson told me in his office in Mountain View, California. "Our philosophy was relentless positivity. We set limits, but within those boundaries we let the kids run free. Then I came home and my kids were playing sports, and I saw these highly educated parents doing exactly the wrong thing. That's where I got the idea for positive coaching."

The purpose of youth sports, Thompson said, is to create better competitors and to create better people. He often asks parents who they think has the job of accomplishing the first goal. "They get it right away," he said. "Coaches and kids." Parents have a more important job, he tells them. "You focus on the second goal, helping your kids take what they learn from sports into the rest of their lives." Let's say your kid strikes out, and his team loses the game. "You can have a first-goal conversation about bailing out of the batter's box, keeping your eye on the ball, etc. Or you can have a second-goal conversation about resilience, character, and perseverance."

What are some tips for how best to accomplish that objective? Thompson divided his recommendations into three phases: before the game, during, and after it's over.

Before the Game

Be driven, don't drive. Don't push sports on your kid; wait for them to push you. Thompson said he recently held a coaching workshop with Peyton Manning. Somebody asked Manning who the best coach he ever had was, and he said his dad. "My dad told me he could teach me how to be a quarterback, but I had to ask. So when he came home, I would immediately badger him, 'Hey, let's go out and work on my three-step drop.'" Once the child shows initiative, the parents can get involved. As Thompson summed it up, "It's hard for a child to be driven when he's been driven all the time by his parents."

Define your goals. Thompson likes to ask parents to identify their goals for their kids in doing athletics. He gives them a list of choices and 100 "points" to divide across the goals.

_____ Become a good athlete.
_____ Learn to play the sport.
_____ Learn teamwork.
_____ Win.
_____ Gain increased self-confidence.
_____ Learn "life" lessons.
_____ Have fun.
_____ Make friends.
_____ Earn a college scholarship.
  100 TOTAL

"Almost never does anyone put more than five or ten points in winning," Thompson said. He encourages parents to have their children fill out the same form, then compare answers.

During the Game

No verbs. "Our advice is to cheer, but don't give directions," Thompson said. "You can say 'good pass,' but you can't say 'pass it to her.' You can say 'nice shot,' but you can't say 'shoot.'"

Flush the toilet. One thing I heard a few times from Fury players was they hated when their parents said "Keep your chin up!" or "Don't worry, you'll get 'em next time." Geez, I thought. Parents can't catch a break. Even pick-me-ups aren't allowed.

Thompson has an innovative solution. He suggests parents

devise a "mistake ritual" with their kids, which parents or kids can do whenever the child makes a blunder. Some examples he's seen work:

- When a player makes a mistake, she removes her cap; as soon as she puts her cap back on, she forgets the last play and focuses on the next.
- When an athlete slips up, he taps his helmet twice. If the child forgets to perform the ritual, Dad taps his head twice to remind him it's okay to make mistakes.
- "What do we do with stinky things?" a trainer once asked Thompson. "We flush them down the toilet." The trainer does the same with his student athletes. Whenever one child makes a blunder, the entire team makes a flushing movement with their hands to indicate the mistake is gone and forgotten.

After the Game

No PGA. Thompson said the number one thing that parents should avoid after games is the deconstructing of mistakes. Your job is not to play jock radio host and chomp on every missed kick, whiffed catch, or dropped ball. Thompson's way of expressing this is "No PGA. No postgame analysis."

You're the type of person who . . . Ask your child for three things they remember about the game, then tell them three things you remember. If your kid mentions something negative, respond with what Thompson calls a *You're the kind of person who* statement.

" 'Sure, you didn't get a hit, but I want you to know, one of the reasons I like you is you're the kind of person who doesn't give up easily or keeps practicing until you get it right.' The kid may be thinking, 'I am?'" Thompson said. "But it's the kind of reinforcement that builds esteem. 'Yes, I screwed up out there, but I'm the kind of person who bounces back.' Suddenly the conversation on the way home is not about feeling negative; it's about feeling positive."

THE WORLDWIDE LEADER IN SPORTS

ESPN's headquarters are located on a former garbage dump in a backwoods Connecticut town that used to be known as "Mum City" because it was a leader in chrysanthemum production. Today it's the epicenter of American sports, a Hogwarts for guys. Half of all Americans age twelve to sixty-four spend time on an ESPN platform every week, including two-thirds of men ages eighteen to thirty-four, who spend an average of one hour a day. "Oprah is to women as ESPN is to men," Tom Shales, the Pulitzer Prize–winning television critic, told me.

As one of those ESPN-centric guys, I was thrilled to spend a day on campus, speaking with athletes, anchors, and Super Bowl champions about how sports can enhance families. Can cultivating a culture of play make families happier?

At its core, play *is* happiness. The *Oxford English Dictionary* contains more than a hundred definitions of *play*, from *cavort* to *giggle* to *galumph*. It's a "soup of behavior," one Harvard anthropologist concluded. "We play because we have an exuberance of spirit and energy," wrote psychologist Kay Redfield Jamison, "but we are also exuberant because we play."

Long before the business of sports took over, play was largely a family-based activity. As recently as a century ago, when families were more isolated, children were not segregated into age groups and instead played primarily with siblings and cousins of different ages. Parents, too, were less self-conscious about what types of play were appropriate for adults versus kids. If you wanted to play games, you played with your family. The typical repertoire included cards, jigsaw puzzles, tag, rolling the hoop, horseshoes, and leapfrog.

What was striking about my visit to ESPN was how everyone had a story about a time when families and sports were more connected. Mike Greenberg, the cohost of the network's signature morning show, told me the overwhelming majority of his family bonding as a child took place over sports. Now a father himself, he leaves inspirational notes for his children taken from legendary UCLA coach John Wooden's motivational handbook, *Pyramid of Success*. "My favorite is 'Be quick, but don't hurry,'" he said. "I have used it with my kids a million times. Like when they're doing homework. You want to do that fast, I tell them, because when you're done you can play, but you don't want to hurry. That defeats the purpose."

Greenberg's cohost, Mike Golic, a former NFL lineman, said he learned to love football from his father, Lou, who ran backyard drill sessions for his three sons. At one point he even had them push trucks down the road. When Golic's brother Bob announced he wanted to play football in high school, his dad, a former Canadian player, warned him about punches, kicks, and torn ligaments. When Bob said he still wanted to play, Lou took him to school, marched up to the coach, and said, "I am your new head coach." "My dad was a big guy," Golic remembered, "so the coach said, 'Sure thing.'"

Josh Elliot, an anchor (who later moved to ABC News), believes that in many families sports provide a common language between generations. "I will never forget what Dodger Stadium looked like the first time I saw it," he said. "Not ever, ever, ever. And my father just knew I would react that way, so he took me to a game when I was six. And I loved him for it. And that love had nothing to do with sports, but it was transmuted through sports.

"Look, I'm in no place to discuss successful families," he went on. "I'm adopted. My father came out of the closet when I was fourteen. My brother and sister, both adopted, are completely unlike me. Yet I totally am qualified to talk about this, because being connected to something larger than myself is what kept me going."

So how can parents cultivate that feeling? Rich Luker, the founder of the ESPN Sports Poll and one of America's big thinkers about sports, agreed that games, at their heart, are low-intensity ways for different generations to play together. "If you look at the most popular intergenerational games," he said, "they've all been around for centuries: poker, bowling, golf."

By playing these games first at home, you ensure your family is at the heart of your child's sporting life. "You start by having a kid go out for a pass, thrown by mom or dad," Luker said. "So the act of catching a pass or shooting a basketball is associated first with Mom and Dad." Then, when that kid gets a hit at Little League, he continued, the child comes running up to you to celebrate. "And that becomes a pinnacle moment you share as a family," he said.

The next time you go out back with your child, he went on, you look for opportunities to encourage the child to take a little more risk. Run a little farther to catch the pass; take a few steps back before throwing the Frisbee. "You look for that teachable moment," he said. "'See what happened? You didn't think you could do this, but you did it! How did you feel?'

"'I liked it.'

"And suddenly the kid is deciding how far she wants to go," Luker said. "Sure, she's learning all sorts of important skills— confidence, competitiveness, risk. But all that can come later. What matters now is a parent and a child are playing for fun. Sports, at that moment, are not a source of division in families. They're a source of connection."

So years later, whether your child's team goes on to become number one in the state, as happened with the Fury after the tournament I witnessed, or your child's team goes on to lose every game of the season (except one!), as happened with my daughters' soccer team that year, the outcome doesn't really matter. What matters more is what happens before and after the game. The battle of Waterloo may have been won on the playing fields of Eton, but for families, the battle for character is won in the backyard.

13

GIVE WAR A CHANCE

The Green Beret Guide to the Perfect Family Reunion

THE LOOK IN their eyes was eager yet afraid. They were gulping down Gatorade and ripping open PowerBars. There were twenty-nine of them: a schoolteacher and her twenty-three-year-old daughter who were hoping to reconnect after some estrangement; a sixty-two-year-old U.S. Army colonel who was blinded in a roadside bomb in Iraq and was walking with the aid of a comrade; a retired firefighter who wanted to pay tribute to the forty buddies he lost on 9/11. Each had paid a sizable entry fee to be here and was lugging a military-grade black rucksack with thirty pounds of bricks inside.

"Welcome to the Goruck Challenge," said Jason McCarthy, the leader of the group. "Ten to twelve hours. Fifteen to twenty miles. Good livin'!"

McCarthy was standing on a darkened corner of Broadway in the heart of New York's Chinatown. It was 8:00 P.M. on Saturday, September 10, and over the next dozen hours, McCarthy, a toothy, slender, six-foot-five former Green Beret from Ohio, would lead the group on a brazen obstacle-course-cum-death-march through the streets and over the bridges of New York City, ending at Ground Zero at the exact hour the first plane crashed into the North Tower.

"Be sure and wrap those bricks well," McCarthy barked. "I got plenty of duct tape and bubble wrap. I know you're thinking, 'Oh, mine are wrapped,' but an hour and a half from now, clank, clank, clank. Then we'll have to come back to the starting line."

McCarthy, a thirty-two-year-old Iraq War veteran, looks like a lankier, more devilish version of Tim Tebow. He started Goruck as a company in 2008 (the name is a variation on *rucksack*), and nearly every week they hold sold-out challenges from Montana to Georgia. This was the group's sixty-third event.

"People wonder why guys in the military have such a strong bond," McCarthy told me earlier. "It's because they suffer together, and they do things as a group they could never do as individuals.

"And that sense of camaraderie is lost on too many people," he continued. "The world tells people what they cannot do. The Goruck Challenge shows them what they can do. But in order to do that, you first have to break them down as individuals."

Goruck is part of the booming business of extreme bonding recreational activities that includes other races with names like Tough Mudder, Muddy Buddy, Beach Palooza, and Warrior Dash. Collectively, these companies bring in more than $250 million a year.

All this interest in team building led me to wonder if I could learn a few tips from this world of extreme play about how to make family gatherings more successful. Maybe the Green Berets could improve our week at the beach with my extended family or the Rottenbergs' annual July Fourth weekend on Cape Cod.

"Okay, everybody," McCarthy shouted. "We're going to be in formation. Break down into two columns. Whenever I say 'Go!' you say 'Ruck!'"

"Go!"

"RUCK!"

"Go!"

"RUCK!"

"Remember," he called out. "Everything is done as a team. You'll mess up soon enough, but don't worry, you'll pay for it later. Now, follow me.

"Go!"

"RUCK!"

"Go!"

"RUCK!"

And with that McCarthy took off sprinting down Broadway.

KEEPING TIME TOGETHER

The night my mother met my future mother-in-law the two of them disappeared into the other room and returned five minutes later with smiles on their faces: The Feilers would get Thanksgiving and Labor Day; the Rottenbergs Passover and July Fourth. In the years that followed, those summer gatherings became marquee occasions for grandparents, siblings, cousins, and others. At Camp Rottenberg, the seminal events are long bike rides, competitive board games, and a campfire. At Camp Feiler, the high points are homemade ice cream, tie-dye, and a watermelon seed spitting contest.

Forty percent of Americans attend a family reunion every year, with another quarter attending one every two or three years. Reunions usually involve a core family whose descendants bring their own families to a joint event. These gatherings can range from under thirty people, as happens with both the Feilers and Rottenbergs, or up to a thousand. The editor of *Reunions* maga-zine, Edith Wagner, told me at least two hundred thousand family reunions are held every year, involving as many as a hundred million people.

Some reunions are long-standing. The descendants of Samuel and Hannah Rockwell have held a reunion annually since 1847, believed to be the oldest in the United States. They gather outside Canton, Pennsylvania, on the first Saturday in August. Highlights include a presentation of historical meaning to the family, such as the role of women in nineteenth-century Pennsylvania or how the Civil War affected the family. One year they learned how to build a barn and toured one built by family members in 1883.

Other reunions are elaborate. More than a thousand members of the Whiting family have gathered every year since 1948 in a remote area of Arizona to celebrate the family's role in building a Mormon homestead in the 1870s. Descendants re-create the original village with hands-on activities including a barbershop, chair factory, chicken coop, and ice cream parlor.

Many reunions have themes. One hundred fifty members of the Rosebeary family have gathered annually for thirty-five years on Lake Tenkiller in Oklahoma. "Survivor" was their funniest theme, they say. The "70s Flashback" included disco and The Newlywed Game. Each family wears a different color T-shirt; they have relay races and toss horseshoes. The weekend opens with "doughnut decorating" and closes with "see you later burgers."

And an extraordinary number of reunions involve African American families. Inspired by Alex Haley's *Roots*, many black families began tracing their lineage back to slavery. The Guy family dates its origins to the birth of a slave girl named Millie in

1810 in Raleigh, North Carolina. Nearly seven hundred people attended a recent reunion, which featured historical tours, roller-skating, a talent show, and lots of prayers. One reason for their success: The reunion's committee chair calls four hundred relatives once a month just to chat (and to badger them to attend the event).

The stories behind these reunions are often similar. Wagner told me she once assigned a young staffer to call a number of families to find out how their reunions got started. "After half a day she slammed down the phone and said, 'I can't do this anymore. Every story is the same.' Family members met up at a funeral and decided they wanted to gather in happier times."

From that beginning, gatherings slowly became more involved. On the Web sites and Facebook pages where organizers gather, they chat about how many frozen hot dogs to order, renting Porta Pottis, and the proper rope length for tug-of-war. I can relate. Over the years, both our summer gatherings have become more ornate. One year my mother-in-law initiated a campfire with s'mores; the next year we added T-shirts and a cheer; the following year we included a skit and carved a wooden sign. My mother loves charts, so we have spreadsheets for who's cooking; detailed maps for geocaching; and minute-by-minute schedules for carving sand castles and catching crabs. Our vacations began to seem like scout camp.

And that's when it hit me: Who's more expert at turning assorted lie-abouts into close-knit, supportive teams than the military? They've been doing it for thousands of years. As historian William McNeill wrote in his charming book *Keeping Together in Time*, humans have the unique ability to bond through mass dancing, drilling, drumming, marching, clapping, singing, and chanting. The "I" passes into "we," he said. The "my" shifts to "our."

Goruck and its kin are just the latest attempts to apply those techniques to civilians. I didn't expect we would directly copy their stunts. The idea of asking my in-laws to carry thirty pounds of bricks to the beach would go over like, well, a ton of bricks. But surely we could pick up a few tips to make our gatherings more fun and our family more unified.

GET YOURSELVES A LOG

Jason McCarthy had barely sprinted a block and a half down Broadway before the camaraderie of Team 63 evaporated. Some people sagged under the weight of the bricks. Others took off at a hyperpace. The once tightly huddled team looked like a string of Morse code stretched out on the sidewalk, dotted and dashed in clumps of one, two, or three.

"Hey, keep up!" someone shouted.

"Pick up the pace!"

"What tends to happen," McCarthy explained, "is people show up with their own individually wrapped lives. 'Oh, I've got my water. I've got my food. I can take care of myself.' But this is not an individual-serving-size type of thing. We have to show them they're going to have to stick together."

McCarthy led the group to the paved plaza along the southern tip of Manhattan, overlooking the Statue of Liberty.

"Jersey represent!" someone called.

McCarthy did not look pleased. "When I hear you boasting about where you're from or shouting 'Hurry up,'" he said, "I hear you saying, 'Aren't I cool?' or 'Screw you in the back.' If you want that kind of bravado, go run a marathon for time. I think we need to slow this down." He paused. "Everybody on the ground, we're doing bear crawls."

The twenty-nine members of Team 63 dropped to the pavement and began crawling alongside the balustrade. The rhythm was imprecise and jerky. Unsatisfied, McCarthy had the team sink to the ground and do commando crawls. Still unsatisfied, he had them put their toes up on park benches and do push-ups facing the water. "I want you to have a better view of the Statue of Liberty," he said.

At this point, a few people started collapsing. I heard audible moans. One person got up, hobbled over to McCarthy, and ran off into the night.

"We're down to twenty-eight," McCarthy cried. "How's Jersey looking to you now?"

After an hour and a half, McCarthy finally gave the group some relief. He invited them to stand and drink some water. Then he dropped the hammer. He told them they could no longer use their shoulder straps. That meant as they set off jogging north in double file, they had to carry their rucksacks in their arms.

This new rigidity had some effect. The group stopped in front of the New York Stock Exchange and did the cycle of crawls and push-ups again. This time they were more in sync. Next they jogged across the Brooklyn Bridge and down to the East River, where McCarthy had them wade into the water and start doing push-ups, with their faces plunging into the black current.

"At this point, they're thinking, What did I get myself into?" McCarthy told me. "They're grown men and women. Every part of their body is telling them 'Don't do this.'

"It's like jumping out of an airplane," he continued. "Every time I did it, I was sick to my stomach. But the army's concept is that while you don't necessarily need people to jump out of airplanes, you need the type of people who are willing to jump out of airplanes. The only way to make that happen is to let them work out a system."

McCarthy has one fail-safe method for forcing a group to create that system. It's a technique that works with families, he added. And it was waiting for Team 63 in the middle of the Manhattan Bridge.

It was a log.

"This log is now part of your team," McCarthy told the group as they gathered around the gnarly tree trunk. He estimated it weighed a thousand pounds. "You're going to become intimately familiar with this teammate. Work out a system. But remember, if your new teammate here touches the ground, that's twenty-five push-ups."

The group snapped into action. "Rest it on your knees!" someone cried. "I need more help," cried another. "DO NOT drop the log," added one.

Ten minutes later, the log hadn't moved ten feet.

"The log is perfect for team building," McCarthy said, "because it forces everyone to get involved. You can't lift it by yourself. You're what the military calls 'nut to butt' with everyone else, and you're thinking, Oh, we're going to have this for a few minutes. But they're going to keep it for the next three hours.

"And here's the lesson for families," he continued. "Think about all those great moments in your family that nearly got ruined. The day it rained on vacation, the picnic that got inundated with bugs, the wedding where someone got drunk. There's always a moment when the demons come out. In that instant, you have a choice to make. You can either turn against one another, or you can turn toward one another. The best way to do that is to get yourselves a log."

For what seemed like forever, the members of Team 63 struggled to find a rhythm. They tried taking a break every thirty steps, then twenty, then fifteen. They tried having everyone under the log, then rotating people in and out. They tried screaming. After nearly an hour, they were still on the bridge.

"We're getting close," McCarthy whispered to me. "The vultures are circling."

It was 4:23 A.M.

And then, just as the group stepped onto Canal Street and the first hint of light appeared in the sky, the most remarkable thing happened. Shoulders started to align. Legs began working in unison. Eyes looked forward. Team 63 suddenly looked like an army of ants effortlessly carrying a peanut.

"Are you good, Lauren?" someone called out.

"I feel like I'm not doing enough," she said.

"You're doing great," someone answered.

A young woman in heels staggered out of a bar, jolted upright at the sight of the Goruckers, and applauded.

"We bought this," a team member called out, "but they wouldn't deliver."

Everyone laughed. *Laughed!* With a thousand pounds of lumber on their shoulders, thirty pounds of masonry on their backs, and ten hours of blood, sweat, and sadism in their soles.

"People reach a certain point, and suddenly they get it," McCarthy said. "They've seen people help them. They've felt their needs answered. And they start to think of themselves last. Their bodies are weaker, but their system is better."

McCarthy's words echoed the more memorable lessons I had learned. In families, some of our greatest demons arise when the needs of the group conflict with those of the individual. We need more sleep, but we have to get the kids up and out the door. Someone wants to pull the plug on Grandma; others do not. In that moment, you can flee. You can fight. You can pout. But you only truly succeed when you break through the conflict and work out a system with the others on your team.

Just before 7:30 A.M., the snaking centipede of Team 63 hobbled to the outskirts of Ground Zero. By this point, they had already said good-bye to the log in Times Square, then sprinted down Fifth Avenue. They were exhausted, haggard, and completely pumped.

"As far as I'm concerned, the Goruck Challenge starts here," McCarthy said. "From here on, it's all your heart."

He asked the team to pair off and do body-carries across the finish line. The smaller person, he said, must carry the bigger person. And they did it. Some used the fireman's carry, where one person is draped over the other's shoulders. Some turned the second person upside down. The daughter carried her mother on her back. And just after 8:00 a.m., on a crystalline morning in New York, fourteen teams crossed the finished line.

"I feel much more emotion than I would have expected," the mom said to me moments later. "My daughter wants to join the military, and I was nervous. Now I understand. This is a very powerful feeling. The connection you feel with others is unlike anything I've ever experienced. No wonder all the Goruckers on Facebook call themselves brothers and sisters."

The firefighter was leaning on a fence. He was sobbing. "I feel so attached to my buddies on 9/11 right now," he said. "But I couldn't have made it through the night without these guys here." He gestured to Team 63 around him. "I'm coming back next year."

Standing off to the side, Jason McCarthy was also looking contemplative.

"I came from a broken family," he continued. "I was basically raised by my grandparents. I went through a period when I thought the individual doesn't need anybody else to survive. I didn't need family.

"But I've realized I was wrong," he continued. "Life is meant to be shared. Ultimately, the greatest experiences I've had have all come with other people. That's what I want people to experience with Goruck. We all need family, but that family has to be earned."

THE OLYMPICS OF STICKY BUNS

So which of these techniques (if any) might apply to families? To answer that question, I went to someone who would know.

The U.S. Naval Academy is located in Annapolis, Maryland. The 340-acre campus has four thousand midshipmen and five hundred professors. One of those instructors is Commander David Smith, the chair of the Department of Leadership, Ethics, and Law, and one of the country's leading experts on building unit cohesion. He's also the spitting image of Alec Baldwin in his role as the naval historian in *The Hunt for Red October*, which was filmed at the Naval Academy. When the Pentagon decided recently to review how it builds morale among troops, it called Commander Smith.

"We know that being a member of a group is something all humans strive for," Smith told me. "Feeling kinship. The number and types of relationships you have. All these are central to having a happy life."

It's amusing to hear that U.S. military leaders are sitting around reading books about happiness, but the sentiment is hardly new. Lao-tzu first talked about military morale two thousand years ago; Shakespeare's Henry V spoke of soldiers as a "band of brothers." But it wasn't until after World War II that the military began to systematically study the concept of unit cohesion, which it defined as "the capacity of any group of people to pull together consistently for a common purpose."

Until recently the military taught unit cohesion by "dehuman-

izing" individuals, Smith said. Think of the bullying drill ser-
geants in *Full Metal Jacket* or *An Officer and a Gentleman.* But these
days the military spends more time building up identity through
communal activities like the ones used by Goruck. Smith sketched
out a few recommendations that could work at family gatherings.

Tell Your History

A key technique in building a group is what sociologists call
"sensemaking," the building of a narrative that explains what the
group is about. At the Naval Academy, Smith advises graduating seniors to take incoming freshmen, or "plebes," on history-
building exercises, like going to the cemetery to pay tribute to
the first naval aviator or visiting the original B-1 aircraft on display on campus.

Many families employ similar techniques at their reunions,
from cleaning gravestones to gathering an oral history. The Neal
family of California includes a family history trivia contest in their
reunion. Questions include:

- Eleazar and Ollie Neal had seven children. Name them in
  order.
- Stephen and Francis earned a living by farming cotton,
  until boll weevils became a problem. Where did they
  move?
- Which Neal brother was known for offering to buy his
  children a "nickel dip of cream"?
- Which cousin is a diehard San Francisco Giants fan?

The Murphys of Ohio are among the growing number of
families using reunions to take medical histories. Attendees work

together to fill out a family tree, not just with date and place of birth, but also cause of death, to detect patterns. They've even brought in doctors to discuss illnesses common to the family.

Compete

Summer camps have it right: Color wars are great morale-building exercises. Research shows that having a "them" is one of the best ways to get an "us," Smith said. Even friendly competition can breed in-group identity, which can unite people from different generations and families. Adopting team colors, cheers, and flags is also a huge boost to morale, which is why armies have been employing them for millennia.

The Cowans held a family Olympics near Rochester, New York. Activities included the Great Paper Boat Race with origami boats in a nearby creek; a pie-eating contest with hands behind the back and lots of whipped cream; an Oreo-stacking contest; and a competition where blindfolded teammates stand around a field and call out to one another until everyone is reunited.

At the Dominique family reunion in Ohio, participants formed four teams of fifteen. One competition included staring at a table of family items for several minutes (Grandpa's old pipe, the vase from Grandma's kitchen, and so on) then answering questions about the items (*How long was the pipe? Name three elements in the design on the vase*). Other games involved laying out a board that was two feet wide by fourteen feet long and timing people as they arranged themselves first by height, then by alphabetical order, then by age— all without falling off.

At the Rottenberg gathering over July Fourth, we started a kids-only "Cape House Challenge," a morning of competitive games. I was amazed by how much the children loved coming up with names for their teams and how much effort they put into creating cheers. Long after the games were over, the cheers still echoed around the house.

Play

The military has studied the impact of different types of activities on bonding. Solo games (bowling, golf) have the least impact. Relay races are next, because they have both individual and team components. The most effective are full-blown games (volleyball, touch football, ultimate Frisbee) in which everyone depends on one another.

"Start by asking what it means to be a Feiler," Smith advised. "Then pick an activity based on what you like. 'Okay, we're lifelong learners; we're going to try something new.' 'We're risk takers, so we're going to go hang gliding.' 'We're really outdoorsy, so we never stay inside. I don't care if a hurricane is coming, we're still going surfing.'"

The Carneys of North Carolina are nature lovers, so at their winter gathering, three generations were sent into knee-deep snow on a scavenger hunt. Teams were expected to find three different kinds of leaves, three seeds, three birds, three animal tracks, an insect, something more than a hundred years old, and something less than a month old—all in under thirty minutes. What they couldn't collect, they could take a picture of. Winning items included two goldenrod gall flies, chickadees, blue jays, Canada geese, and tracks from cottontail, coyotes, and dogs. Snow was turned in both as something more than a hundred years old and as something less than a month old.

Decorate the Winners

No surprise, the military loves medals, pins, ribbons, and bars. And they have proof these decorations work. Smith recommends abundant recognitions for team spirit, from coins to award ceremonies.

The Sedemann family of Wisconsin has held reunions since 1933. What began with forty people now tops four hundred. The family holds an annual high-stakes Bake-Off featuring cakes, pies, cobblers, and, in honor of its German roots, sticky buns, or kuchen. A panel of judges awards the "Official Kuchen of Sedemann Games." Family members then bid at auction for the treats, with teenagers intentionally bidding up prices on their parents' submissions to help pay for the event.

In the Cape House Challenge I ran with my sister-in-law, we promised to give the kids awards but quickly forgot. The winners didn't forget! They bugged us for twenty-four hours. Finally we crafted homemade certificates and let the winners decorate theirs first, followed by the runners-up. The kids cradled them in bed that night.

So what happens if some family members resist these activities? In my experience, there's always someone who would rather do a crossword or who generally complains about too much togetherness. "There's always going to be some tension, particularly at the beginning," Smith said. Groups, he explained, tend to follow a typical pattern:

Forming
Storming
Norming
Performing

First the group convenes, he said. Then it quickly disintegrates into squabbling as people try to figure out their roles. Then you begin to establish norms. *Each person gets only five minutes in the bathroom. Grandma has a system for hanging up towels.* "Eventually we all get our roles, and at that point we start performing," Smith said.

That pattern rang true for me. The Feiler family reunion every August is often marred by early storms. As happened at that explosive dinner that first sent me exploring happy families, each family brings preset tensions and sore points. But then things settle down, routines emerge, and moments of genuine connection occur. One lesson I took from studying family reunions is to push occasions for members of different families and generations to work together—from making pancakes to setting up a volleyball net. The task matters less than the shared effort.

Finally, Smith stressed, it's important to have an emotional conclusion. On Tybee we introduced a family play. The children play the leads; aunts and uncles wear silly costumes; my mother paints a backdrop; and everyone bakes cookies for the cast party. The dustups that dot other days don't disappear; they're just overshadowed. That's a common theme in happy families, I now realized. All families have conflict; strong families have enough communal high points to outshine the low ones.

The best example I heard of a rousing climax comes from the Mellenbruchs of Kansas. At the end of their three-day gathering, the family holds a church service featuring a fifty-voice choir singing favorite hymns of patriarch Henry Frederick Mellenbruch. For the sermon, someone reads excerpts from the final letter Mellenbruch sent to his wife and nine children in February 1898.

My dear children, I cannot leave you each a fortune in dollars and cents. If you love me and revere my memory, give heed to the follow-

ing advice: Love one another. Be forgiving one toward another. Bear
with each other's shortcomings. Be always willing to give way or
meet the other [person] more than halfway. Be kind and courteous to
outsiders. Make you each a copy of this last advice and read it once a
year.—H. F. Mellenbruch, Fairview, Kansas

The family has followed his wishes. This letter has been read
out loud every summer for more than 110 years.

FAMILY BOOT CAMP

At 10:30 P.M. on a Friday night in late December, Norman Seavers
III led his family onto the driveway of their home in Gainesville,
Florida. At six feet, 180 pounds, Seavers, who grew up in a tight-
knit African American family in Illinois, still has the body of the
elite basketball player he was in high school. Only now, at forty-
two, and the manager of a biotech firm, he also has specks of gray
in his mustache and goatee.

"Okay, listen up everybody," he said to his wife, Natasha, and
their four children, ages fourteen to four. "I want you to put a
brick from the pile in your backpack. This is going to be fun, but
you're going to have to stay together. If you don't, it's going to get
a little less fun for a while."

Norman was doing his best to imitate Jason McCarthy. Having just completed a Goruck himself, Norman shared photos and
details with his kids. "They thought it was crazy cool," he said.
"My twelve-year-old son likes to watch shows about special forces
guys, and my other kids are pretty athletic. Instantly they started
bugging me to take them on a challenge."

Norman is just one of many Goruckers who apply some of its

tricks to their families. Paul Morin, a single dad in Fairfax, Virginia, takes his young son and daughter on training runs carrying kid-size rucksacks and a log. Jeremy Gagne, of Washington, DC, turned his wife's three-mile walk to the farmers' market every Saturday into a Goruck with their kids.

The Seavers were already used to elaborate family workouts. On Saturdays, Norman would take them to a nearby field, let them get a thirty-yard head start, then send their seventy-pound black Lab to chase them. He then asked one kid to do as many push-ups as possible, followed by the next person, until they reached 150. Afterward, he would take them into "The Swamp," the ninety-thousand-seat stadium of the Florida Gators, and have them run four times to the top with the dog.

"You want to take huge vacations," Norman said, "but with four kids, that's not always practical. Saturdays are the time we all do stuff together." The kids love to ask questions during these workouts, he said. "They want to know what their mom and I did while we were in college. We're able to share how we grew up and what we believe. It's a time when we tell them the mistakes we made and what challenges are headed their way."

I was reminded of Stephen Covey's idea that we should articulate our values to our children and Marshall Duke's insight that we should share with them our ups and downs.

"It's the biblical perspective," Norman said. "You tell people where you come from."

Norman was initially resistant to taking his kids on a family Goruck. (His wife refused to join the first one.) But he eventually relented. He purchased four Energizer headlamps and took the kids outside after bedtime. "For kids, just being out that late is a really big deal," he said.

He led them to a nearby bike path, had them do some push-ups and lunges, then dispatched them to find sticks that reached their shoulders. The stick could not touch the ground all night, he told them. After an hour or so, a man appeared on the path. "He was lit up like a Christmas tree," Norman recalled. "He had glowing lights all over his body and bike."

Norman saw an opportunity. This man was their enemy, he told the kids. He was their log. He told the kids to pile into a ditch and camouflage themselves under leaves and debris. "They were completely silent," Norman said. "They couldn't believe they saw the man, but he didn't see them. After the man rode by and didn't detect them, the kids went ballistic. They were so excited they ran home and told their mom over and over again what happened."

Which is why Natasha, a financial planner, agreed to go with the family on the next Goruck. This time, after asking everyone to add a brick to their backpack, Norman directed the family to a nearby park, where he had hidden five clues. The kids had to count their steps, build a tower of pinecones, and construct a shelter out of sticks. He punished them only once, when the group started to lag. He had them hold a push-up pose for nearly a minute. "My older son was laughing at first," Norman said, "but he soon figured it out and got in line."

Finally, the clues led the family to a tree. The older siblings lifted the four-year-old brother into the branches, where he found a bag of candy. "They were happier than Christmas morning," Norman said.

So did he notice any difference around the house after the training?

"I have. My older son understood more about the discipline it requires to be a great athlete or do well in school. My daughter had her competitive fire stoked. And the four-year-old, he's so competitive he does workouts by himself in the backyard."

Something else happened. The kids wanted to bring their friends on the next challenge, or their cousins. I asked Norman whether he thought a Goruck would work with extended families.

"It's certainly not for everybody," he said. "There are some people you couldn't talk into it. There are others you could talk into it who would quit after ten minutes. But for those willing to try, it's great."

So at the end of the challenge, when the kids came down with that bag of candy, did he feel proud?

"When I finished my own Goruck," he said, "I had the most amazing feeling. It was a spiritual sense of being locked into something I was supposed to be doing. I had that same feeling that night I led the one with the kids, though I have that feeling quite regularly, I must say. I'll see them smile when we're doing a workout or helping one another across a creek, and I'll say to my wife, 'We're doing this. Together.' And the lessons about teamwork and commitment will transfer to their academic life, their job, and their own family someday.

"And we're just at the beginning," he continued. "They're young. We're semiyoung. We're passionate about our family. We're going to watch some great things happen in our kids' lives. And that's better than any job, any vacation, or anything else in life."

CONCLUSION

All Happy Families

S TEPPING ONTO A Hollywood soundstage is exciting and a little disappointing. The excitement comes from peeking behind the curtain—in this case, a television show, the most popular one in America, *Modern Family*. Ooh, look at all the food they lay out. Wow, I can't believe the water actually works in the sink on that set. Hey, that actress sure looks hot in her bathrobe.

The disappointment comes from being reminded it's all just make-believe. Wait, those trees outside the window are fake? Boy, he's shorter than I would have expected. Gee, they shoot fifteen takes of every joke.

It's also a lot easier to be a happy family when twenty writers are crafting every line, teams of wardrobe and makeup artists are getting you dressed, and swarms of stagehands, carpenters, and caterers are poised to change every lightbulb, repair every leak, and prepare every meal. No wonder we all want to be like the families we see on television!

The sets for the homes of the three families that make up *Modern Family*'s central clan were clumped together. Eric Stonestreet, who plays Cam, the portly, gay Mr. Dad, was filming a scene in which he learned some bad news. His partner, Mitchell, had failed to mail the invitations to a fund-raiser planned for that night. Cam had ordered the crab cakes and rented the harps, but he had no guests.

"Get me Mitchell!" Cam shouted to his nephew, Luke.

What followed was a high-tech version of "Who's on First?" Luke doesn't know Mitchell's number. Cam grabs the phone and presses speed dial. Mitchell lets the call go to voice mail. Luke doesn't know how to press redial. Cam snatches the receiver and gets twisted in his headset. We've had five back-and-forths in ten seconds and still nobody has managed to communicate.

Shakespeare used mistaken identities to befuddle his lovers. *Modern Family* uses dropped Skype connections.

One of the things that makes *Modern Family* so, well, modern is its dead-on portrayal of the exasperating role technology plays in our lives. Nearly every scene is refracted through a digital fun house: an iPad screen, a cell phone camera, a baby monitor, a YouTube video. Characters spend half their time glancing past one another rather than communicating directly.

"We used to talk about how cell phones killed the sitcom because no one ever goes to anyone's house anymore," said Abraham Higginbotham, one of the executive producers on the show. "You don't have to walk into Rachel and Ross's house on *Friends*, because you can call and say, 'Hey, what's up?' We embrace technology so it's part of the story."

Mark Zuckerberg may be a bigger influence on *Modern Family* than Norman Lear.

For all of its digital make-believe, though, *Modern Family* fits into a long line of comedies that both reflect and help shape the families of the eras they're in. From *Leave It to Beaver*'s suburban white utopia to *All in the Family*'s tense, intergenerational battles to the idealized, throwback warmth of *The Cosby Show*, each generation embraces a family comedy that best captures the moment. So what does *Modern Family* say about modern families? I asked the creators and cast that question and came away with a few impressions.

Everybody wants to be in a happy family. There have been a few family comedies over the years that celebrated dysfunction. *Married . . . with Children* and *Roseanne* come to mind. But, in general, families that overcome their difficulties and manage to reaffirm their connection have been the bedrock of the form. By the 2000s, however, that type of upbeat, profamily comedy was considered passé. The acid humor of *Seinfeld* or *The Office* had prevailed. The family comedy, the backbone of Hollywood since the birth of television, was said to be dead.

That is, until *Modern Family* proved the naysayers wrong. Americans still aspire to be in a healthy, functioning family. "There's been an absence of well-grounded, family comedy on television in recent years," Jesse Tyler Ferguson, who plays Mitchell, told me. "Instead we've had fantastic snarky comedies, like *Seinfeld* and *Arrested Development.* I think people miss shows like *The Cosby Show* and *Family Ties* that showed true family values."

Conflict is the norm. Comedy thrives on conflict. The more tense the standoffs, absurd scenarios, and outlandish schemes characters get themselves into, the funnier a show is. What *Modern Family* captures better than any show in decades is parents' complete bafflement about how to raise their kids. While Mom and Dad in classic shows like *The Brady Bunch* and *Happy Days* had all the answers, now the parents rarely do.

On *Modern Family*, no one has fewer answers than Claire Dunphy, the harried mother of three. Claire is played by Julie Bowen, a mother of three herself. I asked her what is modern about Claire and her goofball husband, Phil. "They still have sex," she said. "That's pretty modern. It's modern that they scheduled the shooting of their child with a toy gun in the pilot episode, thinking that was the best parenting choice.

"But I think what's most modern about them is they admit their children don't poop rainbows 24/7," she continued. "There seems to have been this period for the last decade or so in which everything children did was perfect all the time, and they just needed to be told they were fantastic, gorgeous, and lovable, and they would turn out perfect. And we're all finding out that's not true. Claire and Phil love each other, and they love their kids, but they can also admit when their kids are obnoxious pains in the ass. I think Americans are hungry for that."

Love, American style. Jerry Seinfeld once said his show was built around a simple credo: "No hugs and no learning." *Modern Family* is built around the opposite idea, that no problem is too big it can't be swept under a hug. Even though a few of its families are nontraditional—a divorced older Anglo man and his wife, a divorced younger Latina; a gay couple with an adopted daughter— the values of the show are strictly traditional. *Modern Family* is about the triumph of family over modernity.

"So often comedy is about how we don't like each other," Higginbotham said. "This show is about how we fight with love, how we argue with love, how we cry with love. We're not afraid of those moments when you get caught off guard by a tear. That's what happens in families. Family moves you."

The currency of that emotion is conversation—lots of real, frank talk. "There's a lot of direct communication in our show," said Christopher Lloyd, the cocreator. "There's a lot of talk about problems and feelings, more than in most families, which might be why people gravitate to it. Viewers wish their family communicated a lot more directly, the way our guys do."

Small changes. There's an underlying rule about family comedy

I hadn't fully understood until I talked with the team behind *Modern Family*. And that is: Characters don't really change. They keep reliving the same flaws week after week, year after year.

"Generally, sitcom characters don't grow all that much," said Ty Burrell, who plays Phil. "I hear that from people all the time, 'When are you going to grow?' It's hard to break the news to people that our characters are not going to be growing."

When people do mess up on the show, or realize they erred, the correction is slight—a peck on the cheek, a wry smile, a quick embrace. "That resolution shows a tiny, tiny bit of growth," Burrell said. "But by next week, everybody will be back making the same mistakes all over again."

That is perhaps the biggest lesson for all of us in real families. Conflict happens every day. Mishaps occur. But the microgesture of reconciliation—the hug, the pat on the back, the little object laid out on the bed, or the note tucked into the bag—goes a long way.

Just don't expect the other person to be all that different a few days later.

THE SECRETS OF HAPPY FAMILIES

At the start of this project, I set out to answer a simple question: What do happy families do right and how can the rest of us learn to make our families happier? Everywhere I went, I asked people a version of that question. In the process I learned a number of things about families I hadn't known before.

The first is how central they are to our overall happiness. The last decade has seen a major reevaluation of the role of family in our lives. The big takeaway from all this research: We are not individuals forced to live against our will in groups. We are inherently social beings. Our lives are shaped by our ability to cooperate and coexist with those around us. We function most effectively in teams, networks, or groups.

Sure, some of these groups are made up of strangers, colleagues, or friends. But the most foundational of these groups—the group that's most important to identity, to our self-esteem, to our capacity to love, and to our ability to be satisfied in our lives—is our family. Far from being something we tolerate when we're young, than flee as soon as we're old enough, the sticky, lovable, chaffing extended clan is our natural state.

We are wired to be in families.

So how do we get ours right? Or at least as right as we can? When I set out to find the best practices for family today. I was determined not to force the things I learned into some catchy list of rules you absolutely must follow to have a happy family. I continue to believe there is no such list. As I suspected, my big takeaways differed from Linda's, which differed from my sister's, which differed from those of the other families we shared them with.

I was particularly taken with ideas about sharing family history over dinner (or any other time), sitting on cushioned chairs when disciplining children, and designing elaborate scavenger hunts on family vacations. And I really loved the Law of Two Women, the premortem, and other tips for having difficult family conversations.

Linda became a devotee of the notion that we should switch up routines, pull in ideas from outside sources, and have the kids pick their own punishments, make their own schedules, and generally play a more decisive role in their own upbringings. Also, she's the one who insisted we hang our family mission statement in our dining room and refer to it often when talking with the girls.

Others chose from elsewhere on our list of best practices. My sister rejected the family meeting, but liked having her kids check off there own chores. Linda's brother had no interest in a family mission statement, but loved the ideas about allowance and talking to kids more about sex. The lesson we took from this eclecticism was as reassuring as it was obvious: There is no single formula to make every family happier.

Still, to my surprise, I did keep hearing certain ideas over and over again. A number of overarching themes did emerge. So at the risk of hypocrisy, here is my nonlist list of things that happy families consistently do:

1. Adapt All the Time

The idealized, mid-twentieth-century American family came with preset roles—the father did this, the mother did that, the children behaved in a certain way. There was a clear script, and millions after millions aspired to realize that script, even if few actually did.

That script has been thrown out. Whether we're talking about the makeup of your family, the strategy you use to get your family out the door every morning, the way you feed your family every night, or the techniques you use to discipline, entertain, or inspire your family, the smartest research shows, and the most effective families know, you have to be flexible. You have to be agile.

Agile can mean lots of things. It can mean, like the early adopters of agile family techniques, using more morning lists, chore charts, and other means of being accountable. It can mean, as Linda and I adopted, weekly family meetings to evaluate how your family operates. It can mean simply looking at when you eat meals, how you give out allowance, or where you sit during family discussions and changing things from time to time. Above all, it means your family is capable of evolution and change.

In their detailed studies of American families, Reed Larson, of the University of Illinois, and Maryse Richards, of Loyola, discovered that the most successful families rely on continuous renegotiation. "Collective family well-being depends not on fixed role assignments," they wrote, "but rather on flexible *processes* that allow the family to adjust and adapt."

Management guru Tom Peters, author of *In Search of Excellence*, coined a colorful term that captures this idea of continuous reinvention. The best way to keep up with the ever-changing nature of our times, he said, is to follow what he called "perhaps the only surefire winning formula for success": S.A.V., or screw around vigorously.

Now there's a motto for our age. Want to have a happier family? Tinker with it all the time.

2. Talk. A Lot

Most healthy families talk a lot. From mealtime to long car rides, from disputes between spouses to showdowns among siblings, from money to sex, a key ingredient of successful families is the ability to communicate effectively. As the girls on the Connecticut swim team told me regarding the birds and the bees, "It's no longer 'The Talk.' It's a series of talks. It's a conversation." That credo could apply to nearly every aspect of family life.

But "talking" does not mean simply "talking through problems," as important as that is. Talking also means telling a positive story about yourselves. Specifically, one powerful form of talk families do together is to create a family narrative.

I first heard this idea from Marshall Duke, the Emory psychologist who studied the importance of knowing your family history. Duke showed that the more children know about their parents and grandparents, especially their successes and failures, the more they are able to overcome setbacks. The navy, I learned, uses a similar technique of connecting newcomers with the storied lives of their predecessors.

Jonathan Haidt summed up the importance of storytelling in *The Happiness Hypothesis*. Feeling good about yourself involves stitching experiences into a forward-moving, hopeful narrative. "If you can find a way to make sense of adversity and draw constructive lessons from it, you can benefit." When faced with a challenge, happy families, like happy people, just add a new chapter to their life story that shows them overcoming their hardship. This skill is particularly important for children, whose identities tend to get locked in during their adolescence.

Simply put, if you want a happier family, spend time crafting, refining, and retelling the story of your family's positive moments and your ability to bounce back from the difficult ones. If you tell it, they will come.

3. Go Out and Play

Finally, don't just make adjustments and tell stories. Make fun.

Playing games. Taking vacation. Having get-togethers. Inventing goofy traditions. Cooking. Swimming. Hiking. Singing Dad's favorite song that makes everyone's eyes roll. Tossing a football. Going bowling. Getting lost. Making a giant domino trail on the dining room table. Whatever makes you happy, doing it with other family members will make your family happier.

"Happiness consists in activity," the British writer John Mason Good said nearly two centuries ago. "It is a running stream, not a stagnant pool."

Modern science has backed him up. As happiness expert Sonja Lyubormirsky observed, activities that give us durable happiness are the ones we have a hand in creating. We don't just sit back and receive pleasure. We actually generate the pleasure ourselves. "And you have the ability to make them happen again," she wrote in *The How of Happiness*. When you and the people around you are the source of positive emotion, she continued, the happiness is "renewable."

This idea may not be particularly groundbreaking to families, but it seems to be among the hardest to act on. If you want to have a happier family, find some of those family members, make some time, and play.

WHAT TOLSTOY KNEW

When Leo Tolstoy was five years old, his brother Nikolai told him he had recorded the secret for universal happiness on a little green stick and hid it in a ravine on the family's estate in eastern Russia. Should the stick ever be found, Nikolai said, all humankind would become happy. There would be no diseases; no one would be angry with anyone; everyone would be surrounded with love.

The legend of the green stick became a consuming metaphor in Tolstoy's life. Time and again, in his writings and in his quest for spiritual meaning, Tolstoy returned to the idea of a world free of misery and filled with happiness. In the notebooks he kept for *War and Peace* and *Anna Karenina*, he referenced several times a French proverb, "Happy people have no history." That notion, that happy people don't have a story and unhappy people do, became the inspiration for the opening line of *Anna Karenina*: "All happy families are alike; each unhappy family is unhappy in its own way."

Though Tolstoy may have been dismissive of happy families in his famous maxim, he never stopped searching for happiness himself. In the last years of his life, he returned to the idea of a world purged of pain and overflowing with joy. He asked to be buried in the ravine of his family's estate where he believed his brother had hidden the elusive formula. "There should be no ceremonies while burying my body," Tolstoy wrote. "A wooden coffin, and let anybody who will be willing to take it to the Forest of the Old Order, to the place of the little green stick."

Tolstoy still rests there today, in an unmarked grave, covered in a mound of green grass.

CHOOSE HAPPINESS

Tolstoy's lifelong quest for the little green stick perfectly captures the final lesson I took from this journey. Happiness is not something we find; it's something we make.

All the researchers who've examined well-run organizations, championship teams, or successful groups of any kind have come to pretty much the same conclusion. Greatness is not a matter of circumstance; greatness is a matter of choice. And the best way to make that choice is to take microsteps. There's no grand defining action; no single gesture; no magic lever you can pull or button you can press. There's just a commitment to making incremental changes and accumulating "small wins."

For busy families, this idea of gradual victories is both comforting and energizing. You don't need a wholesale makeover. You just need to get started. I heard this idea repeatedly in my travels: The surest way to have a poorly functioning family is to be content with the status quo. The easiest route to unhappiness is to do nothing.

The opposite of that dictum also holds: The easiest path to happiness is to do something. As the Dalai Lama said, "Happiness is not something ready-made. It comes from your own actions." Tackle the challenge that's been nagging your family, tweak the routine that's not working any longer, have the difficult conversation, pull out the game from the back of the closet.

Reach for the green stick.

You may not find it today, tomorrow, or even next month. You may not discover it until the kids get through this awkward phase. But you can craft a new strategy for the mornings, or make some time to get everyone together in the backyard. And you will reach that point, as long as you make the effort to start. In the end, this may be the most enduring lesson of all. What's the secret to being a happy family?

Try.

ACKNOWLEDGMENTS

I would like to thank the dozens of people who appear by name in this book. They welcomed me into their homes, sat with me in their offices, introduced me to their children, fed me, sometimes even housed me, and, in every case, answered my deeply personal questions with warmth, honesty, and insight. I am deeply grateful for the tremendous amount I learned from them, the worlds they opened up for me, and the countless ways they changed and enriched the lives of everyone around me. This book is a tribute to their inspiring commitment to family.

Countless other people opened doors, submitted to questions, introduced me to unexpected notions, and otherwise provided invaluable assistance to the ideas and stories gathered in this book. A partial list includes Mike Ahearn, Janis Backing, Gina Bianchini, Campbell Brown and Dan Senor, Belle and Wences Casares, Laurie David, Bernie DeKoven, Nadya Direkova, Dani Dudeck, Jo Flattery, Lyn Fogle, Leslie Gordon, Robin Gunn, Bill

Hoffheimer, Sarah Hrdy, Lila Ibrahim, Michael Lazerow, Norman Lear, Susan Levy, Debra Lund, Sheila Marcelo, Beth Middleworth, Mark Pincus, Sophie Politt-Cohen, Marideth Post, Robert Provine, Joanna Rees and John Hamm, Evelyn Resh, Kevin Slavin, and Larry Wente.

I have been enormously honored to explore many of the themes in this book in the Sunday Styles section of the *New York Times*. I would like to thank the always stylish and thoughtful Stuart Emmrich for that singular privilege. Laura Marmor has guided my columns from fledgling ideas into full-fledged pieces. Her daily wisdom and warm companionship have been a delight. Maggie Murphy encouraged me to write about family dinner in *Parade*. Thanks also to fellow writers and toilers on these trails: Lisa Belkin, Randy Cohen, K. J. Dell'antonia, A. J. Jacobs, Jodi Kantor and Ron Lieber, Corby Kummer, Jane Lear, Gary Rosen, Gretchen Rubin, and Bob Wright.

I am thrilled to work so closely with Alan Berger, Craig Jacobson, Brian Pike, and Sally Willcox.

Michael Morrison, Liate Stehlik, and so many others have given me a supportive and enthusiastic home at William Morrow. Special thanks to Lynn Grady, Tavia Kowalchuk, and especially the great Sharyn Rosenblum. Henry Ferris worked around the clock to deeply improve every aspect of this book. Our friendship resounds in these pages. Thanks also to Cole Hager.

David Black is every writer's dream partner, along with Dave Larabell, Susan Raihofer, and the gang at the David Black Literary Agency.

Three cheers for Chadwick Moore, a talented writer and tireless worker.

I am surrounded and uplifted by a buoyant group of encouraging voices: Sunny Bates, Laura Benjamin, Justin Castillo, David

Kramer, Karen Lehrman Bloch, Andrea Mail, Lynn Oberlander, David Shenk, Jeff Shumlin, Lauren Schneider, Max Stier, and Joe Weisberg. Ben Sherwood is a visionary leader and a great dad. Joshua Ramo has been enmeshed in this project from its initial creation, including offering many perceptive comments about the final manuscript.

I am blessed to be at the intersection of two great families. I know no people more devoted to theirs than Debbie and Alan Rottenberg. Thank you for teaching me so much. And for all the games, sleepless mornings, shared journeys, and swapped tactics, a big hug to Elissa and Dan Rottenberg and Rebecca and Mattis Goldman. Have I finally passed the Cape House Challenge?

I grew up in a robust, supportive family that continues to evolve and find new ways to boost and uplift everyone it touches. I pay special tribute to my parents, Jane and Ed Feiler, as well as to Cari and Rodd Bender. My brother, Andrew, devoted precious time and relentless insight to enriching this manuscript. Thank you.

A tearful expression of love and appreciation to the great John Healey. This book marks five years and counting. Every step I take is a testament to you.

With this book, more than any I've written, I felt as if I had a copilot. Linda Rottenberg was a willing participant, an enthusiastic guinea pig, an occasional combatant, a good sport, and an extremely perceptive reader. I am so deeply lucky to be building a family with her. Any benefits we gained from this experience are entirely attributable to her willingness to embrace and improve them. I love you.

From the very beginning, and through every step, this book was inspired by two people, born on the same day, who have brought pleasure, wonder, occasional havoc, intermittent raised voices, and, above all, joy to everyone who knows them. Tybee and

Eden, I dedicate this book to you. When you were very young, I used to tuck you in at night with a little poem: "Wherever you go / Whatever you do / Always remember / Your daddy loves you." But you preferred another version, and always insisted I say it: "Wherever you go / Whatever you do / Always remember / Oops, I forgot . . ." And then you would laugh.

May your lives be filled with laughter, remembering, adventure, and, above all, happy families.

NOTES

This book draws heavily on the abundance of new research and ideas about how groups, teams, organizations, networks, businesses, and, yes, families function most effectively. As described, all the interviews in this book were conducted by me over a several-year period. These notes are an attempt to further flesh out and credit that vast array of research I've tried to bring together in one place. A select bibliography follows.

Introduction: Why We Need New Thinking for Families
The research about how spending time with others is a key ingredient in happiness can be found in many quarters of positive psychology; in particular, see Jonathan Haidt, *The Happiness Hypothesis*; Daniel Gilbert, *Stumbling on Happiness*; and Martin Seligman, *Authentic Happiness*. The two extremes of the parenting wars are Amy Chua, *Battle Hymn of the Tiger Mother*, and Pamela Druckerman, *Bringing Up Bébé*.

1. The Agile Family Manifesto

David Starr's 2009 white paper, "Agile Practices for Families: Iterating with Children and Parents," including photographs of his early-morning lists and flowcharts, can be found at http://pluralsight-free.s3.amazonaws.com/david-starr/files/PID922221.pdf. The original agile manifesto, including photographs of the participants, signatories, and a background on the original meeting, can be found at http://agilemanifesto.org.

The Pew Research Center's numbers on family happiness are included in "The Decline of Marriage and Rise of New Families," from November 2010. Research about the effects of family stress on children was conducted by the National Institutes of Health, January 2010 (childhood obesity); the *Journal of the American Medical Association*, October 2003 (mental illness); and the International and American Association for Dental Research, April 2009 (tooth decay). Ellen Galinsky's research appears in her book *Ask the Children*.

Jeff Sutherland's inspiration, "The New New Product Development Game" by Hirotaka Takeuchi and Ikujiro Nonaka, appeared in *Harvard Business Review* (January-February 1986). Tom Peters's quote on agile organizations can be found at www.tompeters.com/blogs/freestuff/uploads/TP_Purpose083107.pdf.

The research on children setting their own goals comes from multiple studies by Silvia Bunge at the University of California, Berkeley. For an overview, see http://vcresearch.berkeley.edu/news/learning-getting-heads-schoolchildren or *Nurture Shock* by Po Bronson and Ashley Merryman. "The New Science of Building Great Teams" by Alex Pentland appeared in *Harvard Business Review* (April 2012).

2. The Right Way to Have Family Dinner

Portions of my interview with John and Jennifer Besh appeared in *Parade* magazine on June 17, 2012. Laurie David gathers an enormous amount of research about the value of shared meals in her book *Family Dinner.* Additional research is collected at www.thefamilydinnerproject.org and www.barilla.com/share-table?p=research-on-the-benefits-of-family-meals. Data on family mealtimes predicting academic and emotional health appears in Sandra Hofferth and John Sandberg, "Changes in American Children's Time, 1981–1997," from the Population Studies Center at the University of Michigan.

Research on the decline of family mealtime appears in multiple places. The UNICEF report is at www.unicef-irc.org/publications/pdf/rc7_eng.pdf and the UCLA research is in Elinor Ochs and Lisa Capps, *Living Narrative.* Marshall Duke and Robyn Fivush's research on family resilience appears in "Of Ketchup and Kin," May 2003, www.marial.emory.edu/pdfs/Duke_Fivush027-03.pdf. Their work on the intergenerational self appears in Fabio Sani, editor, *Individual and Collective Self-Continuity.*

The story of the Kennedy dinner table comes from Evelyn Lincoln, *My Twelve Years with John F. Kennedy,* and Thomas Reeves, *A Question of Character.* The statistic about family dinners containing around ten minutes of substantial conversation comes from Shoshana Blum-Kulka, *Dinner Talk,* and Lyn Fogle, *Second Language Socialization and Learner Agency,* as well as from my interview with Fogle. Ellen Galinsky's vocabulary research appears in *Mind in the Making.* Qi Wang has done extensive work comparing maternal conversation styles in American and Asian cultures. Her work is summarized here: www.human.cornell.edu/hd/outreach-extension/upload/wang.pdf. Co-narration is outlined in Elinor Ochs, Ruth Smith, and Carolyn Taylor, "Detective Stories at Dinnertime," *Cultural Dynamics* (1989).

3. Branding Your Family

The study written for the Department of Health and Human Services conference in 1989 was called "Identifying Successful Families," by Maria Krysan, Kristin Moore, and Nicholas Zill. Martin Seligman's twenty-four character strengths and other resources can be found on the blog www.authentichappiness.sas.upen.edu, as well as in his book *Character Strengths and Virtues*. For more information about the work of Peter Kruty, please visit www.peterkrutyeditions.com.

Alan Kazdin's parenting advice is gathered in *The Kazdin Method for Parenting the Defiant Child*. Laura King's research about best possible selves appears in "The Health Benefits of Writing About Life Goals," 2001; the comparison of that technique with gratitude journals is found in "How to Increase and Sustain Positive Emotions," by Kennon Sheldon and Sonja Lyubomirsky, 2006.

4. Fight Smart

My overview of the literature on fighting in relationships draws on many sources. The idea that fighting can be contained comes from Reed Larson and Maryse Richards, *Divergent Realities*; the Karl Weick quotation comes from Weick and Kathleen Sutcliffe, *Managing the Unexpected*. The physiological impact of fighting on men is discussed in *Divergent Realities* (page 124) and Tara Parker-Pope, *For Better* (page 155). The impact on women is reviewed in *For Better* (page 115) and *Divergent Realities* (page 167). As for when to fight, see Deborah Tannen, *I Only Say This Because I Love You* (page 88); *Divergent Realities* (pages 32 and 67); and Daniel Kahneman, *Thinking, Fast and Slow* (page 43). On language: James Pennebaker, *The Secret Life of Pronouns*, and Sam Gosling, *Snoop* (pages 109–110). On body language: John Cacioppo, *Loneliness* (page 118). John Gottman's extensive work on analyzing conversations between partners is summarized in his books for popular audiences, including *The Seven Principles for Making Marriage Work* and *Ten Lessons to Transform Your Marriage*.

The best outline of Bill Ury's philosophy on principles negotiation remains *Getting to Yes*, which he wrote with Roger Fischer. Josh Weiss has an extremely helpful series of audiobooks called *The Negotiator in You* that cover work, life, and home. To see the complete array of impressive research I gathered about why it's perfectly okay to ignore expiration dates on food, see the article I wrote on the topic in the *New York Times*, "Take Back the Trash," May 4, 2001. To see how much impact this has had on my life, visit my kitchen.

5. The Buck Starts Here

For my overview of the research on children and allowance, I drew heavily from the work of Adrian Furnham, of the University College of London, who was kind enough to send me a copy of the manuscript for his book, *The Economic Socialisation of Young People*. It's the single best compendium of knowledge on this topic I've seen. I also benefitted from Dan Pink, *Drive*; Daniel Kahneman, *Thinking, Fast and Slow*; and David Owen, *The First National Bank of Dad*. The work of Kathleen Vohs was summed up well in "The Psychological Consequences of Money," *Science* (November 17, 2006). A talk she delivered at Stanford can be viewed at http://www.youtube.com/watch?v=qrMoDJnJeF8.

The study about couples, fights, and money was conducted by Elaine Eaker et al., "Marital Status, Marital Strain and the Risk of Coronary Heart Disease or Total Mortality," 2007. The study of marital status and financial gain is Jay Zagorsky, "Marriage and Divorce's Impact on Wealth," 2005. John Davis is the author of *Generation to Generation*.

6. Talk About the Marshmallows

My discussion of conflict in sibling relationships draws on the work of Hildy Ross, which is discussed at the website of her family studies lab, http://watarts.uwaterloo.ca/~hrosslab/index.html, and of Laurie Kramer, from the Family Resiliency Center at the University of Illinois, http://familyresiliency.illinois.edu/people/Kramer/profile.html. This and other work in the field of siblings is helpfully reviewed in Po Bronson and Ashley Merriman, *Nurture Shock*.

John DeFrain's study of strong families and difficult conversations appears in *Family Matters*, from the Australian Institute of Family Studies (Winter 1999).

Brian Uzzi's study of scientific papers and Broadway musicals appears in Nicholas Christakis and James Fowler, *Connected*. Gary Klein describes his premortem technique in *Harvard Business Review* (September 2007). The paper behind the Law of Two Women, "Evidence for a Collective Intelligence Factor in the Performance of Human Groups," was written by Anita Woolley, Christopher Chabris, Alex Pentland, Nada Hashimi, and Thomas Malone, *Science* (September 2010). More background can be found in Vicki Kramer, Alison Konrad, and Sumru Erkut, "Critical Mass on Corporate Boards," Wellesley Centers for Women's Publications Office, 2006, and Sean Farhand and Gregory Wawro, "Institutional Dynamics on the U.S. Court of Appeals," *Journal of Law, Economics, & Organization* (2004).

I wrote about the conversation with my parents in a different context in my column in the *New York Times*, "The Father Is Child of the Man," July 27, 2012.

7. Lessons from the Sex Mom

An overview of the Guttmacher Institute's extensive research on teen sexuality can be found at www.guttmacher.org/pubs/FB-ATSRH.html. The data about children talking to parents about sexuality, condom use, and other issues comes from Mark Schuster, Karen Eastman, and Rosalie Corona, "Talking Parents, Healthy Teens," *Pediatrics* (October 2006). The study about gender differences in parent-child conversations was Jaccard, Dittus, Gordon was discussed in *Parent-Teen Communication*. Mark Regnerus reviews the literature of teens and sexuality in "Talking About Sex," *The Sociological Quarterly* (2005).

The data about sexuality among European teens comes from Esther Perel, *Mating in Captivity* (page 92). My discussion of the role parents play in delaying boys' sexual onset draws from Melvin Konner, *The Evolution of Childhood* (pages 473–475). My review of the literature on how parental attitude influences girls' behavior is guided by Joyce McFadden, *Your Daughter's Bedroom*, and Evelyn Resh, *The Secret Lives of Teen Girls*. The study about father-daughter closeness and delayed sexuality comes from Mark Regnerus and Laura Luchies, "The Parent-Child Relationships and Opportunities for Adolescents' First Sex," *Journal of Family Issues* 27 (2006).

The American Academy of Pediatrics recommendations for talking to children about sex can be found at www.healthychildren .org/English/ages-stages/preschool/pages/Talking-to-Your-Young-Child-About-Sex.aspx.

The literature about the benefits of male and female orgasms is reviewed in Christopher Ryan and Cacilda Jethá, *Sex at Dawn* (pages 238–248). Tara Parker-Pope provides a helpful analysis of fidelity statistics in *For Better*, as well as a careful overview of declining sexual activity after marriage (pages 36, 75–81). The

Dawes formula for marital happiness appears in Daniel Kahneman, *Thinking, Fast and Slow* (page 26).

8. What's Love Got to Do with It

Portions of my interview with Gary Chapman appeared in "Can Gary Chapman Save Your Marriage?" *New York Times*, November 19, 2011. Jonathan Haidt's discussion of marriage appears in *The Happiness Hypothesis* (page 88). Tara Parker-Pope gathers the data about the positive influence of marriage and reviews divorce statistics in *For Better* (pages 82–100, 11–14). My understanding of the marital enrichment business was influenced by Rebecca Davis, *More Perfect Unions*. The article about couples counseling was called "Who's Afraid of Couples Therapy?" and appeared in *The Psychotherapy Networker* (November/December 2011).

Research about moms, happiness, and religion came from Jeffrey Dew and W. Bradford Wilcox, "If Momma Ain't Happy," *Journal of Marriage and Family* (February 2011). On dads, happiness, and religion, see W. Bradford Wilcox, "Is Religion an Answer?," Center for Marriage and Families, June 2012. The study about how social contacts affect religious institutions was Chaeyoon Lim and Robert Putnam, "Religion, Social Networks, and Life Satisfaction," *American Sociological Review* (2010).

Other studies referred to in this chapter include Shelly Gable, Gian Gonzaga, and Amy Strachman, "Will You Be There for Me When Things Go Right?," *Journal of Personality and Social Psychology* (2006); and "Saying Sorry Really Does Cost Nothing," *Science Daily* (September 2009).

In the marriage enrichment area, researching putting the "me" back in marriage was done by Arthur Aron et al., "Including Others in the Self," *European Review of Social Psychology* (March 2004). On the importance of date night, see W. Bradford Wilcox and Jeffrey Dew, "The Date Night Opportunity," National Marriage Project, 2012; and Tara Parker-Pope, "Reinventing Date Night for Long-Married Couples," *New York Times*, February 12, 2008. On double-dating, see Richard Slatcher, "When Harry and Sally Met Dick and Jane," *Personal Relationships* (2010). On family night, see Jennifer Senior, "All Joy and No Fun: Why Parents Hate Parenting," *New York*, July 4, 2010; and Brad Wilcox, *When Baby Makes Three*, Institute for American Values and The National Marriage Project, December 2011.

9. The Care and Feeding of Grandparents

My discussion about the role of grandparents in families was informed by my interviews with both Sarah Blaffer Hrdy and John Cacioppo, as well as by their extraordinary books—specifically, Hrdy's *Mothers and Others* and *Mother Nature*, and Cacioppo's *Loneliness*. On grandmothers being the "ace in the hole," see Hrdy, *Mothers and Others* (page 69). On Hobbes, see Cacioppo, *Loneliness* (pages 201–203). On traveling chimpanzees, see *Mothers and Others* (page 3). On the grandmother effect, see Melvin Konner, *The Evolution of Childhood* (pages 442–443).

The research about the influence of contemporary grandparents is reviewed in Konner, *The Evolution of Childhood* (pages 444–462). Statistics about grandparents' involvement comes from "Grandma and Grandpa Taking Care of the Kids," *Child Trends* (July 2004), using data from "The National Survey of Families and Households." For the study about the influence of grandparents on children, see Jeremy Yorgason, Laura Padilla-Walker, and Jami Jackson, "Nonresidential Grandparents' Emotional and Financial Involvement in Relation to Early Adolescent Grandchild Outcomes," *Journal of Research on Adolescence* (September 2011).

An overview of Laura Carstensen's work on aging and positive emotion can be found at http://psych.stanford.edu/~jmikels/carstensen_mikels_cd_2005.pdf. Diana Boxer's research on nagging is "Nagging: The Familial Conflict Arena," *Journal of Pragmatics* (December 2010). Clifford Nass has also written about nagging and constructive criticism in *The Man Who Lied to His Laptop.*

10. The Right Stuff

My thinking about the importance of places for families was informed by Christopher Alexander's masterwork, *A Pattern Language: Towns, Buildings, Construction,* as well as Toby Israel, *Some Place Like Home,* and Claire Cooper Marcus, *House as a Mirror of Self.* My discussion about color and happiness grows out of my conversation with Sally Augustin; also see Faber Birren, *Color Psychology and Color Therapy,* and Leatrice Eiseman, *Color.* In the area of light, there's a wonderful overview of the literature in Yoshiko Miwa and Kazunori Hanyu, "The Effects of Interior Design on Communication and Impressions of a Counselor in a Counseling Room," *Environment and Behavior* (May 2010).

For more of Sam Gosling's ideas about how to evaluate spaces, see his book *Snoop.* Eric Abrahamson's studies of the impact of mess on relationships and the types of mess we make can be found in his book (coauthored with David Freedman) *A Perfect Mess* (pages 103–114); on gender and space, see page 149. On spouses' overestimating their contribution to cleanup, see Daniel Kahneman's *Thinking, Fast and Slow* (page 131).

Humphrey Osmond's ideas on socieopetal and sociofugal seating are discussed in Winifred Gallagher, *House Thinking* (page 130). Seating distance is reviewed in Michael Argyle and Janet Dean, "Eye-Contact, Distance, and Affiliation," *Sociometry* (September 1965). Research on seating position around a table is from

Bryan Lawson, *Language of Space* (page 140). Posture and cushioned seating are both explored in Dana Carney, Amy Cuddy, and Andy Yap, "Power Posing," *Psychological Science* (September 2010).

11. The Family Vacation Checklist

Peter Pronovost's checklist has been the subject of two books: Atul Gawande, *The Checklist Manifesto*, and Pronovost's own, *Safe Patients, Smart Hospitals*. My discussion of social games draws on Jane McGonigal's *Reality Is Broken*. For the study of prosocial gaming in the United States and Asia, see Douglas Gentile et al., "The Effect of Prosocial Video Games on Prosocial Behaviors," *Personality and Social Psychology Bulletin* (March 2009).

12. Shut Up and Cheer

My discussion of youth sports was informed by a number of works, including Tom Farrey, *Game On*; Jim Thompson, *The Double-Goal Coach*; and Rich Luker, *Living Simple Community/Building Simple Community*, as well as by my conversations with Thompson and Luker. For participation statistics, see Farrey (page 16); for the study about athletes and Fortune 500 companies, see Farrey (page 71); for the detail about fertility treatment, see Farrey (page 43); for the chart about the mastery of various skills, see Farrey (page 98). The examples of parental violence are discussed in Thompson (page xvii); the story about the boy and snowboarding comes from Thompson (page 221). The studies of wrestlers and skiers come from Ryan Hedstrom and Daniel Gould, "Research in Youth Sports," published by the Institute for the Study of Youth Sports, 2004.

For the study of children and mastery of talent, see Benjamin Bloom, *Developing Talent in Young People*. Thompson's 100-point test appears in Jim Thompson, *Positive Sports Parenting*. Kay Redfield Jamison's quote comes from *Exuberance* (page 41). I wrote about a different aspect of ESPN in "Dominating the Man Cave," *New York Times*, February 3, 2011.

13. Give War a Chance

The statistics and extraordinary examples about family reunions come from my conversation with Edith Wagner, the editor of *Reunions* magazine, and from the many stories she shared with me, including some that had not been printed. My discussion of unit cohesion is drawn from William McNeill, *Keeping Together in Time*; John Johns and Michael Bickel, *Cohesion in the U.S. Military*; and Geoff Van Epps, "Relooking Unit Cohesion," *Military Review* (November/December 2008).

Conclusion: All Happy Families

For more of my interviews with the creators, writers, and cast of *Modern Family*, see my *New York Times* column, "What 'Modern Family' Says About Modern Families," January 21, 2011. Reed Larson and Maryse Richards write about continual renegotiation in *Divergent Realities* (page 219). Jonathan Haidt's thoughts on storytelling appear in *The Happiness Hypothesis* (pages 144–150). For more on Tolstoy and his little green stick, including an image of the original letter he wrote, see www.tolstoy.org.uk/biography .html.

SELECT BIBLIOGRAPHY

Abrahamson, Eric, and David H. Freedman. *A Perfect Mess: The Hidden Benefits of Disorder.* London: Phoenix, 2007.

Ackerman, Jennifer. *Sex Sleep Eat Drink Dream: A Day in the Life of Your Body.* Boston: Houghton Mifflin, 2007.

Andreasen, Nancy C. *The Creative Brain: The Science of Genius.* New York: Plume, 2006.

Apter, Terri. *What Do You Want from Me?: Learning to Get Along with In-Laws.* New York: W. W. Norton, 2009.

Ariely, Dan. *The Upside of Irrationality: The Unexpected Benefits of Defying Logic at Work and at Home.* New York: Harper, 2010.

Baskin, Julia, Lindsey Newman, Sophie Politt-Cohen, and Courtney Toombs. *The Notebook Girls: Four Friends, One Diary, Real Life.* New York: Warner, 2006.

Berreby, David. *Us and Them: The Science of Identity.* Chicago: University of Chicago Press, 2008.

Blau, Melinda, and Karen L. Fingerman. *Consequential Strangers: Turning Everyday Encounters into Life-Changing Moments.* New York: W. W. Norton, 2010.

Bloom, Paul. *How Pleasure Works: The New Science of Why We Like What We Like.* New York: W. W. Norton, 2010.

Blum-Kulka, Shoshana. *Dinner Talk: Cultural Patterns of Sociability and Socialization in Family Discourse.* Mahwah, NJ: Lawrence Erlbaum Associates, 1997.

Blyth, Catherine. *The Art of Conversation: A Guided Tour of a Neglected Pleasure.* New York: Gotham, 2009.

Brizendine, Louann. *The Female Brain.* New York: Morgan Road, 2006.

Bronson, Po, and Ashley Merryman. *Nuture Shock: New Thinking About Children.* New York: Twelve, 2009.

Browning, Don S. *Marriage and Modernization: How Globalization Threatens Marriage and What to Do About It.* Grand Rapids, MI: William B. Eerdmans Publishing Company, 2003.

Bryson, Bill. *At Home: A Short History of Private Life.* New York: Doubleday, 2010.

Cacioppo, John T., and William Patrick. *Loneliness: Human Nature and the Need for Social Connection.* New York: W. W. Norton, 2008.

Carter, Christine. *Raising Happiness: 10 Simple Steps for More Joyful Kids and Happier Parents.* New York: Ballantine, 2010.

Chabon, Michael. *Manhood for Amateurs: The Pleasures and Regrets of a Husband, Father, and Son.* New York: Harper, 2009.

Chapman, Gary. *The Family You've Always Wanted: Five Ways You Can Make It Happen.* Chicago: Northfield Publishing, 2008.

———. *The 5 Love Languages: How to Express Heartfelt Commitment to Your Mate.* Chicago: Northfield Publishing, 1995.

————. *The 5 Love Languages of Teenagers: The Secret to Loving Teens Effectively.* Chicago: Northfield Publishing, 2010.

————. *Things I Wish I'd Known Before We Got Married.* Chicago: Northfield Publishing, 2010.

Chapman, Gary D., and Ross Campbell. *The 5 Love Languages of Children.* Chicago: Moody, 1997.

Christakis, Nicholas A., and James H. Fowler. *Connected: The Surprising Power of Our Social Networks and How They Shape Our Lives.* New York: Little, Brown, 2009.

Chudacoff, Howard P. *Children at Play: An American History.* New York: New York University Press, 2007.

Cialdini, Robert B. *Influence: The Psychology of Persuasion.* New York: HarperCollins, 2007.

Cohen, Jon. *Almost Chimpanzee: Redrawing the Lines That Separate Us from Them.* New York: Times Books, 2010.

Collins, James C. *Good to Great: Why Some Companies Make the Leap . . . and Others Don't.* New York: HarperBusiness, 2001.

Collins, James C., and Jerry I. Porras. *Built to Last: Successful Habits of Visionary Companies.* New York: HarperBusiness, 1994.

Coontz, Stephanie. *The Way We Never Were: American Families and the Nostalgia Trap.* New York: Basic, 1992.

Cooper, Wyatt. *Families: A Memoir and a Celebration.* New York: Harper & Row, 1975.

Covey, Sean. *The 7 Habits of Highly Effective Teens.* New York: Fireside, 1998.

————. *The 6 Most Important Decisions You'll Ever Make: A Guide for Teens.* New York: Fireside, 2006.

Covey, Stephen R. *The 7 Habits of Highly Effective Families: Building a Beautiful Family Culture in a Turbulent World.* New York: Golden, 1997.

———. *The 7 Habits of Highly Effective People: Powerful Lessons in Personal Change.* New York: Fireside, 1989.

Csikszentmihalyi, Mihaly. *Creativity: Flow and the Psychology of Discovery and Invention.* New York: HarperCollins, 1996.

———. *Flow: The Psychology of Optimal Experience.* New York: Harper & Row, 1990.

Damasio, Antonio R. *Looking for Spinoza: Joy, Sorrow, and the Feeling Brain.* Orlando, FL: Harcourt, 2003.

Davis, Rebecca L. *More Perfect Unions: The American Search for Marital Bliss.* Cambridge, MA: Harvard University Press, 2010.

De Waal, Frans. *Our Inner Ape: A Leading Primatologist Explains Why We Are Who We Are.* New York: Riverhead, 2005.

Deak, JoAnn M., and Teresa Barker. *Girls Will Be Girls: Raising Confident and Courageous Daughters.* New York: Hyperion, 2002.

DeKoven, Bernie. *The Well-Played Game: A Playful Path to Wholeness.* San Jose: Writers Club, 2002.

Diamandis, Peter H., and Steven Kotler. *Abundance: The Future Is Better Than You Think.* New York: Free Press, 2012.

Drexler, Peggy. *Our Fathers, Ourselves: Daughters, Fathers, and the Changing American Family.* New York: Rodale, 2011.

Duke, Marshall, and Sara Duke, eds. *What Works with Children: Wisdom and Reflections from People Who Have Devoted Their Careers to Kids.* Atlanta: PeachTree, 2000.

Estroff, Sharon. *Can I Have a Cell Phone for Hanukkah?: The Essential Scoop on Raising Modern Jewish Kids.* New York: Broadway, 2007.

Fadiman, Anne. *Ex Libris: Confessions of a Common Reader.* New York: Farrar, Straus and Giroux, 1998.

Farrey, Tom. *Game On: The All-American Race to Make Champions of Our Children.* New York: ESPN, 2008.

Feldman, Robert S. *The Liar in Your Life: The Way to Truthful Relationships.* New York: Twelve, 2009.

Fernández-Armesto, Felipe. *Near a Thousand Tables: A History of Food.* New York: Free Press, 2002.

Fischer, Claude S. *America Calling: A Social History of the Telephone to 1940.* Berkeley: University of California Press, 1992.

———. *Made in America: A Social History of American Culture and Character.* Chicago: University of Chicago Press, 2010.

Fish, Joel, and Susan Magee. *101 Ways to Be a Terrific Sports Parent: Making Athletics a Positive Experience for Your Child.* New York: Simon & Schuster, 2003.

Fisher, Roger, William Ury, and Bruce Patton. *Getting to Yes: Negotiating Agreement Without Giving In.* New York: Penguin, 1991.

Fliegelman, Jay. *Prodigals and Pilgrims: The American Revolution Against Patriarchal Authority, 1750–1800.* Cambridge, UK: Cambridge University Press, 1982.

Freud, Sigmund. *Group Psychology and the Analysis of the Ego.* Mansfield Centre, CT: Martino, 2010.

Galinsky, Ellen. *Ask the Children: What America's Children Really Think About Working Parents.* New York: William Morrow, 1999.

———. *Mind in the Making: The Seven Essential Life Skills Every Child Needs.* New York: HarperStudio, 2010.

Gallagher, Winifred. *House Thinking: A Room-by-Room Look at How We Live.* New York: HarperCollins, 2006.

———. *Rapt: Attention and the Focused Life.* New York: Penguin, 2009.

Gawande, Atul. *The Checklist Manifesto: How to Get Things Right.* New York: Picador, 2010.

Gazzaniga, Michael S. *The Ethical Brain: The Science of Our Moral Dilemmas.* New York: Harper Perennial, 2006.

———. *Human: The Science Behind What Makes Us Unique.* New York: Ecco, 2008.

Gersick, Kelin E., John A. Davis, Marion McCollom Hampton, and Ivan Lansberg. *Generation to Generation: Life Cycles of the Family Business.* Boston: Harvard Business School, 1997.

Gladwell, Malcolm. *Blink: The Power of Thinking Without Thinking.* New York: Little, Brown, 2005.

Glickman, Elaine Rose. *Sacred Parenting: Jewish Wisdom for Your Family's First Years.* New York: URJ Press, 2009.

Godin, Seth. *Tribes: We Need You to Lead Us.* New York: Portfolio, 2008.

Gosling, Sam. *Snoop: What Your Stuff Says About You.* New York: Basic Books, 2008.

Gottman, John M., and Joan DeClaire. *The Relationship Cure: A Five-Step Guide to Strengthening Your Marriage, Family, and Friendships.* New York: Three Rivers Press, 2002.

Gottman, John M., and Nan Silver. *The Seven Principles for Making Marriage Work.* New York: Three Rivers Press, 1999.

Graff, Gerald, and Cathy Birkenstein. *They Say, I Say: The Moves That Matter in Academic Writing.* New York: W. W. Norton, 2010.

Gray, Peter B., and Kermyt G. Anderson. *Fatherhood: Evolution and Human Paternal Behavior.* Cambridge, MA: Harvard University Press, 2010.

Gurian, Michael. *The Wonder of Girls: Understanding the Hidden Nature of Our Daughters.* New York: Atria, 2003.

Haidt, Jonathan. *The Happiness Hypothesis: Finding Modern Truth in Ancient Wisdom.* New York: Basic Books, 2006.

Hall, Edward T. *The Hidden Dimension.* New York: Anchor, 1990.

Hall, Stephen S. *Wisdom: From Philosophy to Neuroscience.* New York: Alfred A. Knopf, 2010.

Higley, Jim. *Bobblehead Dad: 25 Life Lessons I Forgot I Knew.* Austin, TX: Greenleaf Book Group, 2011.

Hrdy, Sarah Blaffer. *Mother Nature: A History of Mothers, Infants, and Natural Selection.* New York: Pantheon, 1999.

———. *Mothers and Others: The Evolutionary Origins of Mutual Understanding.* Cambridge, MA: Belknap Press, 2009.

Israel, Toby. *Some Place Like Home: Using Design Psychology to Create Ideal Places.* Chichester, UK: Wiley-Academy, 2003.

Iyengar, Sheena. *The Art of Choosing.* New York: Twelve, 2010.

Jamison, Kay Redfield. *Exuberance: The Passion for Life.* New York: Vintage, 2004.

Johns, John H., and Michael D. Bickel. *Cohesion in the U.S. Military.* Washington, DC: National Defense University Press, 1984.

Johnson, Steven. *Mind Wide Open: Your Brain and the Neuroscience of Everyday Life.* New York: Scribner, 2004.

Judson, Olivia. *Dr. Tatiana's Sex Advice to All Creation.* New York: Henry Holt, 2002.

Jung, C. G. *The Essential Jung.* Edited by Anthony Storr. Princeton, NJ: Princeton University Press, 1997.

Kahneman, Daniel. *Thinking, Fast and Slow.* New York: Farrar, Straus and Giroux, 2011.

Kaplan, Michael, and Ellen Kaplan. *Bozo Sapiens: Why to Err Is Human.* New York: Bloomsbury, 2009.

Konner, Melvin. *The Evolution of Childhood: Relationships, Emotion, Mind.* Cambridge, MA: Belknap Press, 2010.

Krasnow, Iris. *The Secret Lives of Wives: Women Share What It Really Takes to Stay Married.* New York: Gotham, 2011.

Larson, Reed, and Maryse Heather Richards. *Divergent Realities: The Emotional Lives of Mothers, Fathers, and Adolescents.* New York: Basic Books, 1994.

Levine, Madeline. *The Price of Privilege: How Parental Pressure and Material Advantage Are Creating a Generation of Disconnected and Unhappy Kids.* New York: HarperCollins, 2006.

Ling, Rich. *The Mobile Connection: The Cell Phone's Impact on Society.* San Francisco: Morgan Kaufmann, 2004.

———. *New Tech, New Ties: How Mobile Communication Is Reshaping Social Cohesion.* Cambridge, MA: MIT, 2008.

Luker, Rich. *Living Simple Community/Building Simple Community.* St. Petersburg, FL: Tangeness, 2009.

Lyubomirsky, Sonja. *The How of Happiness: A Scientific Approach to Getting the Life You Want.* New York: Penguin, 2008.

Marcus, Clare Cooper. *House as a Mirror of Self: Exploring the Deeper Meaning of Home.* Berkeley, CA: Conari, 1995.

McFadden, Joyce T. *Your Daughter's Bedroom: Insights for Raising Confident Women.* New York: Palgrave Macmillan, 2011.

McGonigal, Jane. *Reality Is Broken: Why Games Make Us Better and How They Can Change the World.* New York: Penguin, 2011.

McNeill, William Hardy. *Keeping Together in Time: Dance and Drill in Human History.* Cambridge, MA: Harvard University Press, 1995.

Meeker, Margaret J. *Strong Fathers, Strong Daughters: 10 Secrets Every Father Should Know.* Washington, DC: Regnery Publishing, 2006.

Mintz, Steven. *Huck's Raft: A History of American Childhood.* Cambridge, MA: Belknap Press, 2004.

Minuchin, Salvador. *Families and Family Therapy.* London: Routledge, 1991.

Mitchell, Stephen A. *Can Love Last? The Fate of Romance Over Time.* New York: W. W. Norton, 2002.

Mogel, Wendy. *The Blessing of a Skinned Knee: Using Jewish Teachings to Raise Self-Reliant Children.* New York: Scribner, 2001.

Mortimer, Jeylan T. *Working and Growing Up in America.* Cambridge, MA: Harvard University Press, 2003.

Nass, Clifford, and Corina Yen. *The Man Who Lied to His Laptop: What Machines Teach Us About Human Relationships.* New York: Current, 2010.

Nass, Clifford Ivar, and Scott Brave. *Wired for Speech: How Voice Activates and Advances the Human-Computer Relationship.* Cambridge, MA: MIT, 2005.

Notkin, Melanie. *Savvy Auntie: The Ultimate Guide for Cool Aunts, Great-Aunts, Godmothers, and All Women Who Love Kids.* New York: William Morrow, 2011.

Nowicki, Stephen, Marshall P. Duke, and Amy Van Buren. *Starting Kids Off Right: How to Raise Confident Children Who Can Make Friends and Build Healthy Relationships.* Atlanta: Peachtree, 2008.

Owen, David. *The First National Bank of Dad: The Best Way to Teach Kids About Money.* New York: Simon & Schuster, 2003.

Parker-Pope, Tara. *For Better: The Science of a Good Marriage.* New York: Dutton, 2010.

Pasanella, Marco. *Uncorked: My Journey Through the Crazy World of Wine.* New York: Clarkson Potter, 2012.

Patterson, Kerry, Joseph Grenny, Al Switzler, and Ron McMillan. *Crucial Conversations.* New York: McGraw-Hill, 2012.

Perel, Esther. *Mating in Captivity: Unlocking Erotic Intelligence.* New York: Harper, 2007.

Phelan, Thomas W. *1-2-3 Magic: Effective Discipline for Children 2–12.* Glen Ellyn, IL: ParentMagic, 2003.

Pink, Daniel H. *Drive: The Surprising Truth About What Motivates Us.* New York: Riverhead, 2009.

———. *A Whole New Mind: Why Right-Brainers Will Rule the Future.* New York: Riverhead, 2006.

Pinker, Steven. *The Language Instinct.* New York: William Morrow, 1994.

Powers, William. *Hamlet's Blackberry: A Practical Philosophy for Building a Good Life in the Digital Age.* New York: Harper, 2010.

Pronovost, Peter J., and Eric Vohr. *Safe Patients, Smart Hospitals: How One Doctor's Checklist Can Help Us Change Health Care from the Inside Out.* New York: Hudson Street, 2010.

Provine, Robert R. *Laughter: A Scientific Investigation.* New York: Viking, 2000.

Quartz, Steven, and Terrence J. Sejnowski. *Liars, Lovers, and Heroes: What the New Brain Science Reveals About How We Become Who We Are.* New York: William Morrow, 2002.

Quindlen, Anna. *Living Out Loud.* New York: Random House, 1988.

Rathje, William L., and Cullen Murphy. *Rubbish!: The Archaeology of Garbage.* New York: HarperCollins, 1992.

Remen, Rachel Naomi. *Kitchen Table Wisdom: Stories That Heal.* New York: Riverhead, 1996.

Resh, Evelyn K., and Beverly West. *The Secret Lives of Teen Girls: What Your Mother Wouldn't Talk About But Your Daughter Needs to Know.* Carlsbad, CA: Hay House, 2009.

Restak, Richard M. *The Naked Brain: How the Emerging Neurosociety Is Changing How We Live, Work, and Love.* New York: Harmony, 2006.

Ridley, Matt. *The Red Queen: Sex and the Evolution of Human Nature.* New York: Macmillan, 1994.

Ripken, Cal, and Larry Burke. *The Ripken Way: A Manual for Baseball and Life.* New York: Pocket, 1999.

Rubin, Gretchen Craft. *The Happiness Project.* New York: Harper-Collins, 2010.

Ryan, Christopher, and Cacilda Jethá. *Sex at Dawn: The Prehistoric Origins of Modern Sexuality.* New York: Harper, 2010.

Sapolsky, Robert M. *Why Zebras Don't Get Ulcers.* New York: Henry Holt, 2004.

Sargent, Ted. *The Dance of Molecules: How Nanotechnology Is Changing Our Lives.* New York: Thunder's Mouth, 2006.

Sawyer, R. Keith. *Explaining Creativity: The Science of Human Innovation.* Oxford: Oxford University Press, 2006.

Schnarch, David Morris. *Passionate Marriage: Keeping Love and Intimacy Alive in Committed Relationships.* Brunswick, Australia: Scribe Publications, 2012.

Seligman, Martin E. P. *Flourish: A Visionary New Understanding of Happiness and Well-Being.* New York: Free Press, 2011.

Sherwood, Ben. *The Survivors Club: The Secrets and Science That Could Save Your Life.* New York: Grand Central Publishing, 2009.

Siegel, Daniel J., and Tina Payne Bryson. *The Whole-Brain Child: 12 Revolutionary Strategies to Nurture Your Child's Developing Mind.* New York: Delacorte Press, 2011.

Sommer, Robert. *Personal Space: The Behavioral Basis of Design.* Bristol: Bosko, 2007.

Soueif, Ahdaf. *The Map of Love.* New York: Anchor, 2000.

Stiffelman, Susan. *Parenting Without Power Struggles: Raising Joyful, Resilient Kids While Staying Calm, Cool and Connected.* New York: Atria Books, 2012.

Stone, Douglas, Bruce Patton, and Sheila Heen. *Difficult Conversations: How to Discuss What Matters Most.* New York: Viking, 1999.

Surowiecki, James. *The Wisdom of Crowds.* New York: Anchor, 2005.

Szalavitz, Maia, and Bruce Duncan Perry. *Born for Love: Why Empathy Is Essential—and Endangered.* New York: William Morrow, 2010.

Taffel, Ron. *Childhood Unbound: Saving Our Kids' Best Selves—Confident Parenting in a World of Change.* New York: Free Press, 2009.

Taffel, Ron, and Melinda Blau. *Parenting By Heart: How to Stay Connected to Your Child in a Disconnected World.* Cambridge, MA: Perseus, 2002.

Tannen, Deborah. *I Only Say This Because I Love You: Talking to Your Parents, Partner, Sibs, and Kids When You're All Adults.* New York: Ballantine, 2002.

Tannen, Deborah, Shari Kendall, and Cynthia Gordon. *Family Talk: Discourse and Identity in Four American Families.* Oxford: Oxford University Press, 2007.

Taylor, Ella. *Prime-Time Families: Television Culture in Postwar America.* Berkeley: University of California Press, 1989.

Thaler, Richard H., and Cass R. Sunstein. *Nudge: Improving Decisions About Health, Wealth and Happiness.* London: Penguin, 2009.

Thompson, Jim. *The Double-Goal Coach: Positive Coaching Tools for Honoring the Game and Developing Winners in Sports and Life.* New York: Harper, 2003.

———. *Elevating Your Game: Becoming a Triple-Impact Competitor.* Portola Valley, CA: Balance Sports, 2011.

———. *Positive Sports Parenting: How "Second-Goal" Parents Raise Winners in Life Through Sports.* Portola Valley, CA: Balance Sports, 2009.

Thurman, Robert A. F. *Inner Revolution: Life, Liberty, and the Pursuit of Real Happiness.* New York: Riverhead, 1998.

Turkle, Sherry. *Alone Together: Why We Expect More from Technology and Less from Each Other.* New York: Basic Books, 2011.

Underhill, Paco. *Why We Buy: The Science of Shopping.* New York: Simon & Schuster, 2009.

Ury, William. *The Third Side: Why We Fight and How We Can Stop.* New York: Penguin, 2000.

Viscott, David S. *Emotional Resilience: Simple Truths for Dealing with the Unfinished Business of Your Past.* New York: Three Rivers Press, 1996.

Vonnegut, Kurt. *Slapstick.* New York: Delta Trade Paperbacks, 1999.

Weick, Karl E., and Kathleen M. Sutcliffe. *Managing the Unexpected: Assuring High Performance in an Age of Complexity.* San Francisco: Jossey-Bass, 2001.

Wolpe, David J. *Teaching Your Children About God: A Modern Jewish Approach.* New York: HarperCollins, 1993.

Wrangham, Richard W. *Catching Fire: How Cooking Made Us Human.* New York: Basic Books, 2009.

Wright, Robert. *The Moral Animal: Why We Are the Way We Are: The New Science of Evolutionary Psychology.* New York: Random House, 1994.

Yalom, Marilyn. *A History of the Wife.* New York: HarperCollins, 2001.